THINKING
ALLOWED

C O N V E R S A T I O N S

ON THE LEADING EDGE OF KNOWLEDGE

WITH JEFFREY MISHLOVE, PH.D.

C O U N C I L   O A K   B O O K S

Thinking Allowed Video Collection

All of the interviews featured in this book, plus more than 100 more, are available on videocassette as part of the Thinking Allowed and InnerWork video collections. For a complete list of titles and special package offers, please write to:

Thinking Allowed
2560 Ninth Street, Suite 123
Berkeley, California 94710
or phone toll free: 1-800-999-4415

Thinking Allowed on Public Television

The Thinking Allowed series is broadcast every week on more than 75 public television stations across the country. For availability in your area, check your local listings or contact your local PBS station.

Published and Distributed by
Council Oak Books
1350 East Fifteenth Street
Tulsa, Oklahoma 74120
1-918-587-6454
FAX 1-918-583-4995
1-800-247-8850

ISBN 0-933031-64-5
Library of Congress Card Catalog Number 91-77972

Edited by Kathleen Goss
Designed by Carol Haralson

150
T

CONTENTS

My partner, producer and director, Arthur Bloch, an inveterate wordsmith, created the title of our television series, *Thinking Allowed*. Naturally, it has multiple meanings. Our intention has been to scrutinize areas that are generally relegated to skeptical contempt or uncritical reverence. (At one conference a woman solemnly informed us that her guru had told her to "stop thinking.") We have also attempted to address the fundamental issues of meaning and purpose in our lives. Such discussions are sometimes dismissed as "sophomoric," a code word that suggests adults often do stop thinking about these basic questions. Finally, we have attempted to portray our guests (at least occasionally) in the actual *act of thinking*, rather than in the process of travelling well-trodden paths of belief.

People often ask how the television series got started. For me, it has been a magical experience which I would like to share with you to convey a sense of the background for the discussions that appear in this book. When I search within myself for the answer, I always remember a dream I had in 1972. I was a graduate student at that time, having recently received a Master of Criminology degree from the University of California at Berkeley. I had been interested in human deviance, but I wanted to focus on forms of deviation other than crime and mental illness.

I had become a student of psychodrama and yoga and a health food eater. I developed good friends among colorful local groups like the Reformed Druids of North America, the New Order of the Golden Dawn, and the Order of Wizard Lore (a division of the Society for Creative Anachronism). I attended lectures on brainwave control, UFOs and psychic healing. Much of the time, my partner in these explorations was Saul-Paul Sirag, then a science writer whose "New Alchemy" column was syndicated for college newspapers throughout the country.

While I was fascinated with the study of deviant behavior, I had come to the conclusion that the criminals I had studied were much less interesting than the many unusual characters I had met among scientists, yogis and intuitives in the Berkeley area. In fact, at that time, I already had a strong interest in the synthesis of the Asian traditions with western psychology and science. I was fascinated by the pioneering work in this area by scholars such as William James, Petirim Sorokin, Gardner Murphy, J. B. Rhine, Abraham Maslow and Charles Tart. However, these important efforts were virtually ignored in academia, and I knew of no way to pursue this interest within the confines of the university.

I felt disconnected from my life's work and purpose, floating without a clear aim. It was my fervent hope that I could begin to develop a new, uplifting career direction for myself. Yet months went by and nothing materialized. This was a source of anxiety, as a desperation grew within me to refocus my life.

One October evening in 1972, I was inexplicably filled with the conviction that the answer to my searching would come to me in a dream. And dream I did:

I am visiting my close friends Peter and Marcy Hartman, who live in the married student housing complex in Albany. When I arrive at their apartment, nobody is home. However, knowing where they keep a hidden key, I let myself in. Entering the living room, I find a magazine sitting in the middle of the floor. It is called Eye. *Paging through the magazine, I am immediately filled with a "Eureka!" sensation – "I have found it!" Then I awake.*

Upon waking, I was possessed with the certainty that I had, indeed, found the answer I had been seeking so earnestly – however, I had no idea what the answer was. There was nothing else to do but jump out of bed, put on my sneakers (this was in the days before running shoes), and jog across Berkeley to married student housing.

Arriving at Peter and Marcy's apartment, I found nobody at home. But, in fact, I did know where they kept a spare key. Like a thief, I let myself into the living room (something I would never have done ordinarily); and there I found, to my delight and amazement, a single magazine sitting conspicuously in the middle of the floor.

And here is a wonderful example of dream distortion: the magazine I found was not called *Eye* (a popular magazine at that time) – rather it was *Focus*. And that magazine literally brought focus into my life.

It was the magazine of KQED television and radio in San Francisco. As I glanced through its pages it dawned on me, literally for the first time in my life, that I might develop a career in educational media. This was truly a shocking thought, for at that time I owned neither a radio nor a television. I was convinced that the only worthwhile human interactions were of the face-to-face variety. I was, in fact, prejudiced against electronic media as embodying the worst aspects of a decadent, depersonalized culture. But at that moment, I changed my mind and set out upon a journey that has lasted to this day.

Since I lived in the East Bay, I applied to work as a volunteer at KPFA-FM, Pacifica radio in Berkeley, where I was accepted as a receptionist and encouraged to learn the basics of radio production. Within three weeks, I had produced two investigative programs. The station manager was so impressed that he offered me the position of host of the *Mind's Ear* program.

Now my life was transformed! Every Tuesday and Thursday found me sharing an intimate noon-hour conversation with a leading visionary thinker and ten thousand radio listeners. I soon discovered that almost everyone of importance in the burgeoning social transformation and consciousness movements eventually passed through the San Francisco Bay Area and that most were happy to appear on my program. These wonderful individuals proved in many ways to be as interesting and knowledgeable as my professors at the University of California.

My curiosity about my own synchronistic dream experiences prompted me to explore questions of human potential further. I quickly learned that there were almost no experts on the far reaches of intuition within the university community, so I resolved to become my own authority. At the same time, I had to decide whether to enter the doctoral program in criminology or to shift my major. A bulletin board announcement caught my eye, indicating that the university would admit graduate students in good standing to individual, interdisciplinary programs if they wished to do research in an area that would not fit within the boundaries of any single department.

Taking advantage of this opportunity, I assembled a committee of five professors who were willing to support my work toward a doctoral degree exploring extraordinary mental abilities. I was fortunate to have the good offices of Professor Charles Tart (whose interview on "Cultivating Mindfulness" may be found in this book). Eventually I gave up my radio program in order to complete my doctoral degree at Berkeley.

As preparation for qualifying as a doctoral candidate, I wrote my first book, an overview of intuition through history, science and experience titled *The Roots of Consciousness*. It remained in print for over a decade and is scheduled for release in a revised edition by Council Oak Books in 1992.

Through a group of graduate students and professors at Berkeley who met to consider the scientific questions raised by the problem of consciousness, I met Arthur M. Young, an inventor and cosmologist, who was to become a mentor in my pursuit of the unknown. Young actually held the patent on the first commercially licensed helicopter, the Bell Model 47. Upon completing this project in 1947, he devoted his life to developing a theory that could integrate modern science with the teachings of ancient mythology and the elusive realities of psychic experience.

Saul-Paul Sirag and I attended one of Young's seminars that was offered informally to a number of graduate students at U.C. Berkeley's psychology clinic. After Young and his wife decided to purchase a home on Benvenue Avenue in Berkeley to house his new Institute for the Study of Consciousness, Saul-Paul and I were offered the opportunity to move into the upstairs bedrooms. We did not hesitate to accept. Young still resides there for six months of the year and, in his eighty-seventh year, continues his explorations.

At the Institute for the Study of Consciousness, we engaged in many seminars and discussions focusing on the quantum mechanical principle of uncertainty and its relationship to free will. Young maintained that the basis for consciousness itself could be found in what physicists called *the quantum of action*. His theory traced the evolution of the quantum of action from the photon to elementary particles, atoms, molecules, plants, animals and the human kingdom. He claimed that his approach was basically an updated version of that promulgated by Pythagoras some 2,500 years ago. The depth of his thought is expressed in the interview with him, titled "Evolution: The Great Chain of Being."

Young's influence upon Saul-Paul Sirag was significant. He would assign to Sirag various logical problems relating to Eddington's attempts to develop a unified field theory. This led Sirag to give up his writing career and devote himself full-time to theoretical physics. Some eighteen years later, his work continues unabated. Don't miss the interview with him in this volume on "Consciousness and Hyperspace."

It was also through Arthur Young that I met Arthur Bloch who was to become my partner in producing *Thinking Allowed*. Bloch is the author of the *Murphy's Laws* series of books (which have sold over two million copies). In spite of his success as one of America's foremost humorists, Arthur Bloch's great loves were the cosmology and philosophy of Arthur Young and video production. He combined these interests in several productions about Young's works, *The Reflexive Universe* and *The Geometry of Meaning*. In one of these, Bloch interviewed me about the implications of Young's thinking in my own life. I also arranged to work with Arthur Bloch in videotaping the "automatic paintings" of Brazilian *espiritista* Luiz Gasparetto. Within one hour, Gasparetto produced over twenty paintings, each in the style of a great early twentieth-century master.

In February 1980, after my dissertation on training intuitive abilities (later published as *Psi Development Systems*) had been approved by the graduate division, I visited Arthur Young in Berkeley to share the news with him. Referring to his ephemerides, he mysteriously told me that it would take six more years for me to overcome the negative and restrictive influences that the university had had upon my spirit.

Young's words proved prophetic, for I began an odyssey that was to last for six years during which I withdrew from almost all research and training work and public appearances. I literally changed professions and acquired a license to practice psychology in California.

One of my dear friends in 1986 was Carol Dryer, a Los Angeles intuitive consultant, whose main claim to fame was probably the work she had done with rock singer Tina Turner, who credits Carol with being a major inspiration in her famous career comeback. Carol's work with Tina helped give her the courage to build a career on her own after suffering years of physical abuse at the hands of her husband.

Occasionally Carol produced cable television programs in Los Angeles. For one of these, she insisted that I fly down at her expense so that she could interview me. Then, after the program, she further *insisted* that I develop a similar program of my own in northern California. She made a point of ensuring that I understood all of the steps involved. Then she went further and forecast that I would find success in television. Her influence was a major inspiration.

After some hesitation, I got together with Arthur Bloch and proposed to him that we produce a series of television interviews with leading social thinkers, psychologists, philosophers and consciousness researchers. He agreed without hesitating. Then the magic began.

We started by producing sixteen local cable programs in Marin County. Then our series was picked up by KCSM-TV 60, public television in San Mateo/San Francisco, where it received one of the largest audience responses in their history. Subsequently, KCSM sponsored us for satellite uplink to PBS stations throughout the United States. For the past four years the program has been available every week via satellite and broadcast by over eighty PBS stations. And it all began in 1972 with a dream that led me to *Focus* magazine.

The interviews that appear in this volume have been selected from over 200 programs. They represent highlights in the quest to reconcile our internal realities with the demands of science and society.

The reader need not sympathize with or accept the validity of my own experiences in order to appreciate the philosophical, scientific and social dimensions of these discussions. For while the study of the reaches of the mind inevitably leads to questions regarding the deeper meanings of life, such questioning has its own value without reference to the motivations of the questioner. I have included my own story in the hope that it may further illuminate your reading of these conversations.

Berkeley, California
February 1992

TRANSFORMING SOCIETY

THE EMERGING NEW CULTURE

WITH FRITJOF CAPRA, PH.D.

Fritjof Capra, physicist and systems theorist, is the founder and president of the Elmwood Institute in Berkeley, California. Dr. Capra is the author of the international bestsellers THE TAO OF PHYSICS, THE TURNING POINT, and UNCOMMON WISDOM, and coauthor of GREEN POLITICS (with Charlene Spretnak) and BELONGING TO THE UNIVERSE. He cowrote the screenplay for MINDWALK, the feature film based on his books.

In this interview, Dr. Capra discusses the new holistic culture that has emerged in the late twentieth century. He argues that the life sciences will replace the physical sciences as the theoretical foundation of our view of reality, and that values and ethics will replace a mechanistic world view as the driving force for change.

Around the turn of the century, many developments happened all at once that really changed our culture – Freudian psychology, modern art, quantum physics. Do you see these things as being somehow related?

FC: Absolutely. I have come to believe that the collective consciousness changes in certain phases. This was one such phase of dramatic shift in the collective consciousness, in art, in science, and in various other fields.

In your book The Turning Point *you describe a new holistic or integral culture that is on the rise now, whereas the old Western culture, with its mechanistic linear models, is in a decline.*

FC: That's right. I follow people like Sorokin and Hegel, for instance, and I follow the I Ching and various traditions and philosophical schools that have seen the development of consciousness and of society as a cyclical process. Cultures and civilizations rise, they reach a culmination point, and then they decline; and as they decline, a new culture will arise and tackle new problems with new ingenuity and new creativity. This is what happened at the turn of the century. The old culture – which was basically the scientific culture of the seventeenth century Enlightenment, of Newtonian physics and the Copernican revolution – this way of seeing the world, in mechanistic terms, in reductionist terms, came to a close and is now declining. And what is rising is a more holistic, more ecological way of seeing things.

You mentioned the sociologist Pitirim Sorokin, who said that cultures are predicated upon ideas or metaphysical principles. The old culture revolved around the metaphysics of materialism. Today the bedrock of our materialistic science is quantum physics; yet quantum physics itself is no longer materialistic in the nineteenth-century sense.

F.C. Quantum physics has brought a dissolution of the notion of hard and solid objects, and also of the notion that there are fundamental building blocks of matter. To study the smallest pieces of matter that we know, the subatomic particles, we must have large instruments – particle accelerators and bubble chambers and detectors. Since quantum mechanics we know that all the laws and regularities at the level of the very small can only be formulated in terms of probabilities. But what are these probabilities of? They are probabilities of making a certain measurement, of the large-scale instruments interacting in a certain way. So whatever we say about the smallest pieces comes back to the large pieces – it can be expressed only in probabilities, in terms of the large pieces. It is sort of a circular situation.

In other words, everything is interconnected.

F.C. Yes, and it is interconnected in such a way that the properties of the smallest pieces depend on the properties of the whole. So whereas before we believed that the dynamics of the whole can be explained by breaking it down and determining the properties of the parts, now we see that the properties of the parts can only be defined in terms of the dynamics of the whole. It is a complete reversal.

And that has become one of the most fundamental scientific insights of our century.

FC: That's right. In fact, if we go even further and ask, "Well, what are these parts?" you will find that there are no ultimate parts – that whatever we call a part is a pattern in an ongoing process; so it is something that is relatively stable. It is like a Rorschach test; or maybe clouds are a better example. You look at clouds, and you may see a chicken up there, or an airplane. You see these things because a cloud formation is relatively stable. But five minutes later it is gone; it changes. Now, with particles the patterns change much faster, but whatever you call an object or a particle or an atom or a molecule, all are patterns in an ongoing process.

So if someone were to ask you, "What is the fundamental building block of the universe?" where we used to have atoms, now we don't have anything.

FC: Yes, there is no such thing. There are no things. And you know, people in other traditions, such as the Buddhist traditions, have been saying that for a long time. There is emptiness, and out of emptiness comes all form. But the forms are not things, not isolated objects. The forms are forms of the whole.

In your book THE TAO OF PHYSICS you make the point that theoretical physics resembles very much the kinds of things that the Eastern mystics have been writing about.

FC: That's right, and that is now coming out in Western science. Physics is a very nice model case, and we know it pretty well because it happened at the beginning of the century. But it is now happening also in biology and psychology and economics and various other fields.

In THE TURNING POINT you suggest that many of the social movements, such as the ecology movement and the women's liberation movement, which are changing our culture so much, are also related to these developments in physics.

FC: Yes, they are not related causally. It's not that physics influenced the feminist movement or the peace movement; but again it is a change of consciousness over maybe fifty years in various fields that is now emerging. We have a definite movement toward wholeness, toward a dynamic view, toward a participatory universe where you don't separate the observer from the observed, and these various characteristics are expressed in science and in society.

How do you think this change in consciousness affects people today in their daily lives?

FC: It affects them very strongly. My starting point in writing *The Turning Point* was the observation that the major problems of today are all interconnected. They are systemic problems; they are all interlinked, and they are in fact reflections of the limitations of an outdated world view. Now, most of our social institutions – the large corporations, the large academic institutions, the large political institutions – subscribe to this outdated world view, and therefore are not able to solve the major problems that we face – the threat of nuclear war, the devastation of the natural environment, the economic crisis, and so on. People who work in these institutions have a very strong sense that things are not going the way they should, or the way they used to, and that we need dramatic change. This is a global phenomenon, and I can even show the direction in which this change has to occur. I find great resonance now in business circles, among managers – interestingly, more so in Europe than here.

What are these managers saying, the ones who are interested?

FC: Well, in the schools they say that they can't teach management the way they used to teach it, because the problems that arise today cannot be neatly pigeonholed as problems of finance, marketing strategy, or research and development. Those are not separate entities; we have to see things holistically. They talk about a holistic approach to management, and they also talk about a corporation or a company not as a machine but as a living organism. So you have to understand living organisms; you can't break them into pieces. You don't design a plan for the organization and impose it from above, as used to be done. You develop it and let it evolve with all the coworkers, with all the teamwork.

It seems that in the United States under recent administrations, there has been more of an effort to rejuvenate the old values and squeeze whatever juice might be left out of them.

FC: That's right. I think there is great materialism and opportunism in the United States. Also, in this country we have the legal requirement of quarterly returns for businesses. In Europe they don't have that; although the corporations are responsible to their stockholders just as they are here, they are responsible to them on a yearly basis and not on a quarterly basis. Part of why we find it so hard to change things in corporations here is that they have this short-sighted view, the bottom line in the next quarter. And so it is very difficult to make changes.

They can't plan the same way.

FC: They don't even have time to think. Nevertheless, changes are occurring in this country, just as everywhere else.

One would think so, because these global changes of consciousness are so implicit in our system. You can't get away from them.

FC: That's right, and the old system is such a spectacular failure that the experts don't understand their fields of expertise any longer. For instance, researchers investigating cancer don't have a clue, in spite of spending millions of dollars, about the origins of cancer. The police are powerless in the face of a rising wave of crime. The politicians and economists don't know how to manage the economic problems. The doctors and hospitals don't know how to manage the health problems and health costs. Everywhere it is the very people who are supposed to be the experts in their fields who don't have answers any longer, and they don't have answers because they have a narrow view. They don't see the whole problem.

One would hope, because of the urgency of all these problems, that the holistic, systems view will emerge, and people will see the patterns.

FC: I think it will. I think there is a very strong desire in the population at large for something new to happen.

And to see things holistically, to see all of the interrelated pieces of the puzzle and come up with new ideas, would seem to require a shift in consciousness to incorporate all the various perspectives.

FC: Not only a shift in consciousness, but also a shift toward consciousness, or toward mind – a mindful universe, a universe of consciousness, of spirit; a spiritual, conscious universe. Even in the new physics – since the new physics is still physics and deals with material phenomena – mind, spirit and consciousness obviously have no room.

The shift that is occurring, and it is going to be very revolutionary, is a shift from physics to the life sciences as the center of our view of reality – that the universe is a living universe, and we are talking about living, mindful systems. The principles of organization of these systems are mental principles. Of course physics and physical phenomena are part of that; there is a part of this whole which is non-living. But the whole is living, and so it is only when you understand life that you will understand that wholeness. I think that is a very important shift.

In other words, the very viewpoint that physics is the bedrock of science will shift.

FC: Right. It's outdated. That is actually a Cartesian viewpoint. Descartes said that knowledge is like a tree. The roots are metaphysics, the trunk is physics, and then the branches are the various sciences. Now we would say that the trunk is life, and the whole tree is alive. You don't split things apart.

For managers, or for people in their daily lives, trying to make this shift as individuals must be a little bit overwhelming – having to integrate all this knowledge from all of these interrelated disciplines.

FC: That's true, and actually it is easier for people who are not intellectuals, who are not scientists, who are not specialists. For simple people it is much easier, because they experience life as a wholeness, and they are much more intuitive rather than analytic and rational. The intuitive mind is a nonlinear mode of functioning, a way of experiencing everything at once and not splitting it up into linear chains of cause and effect. The more intuitive people are, the easier they will find it. So one way of making the shift would be to awaken and cultivate one's intuition.

You have made a transition in your own career from spending a lot of time doing research and writing to getting more involved in social action and other develop-ments.

FC: Yes. THE TURNING POINT started out as a book about conceptual change and ended up being as much about social change as about conceptual change. Recently I have gone further in this direction and founded the Elmwood Institute, which is sort of an ecological think tank; we call it actually "a greenhouse for new ecological visions." We place ourselves between innovative ideas and social action. We are neither lobbyists nor social activists as an institute, nor are we a research institute, but we want to build bridges between the two, and I have been very active in that.

What kinds of areas are you working in?

FC: Those that will facilitate the shift to a new paradigm, a new world view, a new consciousness. We see the various problems coming from an outdated underlying world view, and we want to facilitate change of that world view.

Do you see quantum physics playing a role in this holistic perspective you are inculcating?

FC: Physics will no longer be the model and the metaphor for reality, but it is a very important textbook case of a paradigm shift that can give us a lot of information about how these changes occur in science.

Many people, myself included, get so involved in the notion of the new age, the new culture. And yet when you look at our society today, it seems as if the big institutions – the corporations, the government – have an awful lot of momentum going; they seem so strong. I wonder, how do you see this change occurring?

FC: I see it as an evolution. I see these large institutions getting even larger and more centralized, but at the same time becoming hollow, and in the end they will somehow disintegrate and either change or decentralize or just disappear. I meet so many people inside these organizations who really have a feeling that things have to change, that they are not going to go on.

If you applied the biological model to a corporation as if it were an organism, do you think it would structure itself differently? Are decisions within an organism made any differently than they would be made within a corporation?

FC: A social system is not the same as an individual organism. It is a living system, but it is not an organism. It is more comparable maybe to an ecosystem; that would be a closer comparison. Certainly there are patterns in all living systems – in the individual organism and in the social system – that are very similar and can be studied. Also, the corporation has three levels; any kind of living system where humans are involved has three levels. There is the material level, where you have to talk about resources and money and all these things. Then there is the biological level, or the level of life and mind, and there you talk about the way people organize themselves; you talk about group dynamics and things like that. Then there is the level of consciousness, where you talk about values and ethics. To really understand a corporation and develop it successfully, you have to understand those three levels.

In any kind of organization, and especially in those that work for social change, the level of consciousness, where we talk about meaning and values and ethics, is the one that is really the driving force. If you don't understand that, then you will not understand anything of the organization. If you don't understand the level of meaning and ethics, you won't understand the peace movement or the ecology movement or the women's movement. And of course people who are conservative and in the old paradigm don't understand these movements.

I gather from your work with the Elmwood Institute that you expect these grassroots movements will be the vanguard of this new culture.

FC: Yes. In THE TURNING POINT I call this the rising culture, because they, in the models of Sorokin and Toynbee and others, will rise and eventually take over.

I would assume that they have to base themselves on a solid value system that incorporates internal psychological reality and integrates that with the material world.

FC: That's right. You can almost pinpoint it with a single word, and that word is life. It is the respect for life, the awe of life, the honoring of life, that has to inform our politics, our science, our technology, and our society.

TRANSFORMING HUMAN NATURE

with GEORGE LEONARD

George Leonard is author of a number of prophetic books on human possibilities and social change, including EDUCATION AND ECSTASY, THE TRANSFORMATION, THE ULTIMATE ATHLETE, THE SILENT PULSE, ADVENTURES IN MONOGAMY, and MASTERY. He is a former senior editor for LOOK magazine, a past president of the Association for Humanistic Psychology, and a member of the Board of Trustees of the Esalen Institute. He is also an aikido instructor and founder of Leonard Energy Training (LET), a practice inspired by aikido which offers alternative ways of dealing with everyday life problems.

In the face of our present global crises, this interview explores the question of whether humanity is capable of undertaking the fundamental change that is essential to our survival. Tracing the origins of civilization, Leonard expresses optimism that we can rise to the challenge and begin to realize our vast, untapped human potential.

People make the argument that the more things change, the more they stay the same – that if you look throughout history, we have always had armies, warfare, and oppressed people. You take a more optimistic view. You suggest that if we take a deeper, broader vision and look beyond recorded history, we can see that human beings have made fundamental changes.

GL: Exactly. People always say, "Man was born a builder; he'll keep on building until the whole country is paved over and every river runs in concrete channels. Man was born a fighter; he will have war and conflict and cynicism for all of time." Look at history and you will see that is very true. But as you suggest, we have to look beyond history. Let's open our canvas a little bit; let's look at a longer wave. Certainly what we call civilization, the beginning of the nation-state, didn't go back any further than seven thousand years ago, and probably not that long, whereas hominids, or certainly homo sapiens, have been around probably a million years. It keeps getting longer and longer with every new discovery, every archaeological find. But five thousand years is a wink in time.

Human nature evolved biologically. Our endocrine system, our nervous system, our skeletal and muscular systems, everything, developed while human beings were living for about a million years as hunters and gatherers. As far as we can tell from the archaeological record and from the surviving primitive hunting-and-gathering tribes and bands, in these bands there was no permanent leadership. There was no war as we know it, no standing armies, no bureaucracy, no lawyers. We've got plenty of lawyers now. The human animal was not created biologically for what we call civilization.

Wasn't it in the eighteenth century that Rousseau came up with the image of the noble savage?

GL: I'm kind of sorry he did, because he overdid it so much that now when you say the noble savage, it becomes a sign of naiveté – anyone who thinks of a savage as noble is naive. And that is probably true, because things are always complicated. We should not romanticize the primitive peoples. But in any case we can see that they really lived in what we would call a different human condition, and manifested a different "human nature" – I'll put quotes around that.

There was no specialization in a hunting-and-gathering tribe. Many things that we consider an absolute part of human life and human nature didn't even exist. And then a transformation did occur. Now, a good scientist might say we are being a little careless about the term, but evolution doesn't necessarily mean progress; it goes in both directions. Nevertheless, over these millennia we have seen increasing complexity evolve. We have seen the emergence of conditions in social organization which probably could not have been predicted from what came before.

The first great transformation I am speaking of in this time scale was the transformation between the hunting-and-gathering band and the tribal farmer. That was what we might call the agricultural revolution – when people began planting in the spring and harvesting in the fall. As Professor Skinner would say, that was the beginning of delayed reinforcement. That was a harsh thing for the human being to take, because previously, in hunting-and-gathering bands, individuals had lived in constant equilibrium and harmony with nature. They were part of nature.

You got to eat your food the day you killed it.

GL: That's right. Incidentally, in hunting-and-gathering bands, as far as we know, the food was split with geometric precision. There was no selfishness. Everything was divided up with precision, and in fact the hunter who made the kill was the last to eat.

The tribal farmers were a bit different. To bridge the gap between planting and harvesting, there were religious rites. That was perhaps the birth of serious religion as set apart from the rest of life. The Zuni Indians, for example, spent up to fifty percent of their waking hours in specifically religious ceremonies. The hunters and gatherers had religious ceremonies, but they were part of life. With tribal farmers, religion was split apart from the rest of life. It became specific and separate. Leadership was more by charisma than by heredity, and the society was organized around fraternities, or age-grade societies of men or of women. Now, interestingly enough, the tribal-farmer type of society was often matriarchal and matrilineal; the line went down from the woman rather than the man.

Then we had this huge event, which was the birth of civilization, and which a lot of people think was the only way it ever was. The best we can figure it, this occurred when an agricultural surplus developed, and more specifically, a surplus of cereal crops – the grains of the Middle East, the rice of the Far East, or, eighteen hundred years later, the maize of Mesoamerica. When you have a surplus of crops that you can store, what do you do with this surplus? You've got a problem now; now you need heavy-duty social organization. And wherever and whenever in the world such a surplus arrived, you found a number of developments, including huge and impressive ceremonial centers – great temples, pyramids, and so forth, the earliest WPA projects.

I suppose they also needed language and counting.

GL: Yes, writing. The first writing was used to keep records in the granaries where the grain was stored. They had lawyers, marketplaces, and the beginning of abstract money. They had slavery, territorial war, and standing armies. All of these developments, which we consider part of life, arose at that time – and also caste and classes. How do you deal with a surplus? You create a very small upper class that has access to all of the surplus, and parcel out the rest of it on a scarcity model to the other castes and classes. The development of caste and classes really came about because of a surplus of cereal crops – and also, I would like to say, the development of the human being as a specialized component of a social machine. A component of a machine has to be standardized, specialized, reliable, and predictable. This worked a tremendous hardship on the human individual. We are still doing that; but I think now we are beginning to emerge from it.

And at this point, with the great civilizations, the tribal ethic of being connected and integral and part of nature, of sharing things equally, broke down somehow.

GL: Absolutely. In fact, one of the real hallmarks of civilization is to be able to demonstrate your separateness from nature. On one of Caesar's main campaigns, he had to build a bridge. His troops said, "No, we can't cut down these trees to build a bridge, because they are sacred. They have spirits in them." Caesar himself took his ax and cut down the first tree. The others followed; they built the bridge, and we have been doing that ever since. Today we have bulldozers go to the top of beautiful hills in Marin County, level them out, and take the dirt down to fill up the Bay, and we never stop to think what we are doing to nature. A hunter and gatherer couldn't do such a thing. It would be like whipping his mother.

Freud in his book CIVILIZATION AND ITS DISCONTENTS *says that in order to have a stable civilization it is necessary to repress aspects of the human mind; and thus was born the unconscious mind in Freudian theory. Can we change that situation? Maybe our human nature isn't the way we have lived for the last five thousand years; but to what degree can we get back to our true nature?*

GL: We are talking about a pretty big thing. I wouldn't totally agree with Freud, but certainly with the beginning of the nation-states came the beginning of neurosis; or better, a constant dis-ease – separating ourselves from the present moment; separating ourselves from nature; feeling constantly uneasy within our own skins. The only remedy for this is hard work, going out and killing a few hundred Indians – you know, "The only good Indian is a dead Indian," that kind of thing.

Well, can human beings change? You called me an optimist. I would rather be a possibilist; I will say that it is possible. And it is not just that we would like to change; I would like to say that we must. The basic organizing principles of Civilization with a capital C, which emerged in the pyramid age, included, first of all, a constant growth in the consumption and production of energy. If you had to draw one curve which would be paradigmatic of civilized life, it would be this exponential curve; it goes up, up, up. The other thing was a push/push-back mode of human relations – you push me, I'll push you back. Conflict is inevitable, it is necessary, it is a part of life. Well, not necessarily; but can we make the transition? My question is, can we not make the transition?

I suppose that the fact that we are here speaking about it, and we are not the only ones, indicates that our civilization is self-aware enough to realize that the time is coming when we will either change or possibly face catastrophes beyond which we couldn't recover.

GL: That's right. My book *The Transformation*, which was published in 1972, was one of the first books that brought forward this thesis that we must change. I suggested there that we could have a catastrophe which would wake us up to the necessity of change. In the book I said that perhaps when the first ten thousand people die because of some kind of toxic waste, or pollution, or air pollution, the masters of our present civilization will simply say that science can work up better toxic control methods. It will probably take a death of about a hundred thousand.

We have already had ten thousand.

GL: That's right. This is very pessimistic, but we have already had Chernobyl: there will have to be a disaster which will kill maybe a million people. And then maybe we will wake up to the fact that the mode of organization that keeps developing the material world and the production and consumption of energy in an exponential way, simply reaches certain limits.

Dr. Jonas Salk wrote a book called *The Survival of the Wisest*. It was a very small book. It came out in 1973, one year after *The Transformation*. From an entirely different point of view, the biological, he came up with exactly the same conclusions – in fact, we shared a podium one time. He points out that every time in nature you see an exponential curve, like the growth of a population of fruit flies or bees or wolves or any form of life – whenever you see this, watch out. It is either going to curve off and moderate, or crash out.

You just can't sustain exponential growth.

GL: The system of civilized life, the social system, is running up against a larger constraint, which is the carrying capacity of the biosphere. Another basic organizing principle of civilized life in the nation-state is constant expansion – whether it is through colonization or through conquest of people nearby; but you see, we are running out of people to conquer.

Are we capable of making the necessary adjustments?

GL: Biologically, we certainly are. The human brain-body-mind-spirit system has such tremendous potential. We are mostly unused potential, and nobody can deny that. Some people have posited that the brain itself is improperly organized. I don't think that is true. The brain is mostly unused potential. Both the glory and the damnation of the human individual is its tremendous plasticity.

In Shakespearean tragedy, when confronted with an ultimately tragic, even hopeless situation, that is when the nobility of man is brought out; we reach inside ourselves and come up with the very best that is within us. Perhaps if we are faced with a potentially tragic situation today, we can rise to that challenge. Maybe we will fail; but maybe we will really find within us what it takes.

GL: We are so often conflict-oriented. I think a lot of people kind of hope that UFOs will come down on us. If we could really prove the existence of UFOs, then there would be an other – something that could be rallied against. Who would have thought that the U.S. and the U.S.S.R. might become allies? Who would have thought during World War II that we would become allies with Japan and Germany? Anybody who said that during World War II would have been taken away as certifiably mad. So these things are possible. Human nature can change.

I think the sixties, with all the insanity and shortsightedness and excesses, was kind of a pitiful and glorious attempt to make some kind of transformation. Take the hippie movement, which was a rejection of materialism; it was done by a lot of young people. That is one very important thing about transformation – we need people of all age groups. Just old people can't do it; just kids can't do it. You've got to get the wisdom and the conservatism of age, along with the dash and the impetus of youth.

I think a lot of people are pessimistic today because they got excited during the sixties, and then they felt, "Gee, nothing has happened; in fact, we have gone backwards. The country has become right-wing oriented; social change is not a possibility. We might as well just accept our fate and try and accumulate as much as we can for ourselves in the meanwhile." But I gather that you feel that we can't look at the sixties or the ensuing decades that way.

GL: First, it's not true. Now, politically and in education we have retrogressed since the sixties, and perhaps in some other things. But consider the race situation in 1960; one-fourth of the nation lived in apartheid. People of various races could not even drink water from the same fountain without perhaps losing their lives. Everything was segregated. Look at what is going on now. I mean, it's not perfect; there are some bad situations. But who would have thought of a black mayor of Atlanta, Georgia; or Miss Mississippi in the Miss U.S.A. contest being a black woman?

So we can say we have made gains in civil rights.

GL: We have made fantastic gains. As late as 1967 there was no women's movement. There were no rape crisis centers; there was no equal-opportunity employment; there was no affirmative action whatsoever; there were no battered wives' centers. Now, it is true we didn't get the ERA; we have a long way to go. But we are infinitely advanced from where we were in the glorious Summer of Love in 1967 that was supposed to be so revolutionary. Ecology – in 1967 the word didn't exist. The environmental movement was simply a conservation movement; they were just trying to conserve natural areas. The Sierra Club's membership in 1960 was sixteen thousand; it is now four hundred and eight thousand. In almost every aspect of our lives, we have progressed far beyond the sixties, and we are still dissatisfied. When the extraordinary becomes realized, it becomes commonplace. We take things for granted, and we say, "Oh, but this is not very good." What we've got to do is at least celebrate and acknowledge the gains that we have made since 1960.

What do you think will be the leading edge of transformation in the coming decade?

GL: Well, first of all is the environmental movement, and the ecology movement, the whole way we live – can we coexist with this planet? The human potential movement, or rather, the full development of human resources; they are tremendously underdeveloped. We are running out of material resources to develop; and we're getting more and more pollution and toxic waste associated with the development of physical resources. Human resources are undeveloped; and they are almost infinite. We could start a program for the development of human potential that would create adventures that would make the winning of the West seem pale indeed.

Really we have no idea what the limit of the human being is. If we truly were to experience our full nature, it would be something very surprising to us.

GL: It would scare the hell out of us. It's homeostasis, naturally – society might fly apart if all the human beings started really manifesting all their human potential. Therefore there has to be a certain conservative element. But we can certainly manifest a lot more than we are now. So I would say that is a great area for development.

Also, in the United States certainly, we are going to be beset with a new kind of equal-opportunity challenge – not so much with blacks as with Hispanics and the Asian people, Pacific Rim people. We are going to see what equal opportunity really means.

What are the forces that have held back transformation? Why is there this intransigence at a time of need? Why didn't things move even faster, when they seemed as if they were about to?

GL: Every self-regulating system – whether it is a tadpole, a frog, an individual, a family, or a nation – has a built-in homeostasis. Any change is threatening. And that is true, you know. If your blood temperature or blood salinity changed by ten percent, you would be in big trouble. So whenever any self-regulating system – let's say now a nation, a society – recognizes any real, essential change – and it can be a subconscious recognition, kind of a national subconscious – it will resist that change and fight against it, whether the change is for what we would call the good, or for the bad.

In other words, even if a change is absolutely essential, there will be a force of homeostasis working against that change.

GL: Exactly. I often ask my lecture audiences, "How many of you have at some time made a New Year's resolution, or some other kind of resolution – a good resolution, something that will make you feel better? In fact, you do feel better; and then you backslide." Everybody holds their hands up. Why? It is a natural tendency of every self-regulating organism to remain in the same state. You have to work in increments. So if an idea comes along, and after a while it is resisted severely, it could be for two reasons. One is because it's a lousy idea, and another is because it is a damn good idea. In other words, a really good idea will create the most resistance. Some of the ideas of the sixties really scared people tremendously.

Well, the people who were in their early twenties back in the 1960s are now moving into their forties.

GL: Mid-life crisis, when they reevaluate things. The thirties and early forties are a time of accumulation, materialism, nesting, getting everything together. Now they are having this reflective period: "OK, we've got this Porsche; we've got this BMW. But I don't feel so good. Maybe it wasn't worth it. Let's reevaluate." The nineties are going to be a time when that huge baby-boom cohort begins reevaluating the purpose of life. It is going to be a very thoughtful time. I don't think it's going to be a flamboyant time, because first of all the sixties were a time of tremendous financial affluence; we had enough extra money to make mistakes. We are not going to in the nineties. It is going to be very spare and very disciplined; it will have more of a Zen quality to it. It's going to be less noisy. But I think it is going to be a very significant time of transformation and change.

ANCIENT TRADITION IN MODERN SOCIETY

WITH GAY GAER LUCE, PH.D.

 *Gay Luce is a transformational teacher. With Jean Houston she designed and ran the Human Capacities Program and the Mystery Schools. She now directs and teaches in the Nine Gates Mystery School. She is founder of SAGE, a holistic actualization program for older people, and has been a consultant to the National Institute of Mental Health and the President's Scientific Advisory Committee. She is the author of BODY TIME, SLEEP, YOUR SECOND LIFE, and the forthcoming LONGER LIFE, MORE JOY.*

Ancient societies cultivated a sensitivity to the environment, the body and the inner workings of the mind which is often lost in modern life. In this interview Gay Luce describes the benefits of learning from the native teachings of many cultures and times, connecting with our roots to build a healthier, integrated lifestyle.

I n the Nine Gates Mystery School, you are involved in reintroducing ancient techniques into modern life. You work with shamans and spiritual teachers from many different cultures, and you find that they offer something of value and depth that we can't find with all the quick fixes in our modern culture.

GL: Absolutely, and it is very practical. These traditions evolved at a time when there wasn't a separation between birth and cosmos, between daily life and what is sacred – when people didn't consider that you could cut knowledge in half, and ignore the spiritual side of anything. There isn't anything that doesn't have a spiritual essence, and what these traditions are doing is working with life and our daily problems on a more causal basis. It is much more fundamental, and very useful.

It's a little hard to describe, because I now take it for granted, and I realize that not everybody does. For example, breathing techniques abound. There probably isn't a culture among the ancient mystery schools, or even among any of the traditions today, that doesn't involve attention on breath as a way of changing consciousness and changing health. Some of the things that come up are so simple. For example, if you pay attention to a part of your body, especially a place where there is an energy center like the sole of your foot, wherever attention goes, energy flows; there is a greater flow of energy. This is a fundamental teaching in learning how to heal. It is also fundamental in learning how to sustain energy. For example, Native Americans and many other people walk barefoot on the ground; well, the ground is a source of a tremendous amount of energy. We have these holes, these vortices, in our feet, that just suck up the energy, if we are willing to use them.

And yet the modern view is almost the opposite – that your body works best when you don't notice it at all. The body is not a thing to be felt, except when it's sick. Then you go see a doctor.

GL: We also think our body is very small. We think of our body as in this physical confine, instead of being inside a much larger body – a body of radiant energy, which is also our body. If we thought of our bodies as energy, we would suddenly begin to work with ourselves at a level that is very deep. For example, modern psychiatry and psychology are coming around to the point of view that a lot of disease is caused by one's state of mind. This is a very ancient understanding; it is thousands of years old. People have understood, I would guess since almost the earliest times, that if you are in a bad state of mind, something must happen in the body – that thought and energy come before the congealed or condensed form, which is matter, and that if you shift the mind and you learn how to pay attention, you shift what is going on inside the body.

The ancient people weren't able to fall back on technology, as we do – to the point perhaps where we rely on it too much. They had to use the mind; in a way it was all they had. They had nature, of course, but they didn't have science or technology, the way we do.

GL: They had spiritual science, and it really was a science – that is, knowing exactly how to draw breath up the meridians and around and down. For example, the books of Mantak Chia describe a Taoist breathing exercise that is very healing. This is found all through Asia, and it is related to what we know about acupuncture and about healing.

This is the notion that with each breath you circulate the chi, or life energy, through the body.

GL: Yes. There are many thousands of exercises, each with a particular effect. Some people know how to levitate; other people know how to send energy out through their fingers. In my earlier days, when I played around, trying to figure out how people understood these things, Erik Peper and I did some exploring, and we found karate experts who could drive a nail through the muscle of the forearm and suspend a bucket of water on it without bleeding. As long as this chi energy was going in a certain direction, with a certain force of thought, there would be no wound of the skin. Then they would take the water bucket off, take the nail out, and there would be no sign on the skin that anything had happened. I remember one funny scene in our living room back then, when a young man from Ecuador sat in front of a BBC camera and said, "I'm going to pull this pin through my cheek" – he was talking the whole time – "Would you like it to bleed or not?" And it didn't bleed.

I suppose the fact that we are so astonished by this suggests that we in our modern society really have lost touch with something.

GL: We think of ourselves as very puny, and much more rigid than we are. That is a state of mind. Think of all the people who have learned just recently that they can bend spoons or walk on fire. The limits are in our minds, a lot of them. Now, there are some limits, in the sense that we are part of a whole, and what is really unhealthy is that we don't see that. I think that is where the ancient traditions were really different. People didn't levitate in order to have power in ancient time. Today it gets to be kind of a parlor trick, talking about things like that.

The kinds of things we are doing in Nine Gates are a little more down-to-earth than that. There are ways in which we can begin to be self-conscious about our communication and know that our communication is direct and clear, so that we begin to undo misunderstandings. There are ways in which we can evoke the energy of our hearts to heal each other, actually use emotional hygiene. You know, there are other cultures that are far more civilized than we are in the sense that they don't spray their emotions over each other. They understand that emotions have to be released, and that this is a compressed energy, a labeled energy that has to be given some outlet, and that it is worth looking at. But instead of saying, "You did such and such and you're doing this to me," they say, "I am now going to feel this energy, see these images, and allow this to transform by changing it. It has nothing whatsoever to do with you."

In other words, if I'm angry, rather than take it out on the nearest person, as is often common in our culture, I might hold it until an appropriate moment when I can be alone with myself, and then really process my anger.

GL: And there are specific things you can do; there are a lot of these ancient techniques. You can use breath to charge up, you can do postures as in bioenergetics and in ancient Tibetan traditions, or you can use movements and postures with the breath, so that the emotions begin to come up and through. And then there is a magical moment when all of a sudden the anger turns to sheer energy or excitement, and you go, "Aha!" and you begin to understand that you held that anger in place with a belief, and that you can change that belief voluntarily.

I imagine that some people are driven by anger most of their lives because they haven't allowed themselves to process it to the point of finding that magic moment you've just described.

GL: We all can do that for ourselves. Certainly it is helpful to work with a therapist on problems that one can't see at all, but after a while that's not necessary. I mean, when I go home and I am with my mother and we get into a wrangle, I realize now that all my life I used to blame her. Now I just go in the bathroom and do a little charge-up and release, and suddenly I can be in a conversation that used to be very painful for me, and I'm comfortable. I don't have to be miserable about it. I wish I had learned this a lot earlier in my life.

You seem to see yourself as a child of the planet. I get the sense that you're comfortable drawing on all ancient cultures, as if they are all part of your natural heritage, rather than just one or two select cultures based on your ethnic background.

GL: All is a big word. I wish it were all. I haven't even begun to taste a few of them, but I have been very enriched by the disparateness. For example, for one of our first sessions we have started to work with the Celtic tradition. I had no idea I could experience such depth in English words – that in fact here is a tradition that links us to all of nature, the nature of the triple goddess of creation, which is coming off our tongues at all times.

We speak a language based on ancient Celtic.

GL: Right. The letters all have very deep meanings. They call them oghams, or alphabets, that the bards knew; they were the great prophets and seers. For example, if you say "Hello," you are saying, "I honor God" – L being the letter of God, and O of initiation, H the honorific for what is holy. If you say, "Hi," you are honoring shortness, death. Hello is like namaste – it is an honoring of resting in the initiation of God.

This is the best argument of all for us to search out and return to our understanding of ancient cultures. No matter how much we get involved in this veneer of civilization, everything that we are doing is built on this ancient world and on the ancient understanding, even in something so basic as saying hello.

GL: Padma Sambhava in the seventh century predicted that "when iron birds shall fly and men and women wear the same clothes, the dharma will be brought to the land of the red man in the West."

He was the great Tibetan saint.

GL: That's right; he was the man who brought Buddhism to Tibet, where ancient people were very tuned in to the hologram – the understanding that all of us are a piece of the entirety, and that if we get some decent focus on it and we get good definition, we can see through all time and all things. I mean, "Iron birds shall fly" – what could have seemed stranger in the seventh century?

In other words, the sense that we have of linear time, and of separateness, is a provincial way of looking at things compared to the ancient view.

GL: Look at how we treat death. Instead of the entrance and exit to this life being sacred and valued moments, we avoid death, we anesthetize it, we try to put it out of sight – instead of celebrating it and making it as beautiful as we can. Think of the incredible knowledge of the Tibetan tradition, for example.

We try to make it antiseptic. The Tibetans used to meditate in graveyards.

GL: Right. But you don't have to do that to sit with a dying friend or parent, and do it in a way that makes the experience the most beautiful and deep sharing that is possible in a lifetime. Many of the things we avoid are the best experiences we will ever have. I had a near-death experience, an automobile accident, a couple of years ago, that was one of the high points. I shall never forget what I learned in the two months of recovery. That was the most exquisite experience. I also was privileged, because of SAGE, to be with a lot of people who were dying.

We should mention that SAGE is an organization that you founded, dealing with elderly people.

GL: To let them be all they are. Once people don't have an ego investment in being some particular way, it is a whole lot easier. One of the reasons I did SAGE was that people told me that you couldn't do certain things after a certain age. You can change as much at eighty, if you are ready for it, if you are ripe for it.

I was thinking about how we eat, for example; that's not my best point, because I must say I still eat a little sacrilegiously. The fact is that as we change our consciousness, we can make eating a very different act. What's ironic is that here we are with this terrific technology, with availability of a lot of food, and we are acting very unconsciously, both in the way we farm and treat the ground and the plants, and also in the way we prepare it and eat it. I think all of this is going to change, and is changing.

What is the alternative?

GL: The alternative is to become more conscious of what we are eating, how it tastes. I like to eat with people in silence. When I am working with groups I very often like to have silence, or ask people to feed each other. If we actually have to pay attention to what's going in our mouths instead of talking and shoveling it in automatically, there is an appreciation for what it means to be nurtured, and the various elements that are coming to us through our food, just as they are through television or music.

We are very lucky to have access to all this; think of the wonderful music in all the different traditions that we can hear. These are all messages, just as our very ancient language, English, is a message. It is very thick with dimensionality. When I started working with my name in the Celtic tradition, I suddenly realized that it brought up in me all the qualities that I had been trying to repress, and gave me an opportunity to not only look at them but appreciate them.

What's an example of one of these qualities you were trying to repress?

GL: Well, Gay for example – I always thought of Gay as a name for lightness and joy. But it also means the wild boar – fierce, persistent, brave, but ruthless. The whole name means something like, "I am a wild boar who is pregnant with the killer of death." That is, "I am ruthless in using my persistence and ferocity to bring forth something that goes beyond death."

I never pictured you that way. That's a far cry from your persona.

GL: Or what I like to think of as my persona. But in point of fact, there is that aspect to me, and it has certainly been brought about by doing Nine Gates, because to dream up a program and do it once is one thing; but to actually have a school and a community growing, and all the burgeoning things that happen out of that, is turning me into a general.

One thing that you seem to be suggesting is that the ancient traditions were more in touch with the darker side of human nature and the need to integrate and process it, rather than to separate it out and pretend as if we didn't have this other side.

GL: Exactly. They were much more whole; they had much more power. As a matter of fact, we just did a session on Tantra, and I was thinking that Tantra is really important in daily life. The word comes from an old Sanskrit word that means loom, and it means seamlessness of polarities – bringing the two together.

Dark and light, good and evil are really one.

GL: And when you bring them together, then you have illumination. In some of the ancient Tibetan and Hindu practices, the sexual union of male and female was used not for quick release, but rather for illumination. What you do by bringing polarities together is increase the charge. When you increase the charge in a disciplined way, you create a release that is amazing. I did this once a long time ago with SAGE, simply having people lie foot to foot. It wouldn't matter whether it was finger to finger. What happened was you had two energies coming together, and as long as people put enough disciplined attention on what was happening with their feet, it was an orgasmic and illuminating experience. So the concept of Tantra is very important in our lives, and we also need to do it, in a sense, within ourselves – that is, in our relationship to parts of ourselves. The ruthless part of me and the generous, kind part of me have to come together. When they come together there is real integration. And I think that these ancient traditions are teaching us incredible techniques for living.

One of the ancient traditions I know you have had some experience with is the Native American Church and their use of the peyote ritual.

GL: That is phenomenal. To understand ourselves and allow the things that are in us to come out and be cleansed, before we seek visions – that is very rapid psychiatry. Native Americans have understood all along how to take this sacrament and push individuals with it. It is not always very pleasant.

People often get nauseous.

GL: Quite nauseous; and the sicker they get, the more they get pushed by the wise priest, and a really good shaman can do in one night the kind of therapy that might take therapists a year to do. I just saw a transformation the other night that was extraordinary; I have never seen so much love, or a family so balanced by a process so seemingly simple. We passed the talking stick and sat around the fire; but what happened was that each individual who took the sacrament was in a sense pushed by it, because it has properties that will bring up whatever seems to be repressed. To do this in a supportive way with a wise priest allows family therapy to take place really rapidly.

You mean, when you look inside at what it is that's making you nauseous, at some point you realize it's something I'm holding onto, it's something I'm clutching inwardly.

GL: It doesn't always come out the way it does in our psychological phrasing, but it gets expressed. And a wise priest takes it from the level of psychology into the level of the sacred – that is, it is no longer me, the personal Gay, that is struggling with this little problem. All of a sudden something opens within me, and I feel my connectedness.

It seems logical in a way, since we live in a historical society at least five thousand years old. It seems unlikely that something as important and as basic as psychotherapy would have only been developed in the twentieth century.

GL: Absolutely; it is impossible. Look at Tibetan psychology, which preceded our own modern psychology by fourteen hundred years, or Chinese. I'm wearing an Egyptian symbol of Maat, the goddess with her wings spread, the goddess of truth and consciousness. Look at what the Egyptians had to teach us about architecture, about proportion, long before Greece – about the way that geometry affects our psyches with ancient truths, like the ancient pyramid that we have on the dollar bill.

In a way, we have not necessarily surpassed the Egyptians, when it comes to creating architecture that has the power of inspiring and ennobling human beings.

GL: And that has proportions that are very calculated. There was a science to it; the temples were calculated to affect the minds of the initiates. The hieroglyphics were a language that was dimensional, and that reached farther into what we call the unconscious, or the right brain, than our linear word system. English is not really unidimensional; it's not Flatland, even though it looks like that on the page.

We've been accustomed to speak it in a way that must seem very flat and hollow, even compared to Elizabethan times.

GL: I think that we are in the time of burgeoning now, where these traditions are coming forth. We are going to begin to have respect for our own language, for our bodies, for our breath, hopefully for the world around us, for plant and animal life, and for those people who go into their own consciousness and begin to have these experiences. Some of the experiences that I have had in the Tibetan tradition have led me to understand the words "sentient universe" – meaning that the chair I sit in, and the chrome on my watch, the silver on my ring, are all sentient. Even things that we call inanimate are inhabited by the spirit and by that ineffable organization that creates everything.

It would seem that you are talking about a new renaissance; and this appreciation that you have for the vitality and the spirit of ancient traditions is truly a renaissance idea in our times.

GL: Hopefully we are going to have a renaissance. When I look at people younger than myself, a new generation of people coming in, they take for granted the things that I now need to divest myself of. I started by learning biofeedback and quite mechanical ways of changing. Now I need to start out from where they are, and I do think there is a real renaissance happening.

THE CULT OF INFORMATION

WITH THEODORE ROSZAK, PH.D.

One of America's foremost social critics, Theodore Roszak is Professor of History at California State University at Hayward. He is the author of a number of influential books including THE MAKING OF A COUNTER CULTURE, WHERE THE WASTELAND ENDS, and THE CULT OF INFORMATION.

As an educator, Dr. Roszak warns that our real educational and cultural needs are in danger of becoming lost in the erroneous fascination with the information-processing model of the mind. He delivers a scathing indictment of the over-selling of computer and high-tech ideology to the American public.

T*ell me, what do you have against information?*

TR: Well, I'll tell you a little story that illustrates the problem my book, *The Cult of Information*, is addressed to. A few years back, I was in my office at school, which I was sharing with a professor from the English Department. A student was talking with the English professor about an assignment that had to do with a poem by Robert Frost. I was vaguely aware of the conversation, and I heard my colleague say to the student, "I want you to try to draw all the information out of this poem." She used that phrase several times; this was supposed to be the approach to the assignment. When the student left, I asked her, "What information are you talking about? I know the poem, and I don't think there is much information in it." She said, "Well, I mean the metaphors and the similes and the symbols." I said, "You call all of that information?" She stopped a moment, thought, and said, "Yes." It suddenly struck me that I had been hearing the word information used again and again in various contexts, in more and more ambitious, and perhaps even global ways. And it struck me that information is becoming the "God word" of our time.

It should be pretty obvious why that is happening – because we live in an age when some of the most powerful elements in our culture are the invention of the computer, and research and development on the computer. The computer is an information-processing machine, and if you want to sell a lot of computers in a society, you have to convince people that information is terribly important, and give it the most ambitious definition possible, so that it covers more and more ground and becomes seemingly more and more vital.

It struck me that there is a problem with this sort of development, especially in the field of education, whether you are dealing with kids in kindergarten or students in the university. Certain distinctions are being obscured that are basic to any culture, and among them is the distinction between information and knowledge and judgment and wisdom. These are vital distinctions. They have a kind of hierarchical arrangement, and some are more important than others. Now, as a matter of fact, information is perhaps the least important of them all. And to let the word information simply spread until it covers all intellectual categories seemed to me potentially disastrous for a student's ability to think.

It struck me, as I thought more and more about this, that as a matter of fact what is far more central to what I call in my book the art of thinking is the mastery of ideas. Cultures are based upon ideas, and if you think a moment, you may realize that many of the most important ideas around which our culture is based have no information in them whatsoever. They are not based on information. The ideas are of an entirely different intellectual character.

Let me give you an example of a very familiar idea the importance of which all of us recognize immediately. Take the idea, "All men are created equal." That's an idea we inherit out of the eighteenth century. It is absolutely basic to our political life. It is the basis of our jurisprudence. It has launched revolutions throughout the world. It is a powerful idea. And there is absolutely no information in that idea.

It would be hard to imagine a more powerful idea.

TR: Right. And you can't imagine any body of fact that is related to that idea. So if you ask what that idea is based upon, it is based upon something I would call experience, and especially moral vision. The idea was not created by people who had done research on the subject of human equality; rather it was based upon the moral insight of a generation that had come to find great sympathy for democratic politics, for the natural rights of man. These were the great objectives and goals of that generation, and out of that was born this powerful idea that all men are created equal.

The longer you think about it, the more you realize that what I call the master ideas of any culture have almost no relationship to information: "The Tao that can be named is not the true Tao," "There is but one God, and Allah is his prophet," and on and on. The great religious ideas, the great theological ideas, the great moral ideas have no relationship to information whatsoever.

But science as a whole has never really pretended to offer moral or religious teachings, has it?

TR: Even the great ideas of science usually start as visions, insights, and theories; and once they become theories they sometimes will help generate information. I think most scientists would now agree that you don't create great scientific ideas by putting pieces of information together the way computers put bits of information together. Initially there is some sort of a vision or an insight into the operations of nature. Out of this comes a theory. The theory then directs attention in such a way that it might help people find information that perhaps corroborates the idea. In other words, the relationship between ideas and information is exactly the opposite of what people in the computer sciences seem to believe – namely, it is ideas that generate information; it is not information that generates ideas. And to lose track of that fact is to court disaster in our intellectual lives.

I wonder if you are not putting it a little too strongly, though. Isn't it somewhat reciprocal, actually?

TR: Sure, there is a reciprocity; but you mustn't lose track of the importance of the initial idea, which is often born of experience, and experience is not something that easily reduces to facts and figures. In fact, experience is so deeply metaphysical that it would be difficult for me to define it for you. But we all know what our experience is. It seems to me that what people need to operate in the world successfully, whether they are kids or grownups, is the ability to discriminate among ideas. And what I call the cult of information, which is so focused on information processing and the information-processing model of the human mind popular among computer scientists and people in artificial intelligence research – this evaluation of information as the supreme element in any culture is a very misleading idea. And so I wrote the book primarily as sort of a humanist's approach to the computer and its proper place in our society, and especially in education.

In academic psychology today, the information-processing model of the mind is very big.

TR: Oh, it is one of the biggest ideas going. Let me show you how involuted or tricky this becomes. The very suggestion that the mind is an information-processing instrument is an idea; so it is almost impossible ever to get behind ideas. Ideas are what generate research. They are what finally produce bodies of fact, bodies of evidence. The computer itself is an idea, based upon certain conceptions of numbers and how they can be manipulated. The information-processing conception of thought is an idea, but it is only one idea about the human mind. I tend to think of it as a very poor idea in comparison to the ideas of Plato or Aristotle or Spinoza, who also had ideas about the mind.

But all of these are ideas, and it seems to me that the essence of education is to teach students how to deal with ideas, and especially big ideas or master ideas, as I refer to them, because not all ideas are good ideas; a lot of ideas are bad ideas or toxic ideas.

Even the master ideas might be toxic.

TR: There are cultures, political movements, or social movements that have built themselves around master ideas that are deeply harmful, vicious, negative, and destructive – ideas of a master race, for example. All of these are ideas.

I would challenge people to reflect upon what it means to think, and I suspect that they will discover that for the most part what they are doing is manipulating ideas. Now, they may be doing that well, or they may be doing it poorly, but it seems to me that the function of education is to teach people how to manipulate ideas well – how to compare them with one another, how to discriminate among them, and perhaps even how to invent their own ideas. So it seems to me that it is a major liability of our computerized culture that we are vastly overevaluating the importance of information, which seems to be the lowest level at which the mind functions. Now, the mind does process information; for example, looking up a telephone number is essentially processing information. Buying a plane ticket, choosing which airline to use, which flight to take, and so on, is clearly information processing. That is why things like looking up phone numbers or choosing which flight to take have been computerized, and properly so. I have no dispute about the value of the computer as an information-processing machine. We need to process a lot of information in our lives, and so it is good to have a machine that does that. But to call everything the mind does information processing seems to me deeply misleading and simply warps the art of thinking. It would be a great danger to teach students, for the sake of some manipulation of a computer, that their minds are essentially computers and that when they think they are processing information.

When you describe these master ideas, my sense is that they are not based on information in terms of little bits, but rather on a holistic perception, an intuition of the nature of things as a whole.

TR: Yes, and that might be what I am calling experience, which is a broad, sloppy term that is extremely difficult to define, but we all know what it is. We shouldn't be talked out of the fact that we all experience things; and we tend to experience them in a kind of broad, holistic way. We experience events in our lives; we learn things out of the process of everyday living – out of meeting people, raising children, walking through the world, doing a certain job. All of this becomes the experience out of which we draw ideas, or the various sensibilities that allow us to respond to the ideas we hear – political ideas, religious ideas, and so on. But that is essentially what is going on when we do the most important kind of thinking in our lives. And while the computer is a very valuable instrument for numerous uses, it seems to be one of its great liabilities that it is being overevaluated as a model of the human mind; and in that respect it is doing great pedagogical or educational damage.

I imagine there are many people today who quite literally think of themselves as computers.

TR: You know, if you were to trace the history of the word *information*, you would come to a crucial point where a remarkable coincidence occurred. At about the same time that the computer was gaining visibility on the social scene in the late forties and early fifties, there was a breakthrough in biology

– the discovery of DNA. At that time the biologists were casting around for a model, a paradigm by the light of which they might better understand the function of the double helix of DNA. And they reached out and took the cybernetics information-transfer technology as their model. We now know that might not be an adequate model at all of what actually goes on in the genetic material; but at the time it was an extremely tempting connection to make. And out of that came the image of DNA as a biocomputer – that it has a little string of bits, and somehow if you added up all the bits you got an organism. This lent some credibility to the idea that DNA was an information-processing mechanism; and since we then believed that DNA was the secret of life, it was like saying that information was the secret of life.

It is quite interesting, because this is exactly what happened in the seventeenth century when scientists were looking for a model of the universe and came up with the clock. They said we lived in a clockwork universe, and God was the great watchmaker in the sky. As of the early 1950s, it is almost as if the great watchmaker became the great cosmic programmer, and it became conventional for people to refer to their thinking, or the structure of the genetic material, as being programmed. They should bear in mind this is nothing but an image or a paradigm or a model, and it may or may not be adequate.

Where does it break down?

TR: Well, I'm not enough of a biologist to investigate it, but there have been many findings in contemporary biological research that make it questionable whether this is a good model. If you ask, "Where is the program in this computer called DNA?" that is a very difficult question to answer. So the model may not be a good one.

Historically, however, as of the early fifties, that was a crucial if fortuitous connection – between a field called cybernetics, which had developed independently, and the new biology. At that point the word information took on a luster and a prestige that it had never had before because it seemed to be the very secret of life itself.

Of course the computer industry was quite willing to go along with the idea – yes, information is the secret of life; it is the key to the universe; you need more and more of it; buy a computer. You might almost say that from the fifties on we have had a kind of merchandising project going, the main purpose of which has been to sell computers for more and more uses. And one of the ways you do that is by expanding the meaning, the prestige, the luster of information, and convincing people you need more and more of it, and if you don't know how to manipulate an information-processing machine, you are not a full-fledged citizen of the twentieth century – you won't get a job, you won't make it through school, and so on.

In other words, there is a subtle conspiracy between the world of merchandising and advertising and people who would have us believe in certain mechanistic, materialistic models – that genes can explain our biology, or perhaps that neurons and nerve firing can explain the mind.

TR: I wouldn't call it a conspiracy so much as a marriage of convenience between a couple of different developments in our society that have led more and more people to accept an almost global conception of information as somehow being the secret of life and of the mind – the mind is an information-processing machine; the genetic material is an information-processing machine. This has become so widespread and so commonplace that we don't even reflect upon it anymore. The purpose of my book is to get people to reflect upon exactly what the value and status of information is in their lives, and to recognize that it has a very low level of importance. There are other levels at which the mind functions – and we can't even categorize all those levels, because they may go up to metaphysical insight, ESP, God knows what – but the mind is vastly larger than its information-processing level. Clearly, there are other levels of life that don't respond to information processing.

Just think for a moment the way the news of the day is reported to us; think of our politics – how much is simply the regurgitation of information, of data, numbers, and statistics. We go through elections where it seems that the most vital element to reporters and the public at large is polling. Polling is something that computers do. We place the computer at the center of the entire process and reduce the electoral process to what the computer does so well, which is to generate facts, figures, numbers, statistics. In the midst of all of this what gets lost are issues; and issues are based upon ideas, which in turn lead people to ask questions – questions about justice, fairness, decency, sanity, and so on. These should be the true subjects of debate in our political life. Instead these subjects get swamped in an outpouring of raw data, of information, as if that were the most important thing taking place.

This is a style of the times. We fancy ourselves an age of information in the same way that our forebears, I think much more commendably, thought of themselves as an age of reason. I would much prefer to be in an age of faith, an age of discovery, an age of reason, than an age of information. But it has become the style of the times to try to regurgitate as much information as possible. I think that is one of the things that we find lacking in the general quality of our public life, especially. We are inundated, glutted, with information; whereas often what we need to get a grip on the world we live in are a few good ideas, a few good issues to argue about. And that has nothing to do with mastering information.

In the educational process, what we should do is start with something very traditional – the great books, the great ideas; we should teach students how to handle great ideas which are found in great books. What we need is good old-fashioned literacy rather than computer literacy. It seems to me that computer literacy can wait, because it deals with something much less important in our intellectual life – namely, the collection, storage, and processing of data. That, it seems to me, should play very little part in a true education.

The idea that every student needs to know computer programming seems off base to you.

TR: Yes, and doing that simply crowds out far more vital things that students need to learn. In the modern world, the world we live in from day to day, it is a mistake to believe that you need a bigger and bigger electronic filing cabinet called a computer to keep track of all the data. What you need are ideas that tell you what data matter and what data don't matter. And to sort your way through the jungle of facts, what you need are some good ideas about the world. Education should start with the importance of those ideas; and those things are to be learned in good old traditional ways – out of books, art, music.

What about the current crises we are facing – overpopulation, the potential of thermonuclear war, starvation worldwide? Are we creating some of these problems because we are not focusing on the basic values, because we are losing ourselves in this sea of information?

TR: I'll tell you an excellent example of what the overevaluation of information and computers may lead to. It is now a serious proposition that we should entrust the survival of this country to a weapons system called the Strategic Defense Initiative. This has a great deal of technology associated with it, and at the heart of it there will be computers – the most elaborate, the most densely programmed computers the mind can imagine. What we will be entrusting to those machines, as supposedly thinking machines that supposedly possess something called artificial intelligence, are certain judgments about war and peace, and therefore about human survival. This is far beyond anything that human beings should ever entrust to machines.

We already have computers monitoring our defenses as they exist now.

TR: Oh yes. We are more and more prepared to allocate to those machines crucial judgments about our lives. And if you ask why that is happening, I would suggest that the general public has been sold on the idea that those machines are indeed capable of thinking – that thinking is information processing; that a machine that has a lot of data in it and processes it very quickly is actually thinking, and therefore it can be entrusted with tasks that properly should belong to a human mind. I have read lesson plans for kids that will try to convince them that computers have better minds than they have because they don't make mistakes and they always have the right answer. That is a fatal thing to teach children, because the computer operates only at a certain very minimal level of thinking. The art of thinking vastly transcends that, and when you get to the level of great judgments – in politics, law, social policy – what you need is a fully developed human mind, capable of dealing with issues and ideas. That is far beyond what a computer can do.

We hear from the artificial intelligence establishment that eventually computers will be almost human.

TR: Eventually, they say. In my book I take great issue with the people in artificial intelligence on the grounds that that field has been around since the 1950s, and it has been promising successes, breakthroughs, ever since then – within three years, five years, always just around the corner, right at hand – but these have not yet been accomplished. The field is so filled with an overweening self-confidence – perhaps because it is so richly funded by the government, by the military, by the corporations – that it has been tempted to make promises it cannot fulfill. Artificial intelligence, it seems to me, is one of the most vastly inflated and oversold fields of study in our society today.

Where would you redirect all of that funding? Would you just see it go into the humanities?

TR: Oh, I don't think just into the humanities. But in the field of education, I would simply fund a curriculum that was a little more traditional, that stayed closer to old-fashioned forms of literacy, and that sought to put children as gracefully and as early as possible in touch with the great ideas on which their culture is based, that would ask them to probe those ideas, discuss them, compare them with one another, and reach personal judgments about the great ideas of the culture they live in. I don't see that computers have any role whatsoever to play in that. What we need are sensitive teachers, great books, great art, great music, great science. All of these things play a role in teaching children how to cope with the richness of the ideas they inherit out of their tradition.

COSMOLOGY AND PHILOSOPHY

EVOLUTION: THE GREAT CHAIN OF BEING

WITH ARTHUR M. YOUNG

Philosopher Arthur M. Young is the inventor of the Bell Helicopter and founder of the Institute for the Study of Consciousness. His theory of process, which integrates science with ancient teachings, is elaborated in his books THE REFLEXIVE UNIVERSE and THE GEOMETRY OF MEANING.

Using examples from ancient myths, Young traces the universal pattern of the descent of spirit into matter, and its ascent back to spirit. He distinguishes the physical evolution of the body from the evolution of the individual human soul, a process whose end point has not yet been reached in human evolution.

E*xplain generally what you mean by evolution in the biological sense, in the personal sense, and in the cosmological sense.*

AY: Speaking in terms of biological evolution, animals have developed remarkable powers. An owl uses radar; a bat uses sonar. But man isn't very good at any of these specialties. He makes up for it by making tools. He moves from being something to having it; in other words, instead of being a bird he can have the use of an airplane, or instead of specializing in rapid running he can get an automobile. He doesn't specialize anymore, and that means his being is freed so that it can devote itself to, shall we say, metaphysics – something beyond the immediate needs of sustaining himself. Well, what kind of evolution is that? It's not accounted for by Darwinian evolution; it's not accounted for by evolution of species. It means that there must be some way to account for the increasing competence that we learn as persons. I went through agonies when I first got interested in Buddhism and Zen – reading these remarkable teachings telling me about the egolessness of things, and the egolessness of persons. I just couldn't understand it. What was this helicopter I was making? Did it have no selfhood? Did I have no selfhood? It was a very difficult pill to swallow. I gradually began to recognize then that the helicopter wasn't a thing; it was something you moved toward, it was a goal. Any particular model was already obsolete as soon as you'd made it, and you'd keep moving on. So the real thing is the dynamic that's pushing it on, and this form is something that's peeled off and thrown away when you're finished with it.

When you speak about evolution, you go back beyond biological evolution – beyond the molecule or the atom, don't you?

AY: Well, the whole point of my effort to deal with the problem is to look at the grand sweep of evolution. It's often called the Great Chain of Being, but the Great Chain of Being doesn't include the lower stages – molecule, atom, nuclear particle, all the way back to light, from which everything springs. Everything comes from the initial spark of light.

The photon is the simplest physical unit, isn't it?

AY: Yes, it is the least complicated; but it has a potential for everything else. In any case, I like to look at all these different kingdoms, each one of which has its own sweep of evolution. But those different sweeps are parallel, so that you can learn about one thing from another. In the case of man this is especially important, because we don't know by experience what is beyond us; but we can look in the other kingdoms and see what the later stages of those other kingdoms are.

In other words, the human kingdom might be in some way analogous to the whole animal kingdom.

AY: Yes, but the point is that we are only in the middle. We are stuck in the middle of the human kingdom, and we have a long way to go. To get some idea of what is beyond, we can look at what's beyond the clam in animals.

The clam is about in the middle of the animal kingdom.

AY: Right. So we are like clams in our kingdom.

We're at the turning point, being at the middle.

AY: Yes, there is a turn, because this whole process has to go down into matter to get hold of something to deal with, and then it can evolve.

Many of the ancient myths talk about this notion of the descent of spirit into matter, and then the ascent of matter back up to spirit. This is the basic reflex in your book THE REFLEXIVE UNIVERSE.

AY: Right – it is the turn, and the turning point, which is in all the old myths. In fact, I was able to draw as much from the myths as from science, but science gave invaluable details. The whole sweep was given by the myth.

Could we talk a bit about the notion of the descent of spirit into matter as you see it in this grand evolutionary cosmological scheme?

AY: You can see it in science too, but if you have the myth as a clue, it helps. Take the Egyptian myth, where Set, who is the equivalent of Satan, determines to bring about the fall of Osiris. Osiris is the god that represents man. Set prepares a beautiful casket which is already fitted to Osiris, and then, at the party which he gives for all the gods – they all dance around – he offers it to whoever it will fit. So they all get in, and it doesn't fit any of them until Osiris gets in, and then Set clamps on the lid and bolts it fast and it is sent down the Nile. That is the description of the descent of the monad.

And then there is another myth of Pluto catching Persephone when she was picking flowers. He drags her down into the lower world, where she has to reign half the year. But if you go into the detail of those myths, you find the same things that happen in evolution. You look puzzled.

Well. I'm trying to picture how that works in evolution.

AY: The whole point of the theory is to get something definite to work with, and the stages of the process of evolution are this definite thing. And the first hint of those stages I got from the myths. They all have the fall right at the beginning.

Like the fall of Adam.

AY: The fall of Adam, and the sort of Garden of Eden, like the party. And then comes the tree; the tree seems to occur in all these myths. I equate it to the stage in man when we begin to develop self-consciousness, because until Adam and Eve ate of the tree they weren't even aware that they were naked.

Remember, they put coats of skin on after they ate the fruit of the tree? That's part of this process of self-consciousness, which comes in at the third stage.

It's as if some part of our spiritual essence got tricked, to the point where now we find ourselves in these bodies.

AY: In a way it is a trick, but it also is a necessary plan for our benefit. We might say we are going to school in life, and you'd have to be tricked to get you to go to school. The Popul Vuh myth of the Mayans sounds very much like that. The two brothers fail to pass their initiations, and as punishment they have their heads cut off and stuck in a tree. That's another version of it. Originally they were playing ball and having a good time, but they were called by the owl messengers of the gods to come and take their initiations, and they didn't pass, so then they had to suffer the world.

So we are like those that didn't pass.

AY: Well, we don't pass because we haven't had the benefit of this scale of evolution that goes on for hundreds of millions of years.

Which exists in our very bodies.

AY: Right. Our bodies themselves have evolved, and I think the Darwinian theory is correct, in the sense that we are very close to the apes. But if you go into the Theosophical tradition, they tell in great detail how the ape bodies were improved to the point of receiving human souls. But the fact that our bodies have evolved, in what they call a previous round of evolution, has distracted science from the more important question of what is human evolution. You see, in human evolution we haven't changed our bodies that much since the beginning of recorded history, or before that even. Cro-Magnon man was very similar to the current man.

Let's go back to the Great Chain of Being for a moment and trace that. We began to talk about the spark of light, the photon; from there we go to subatomic particles, atoms, and molecules. Then from molecules, where do we move next?

AY: The molecules are the first things to make the turn, and they begin that by storing energy in what are known as polymers. Sugar, starch, all those things that we eat, are polymers that store energy. Other molecules like salt don't store energy. But as soon as you get to polymers, they supply nourishment. And again, so do proteins.

So in effect that's the turning point in the Great Chain of Being.

AY: Now, that's within the chemical kingdom.

So each kingdom has its own turning point. In the animal kingdom, as we mentioned, it is the clam. Perhaps in the human kingdom it is where we are now.

AY: I believe so, because we are intensely wrapped up in laws, and I think all these machineries teach us laws, how to make things. That's why I wanted to make the helicopter, so I could learn how to make things. It helps in learning how to put a philosophy together.

That is another way of making things.

AY: Right.

With all of these parallels, we could say: as a simple complex carbohydrate is to the whole molecular kingdom, as clams are to the whole animal kingdom, we are to what might be our human potential. If we could see the whole human kingdom in terms of the future evolution of the human being, we might be like a clam.

AY: I am even hesitant to make *man* the key word for the top kingdom, because actually it is to evolve as gods, to become gods. Remember Christ said, "Did I not tell ye that ye are gods?" That is one of the things that has been forgotten recently, in our efforts to get rid of God, and so on. We actually cut off our own heads. We deprive ourselves of this omega point, this thing that we are evolving toward in our own evolution. The whole emphasis in any interaction of persons is to get to something to which both parties agree. And if both parties agree, then there's no need for them to be separate. It is really one mind; and that ultimate union of selves, you could say, is the omega point, where we all understand everything sufficiently so that we don't have to have these wrestling matches to thrash things out. In the same way that the cells in our body have evolved so they all function harmoniously as one organism, perhaps the future evolution of humanity might be to evolve as an organism in and of itself.

Well, I don't buy the idea of the social organism replacing the self. I think the social is a vehicle, just the way the ego is a vehicle.

We're not going to become like a colony of bees.

AY: Right. That is a stage of evolution, but it occurs most powerfully with insects, where the group soul is the most important thing, and all the insects are just cells in that group organism.

It almost seems like the way we think of the Communists, like bees in a hive, and the individual is not important.

AY: Well, I don't want to get into political ideas, but the parallel applies just as much to us – not that we are communists, but we are brought up to group thinking too, and we have to learn to think for ourselves. Each person has to learn to do his own thinking, and that is part of what the turn is.

Let me come back at you from a different angle. You helped build the helicopter. In many ways it has changed our reality, and other forms of technology also are changing the face of the earth. In a way these devices are like extensions of our muscles and our nervous system. It's as if we're building a larger organism as we create our society.

AY: Well, that worries me. I can't buy into that. I mean, America is more mechanized than any other country, and yet is still very powerfully individuated. I think it is more that these machineries are tools or means. You can easily get into the idea that some great computer is going to rule the world, sort of like in *1984*. But we have passed that book. I think the whole point is to use the machine for whatever purpose it is suited for, not to let it boss us.

You began by talking about the myths of our origins and our evolution. We have myths about our future as well.

AY: Well, I don't buy the modern myths, *Star Wars* and that kind of thing. I think there is plenty of richness in the ancient myths, and they go way beyond what we have now.

As regards the future evolution of human beings, in what ancient myths do you find inspiration?

AY: Well, they all say the same thing. In the Popul Vuh, for example, the two brothers fail their initiation; that's the fall, the undoing of the participants. Then we go onto the next stage, where the head of one of the twins is put in a calabash tree, and the princess Xiquic hears about this and comes to pick the fruit of this tree. The head spits in her hand and says, "That is my progeny; now I can die." She goes home, and of course she is pregnant, but her father won't believe this story of how it happened, so he orders that she be executed.

It sounds like a myth all right.

AY: Well, the myth exaggerates everything, so much so that you have to look for the deeper meaning. She persuades the executioners to let her go and to substitute the juice of the calabash tree for the blood, which they do. And she gives birth to twins again, who have the same name as their father, and they conquer; they pass their initiations. The part I like the best is that they become itinerant magicians, and the twelve princes of Xibalba, who brought about this fall, hear about the magicians and invite them to come and perform. They make the palace of the prince disappear and bring it back, and they make the little dog of the prince disappear and bring him back. The princes say, "Could you make us disappear and bring us back?" They say yes. So they make the princes disappear, but they don't bring them back, and then the twins become the sun and moon. That's the climax of this whole evolutionary process. So beyond this stage, a couple of stages beyond us, is the power to deal with magic.

At a deeper level it's talking about the classical cycle of death and rebirth, the development of higher powers, and eventually moving on to a whole other realm of being.

AY: What I did want to say is that most people think of evolution in terms of Darwinian evolution – the evolution of the species, and whether we were descended from apes or not. I would say they are missing the real point, which is not the physical evolution of our bodies; that had already occurred before we even took the bodies. I want to come to the point of the evolution of Jeff Mishlove, the evolution of myself, the evolution of each one of us, which is not a question of species. It is a question of building up more character, more competence, more stature, eventually to become like a god. And that is of direct concern to each one of us, much more concern than what is going on in the zoo.

That's a very powerful point, Arthur.

AY: Well, I am horrified by the fact that it is never touched. This whole cloud of foolishness about Darwin takes its place – you know, the Creationists versus the Darwinists – but the whole point is missed.

They are looking too much at where we came from, rather than where we are going.

AY: Yes, looking back rather than looking ahead. But my point is that evolution of the self is quite different from what's happening with animals, which is evolution of the species.

Doesn't the whole notion of evolution of the self, or even evolution of species, lead you back to a question you must have pondered a great deal – the purpose of creation at all? Why is there any existence?

AY: Well, that's the sixty-four-dollar question; I think at present prices it is way up to six hundred and forty dollars. That is a question we each have to ask ourself, but to me it is God wanting to know himself. We are told by the old myths that we are sparks of God and we have been thrown out into the world to thrive for ourselves, and in this way God becomes more evolved himself. I don't know what God is, but you can't have a comprehensive sense of everything without having some unity of meaning, significance, love, all those things, it has to be somehow unified as is the universe. If it is running under certain principles, then it must be culminating in this unity.

Well, I would say for anybody who is aware of your work if I were God trying to know myself I would look toward the books of Arthur Young.

AY: Oh come on. I'm struggling along just like the rest of us.

But you really address the deep, profound issues.

AY: Because it's wonderful fun. It is the most exciting thing there is.

THE UNIVERSAL ORGANISM

WITH RUPERT SHELDRAKE, PH.D.

Drawing on his research as a cell biologist and plant physiologist, Rupert Sheldrake in his book A NEW SCIENCE OF LIFE articulated a new and controversial hypothesis of biological functioning based on morphic resonance. His more recent books include THE PRESENCE OF THE PAST and THE REBIRTH OF NATURE.

In this interview, Sheldrake suggests that all of creation may be viewed as a living organism, rather than as a great machine with God as the great mechanic, and that the so-called "laws of nature" may actually be more like habits and instincts than immutable and inviolable principles. He discusses the implications of his view of morphic fields for an understanding of human consciousness and the process of evolution.

L et's begin by talking about your hypothesis of morphic resonance and morphic fields .

RS: The hypothesis starts from the idea that the development of organisms – for example, the growth of a baby in the womb, or the growth of a tree from a seed – depends on organizing fields, called morphic fields. The organization of behavior – the instincts of a spider, for example – depends on similar morphic fields, rather than just being in the genes. I think that genes are grossly overrated, and that a lot of inheritance depends on the memory which is carried within these organizing fields of organisms. This memory is a kind of cumulative memory, a kind of habit memory, which is built up through a pool of species experience, depending on a process I call morphic resonance.

You began developing your theory as a way of addressing the great unsolved *problems of biology including the problem of memory itself.*

RS: Memory is indeed one of the great unsolved problems. How you or I remember what we did yesterday, or how we remember people's names, or how we recognize people – all the ordinary facts of ordinary, day-to-day memory are profoundly mysterious. It is usually assumed that all these things are stored inside our brains as physical traces of some kind. Now, none of us has ever seen a physical trace inside our brains, and scientists who have spent many years looking for them inside the brains of people, rats and monkeys, have failed to find them too.

Wilder Penfield found that he could stimulate memories by putting electrodes on different parts of the brain. But he was never able to get the same memory twice that way.

RS: No; even if he could evoke memories by stimulating part of the brain, that doesn't prove they are stored there. If I stimulate the tuning knob of your TV set and it tunes onto a different channel, that doesn't prove that all the programs on that other channel are stored inside the bit that I have stimulated, namely the tuning knob. It could be that it is simply part of the receiving or tuning system. I think the brain is like a tuning system, and that we tune into our own memories by a process of morphic resonance, which I believe is a general process that happens throughout the whole of nature.

Can you define what you mean when you use the terms morphic resonance and morphic fields?

RS: Morphic comes from the Greek word for form, morphe. A morphic field is a field of form, a field of pattern or order or structure. Such fields organize not only the fields of living organisms, but also the forms of crystals and of molecules. Each kind of molecule, each protein for example, has its own kind of morphic field – a hemoglobin field, an insulin field. So does each kind of crystal, each kind of organism, and each kind of instinct or pattern of behavior. These fields are the organizing fields of nature. There are many kinds of them, because there are many kinds of things and patterns in nature. I think our own mental life depends on just this kind of field and through this morphic field theory of organization in nature we can come to a new understanding of the nature of the mind – a field theory of the mind.

That's really intriguing. How do you view creativity, then, and some of the other aspects of the human process?

RS: I'd rather put it in a broader natural framework, because creativity is not confined to people. The evolutionary process shows us that the whole of life, over long periods of time, has involved a great creative process – every new species, every new instinct, all new forms of life. And of course there are millions of them that have come into being throughout the course of history on earth.

And you are suggesting then that it is not merely random mutation and natural selection, but something more creative underlying this process.

RS: I think there are two processes at work. One is the principle of habit, based on morphic fields, through established patterns of activity. The more often they are repeated, the more probable they become. So nature is essentially habit-forming, and all aspects of nature, I think, are based on the principle of habit. Indeed, I would go so far as to say that what we call the laws of nature are more like the habits of nature. So I think habit is one principle. The habits of animals and plants are what give them their habits of growth and their habits of behavior, or instincts. Now, at the same time there's a principle of creativity, because if things all remained in grooves of habit, nothing would ever change.

I think that right through the whole of nature, and then coming back to ourselves, we see these two principles at work. First there is the principle of habit, whereby things through repetition become more and more probable to happen again, and at the same time more unconscious. Our own habits are largely unconscious, and the great majority of our behavior is determined by these unconscious habits. For example, my speaking English is an unconscious habit. I don't have to think how to form each word, or what each word means. If I'm speaking a language I don't know very well, like Telegu, a South Indian language I know slightly, I have to think a lot to try and recall the words. It's not habitual; I'm not fluent.

So habit underlies a lot of our activity, but at the same time there is an openness to the new, which is where creativity comes in. Creativity essentially involves the appearance of new patterns, new forms, new structures – what I would call new morphic fields. For example, at one time there were no bicycles; now there are millions of them in the world. At some stage somebody invented the bicycle. For the first time the bicycle was made. For the first time somebody rode a bicycle. Before that, there hadn't been a habit of bicycle riding. Now tens and hundreds of millions of people in the world have the habit of bicycle riding; and I think precisely because so many people have that habit, it is easier for everybody else to learn to ride bicycles, on average, by morphic resonance from this habitual activity.

In other words, there is now a morphic field for bicycle making and bicycle riding, and it must embrace the whole planet in a way that didn't exist at one time.

RS: Yes. A hundred years ago, or certainly two hundred years ago, this hadn't even been dreamed of, and now it's everywhere. At a certain stage there was a creative step – when the first bicycle was invented, the first bicycle was ridden – and the whole of this came into being. So there is an example of what started as a creative step which then becomes a kind of habit. When people ride bicycles, they are usually not thinking how they ride them, working out which muscles to use; it just happens automatically.

Your emphasis on the notion of habit intrigues me. You were telling me earlier that in the nineteenth century, the mechanistic biologists, who tried to reduce all of biology to a machine-like phenomenon, also felt quite comfortable thinking of human beings as different from biological creation. We could be divine, we could have a soul, but the rest of nature was like a machine. You seem to be saying that we are very much like the rest of nature, but nature itself isn't really a machine either – nature partakes of some of the same soulful quality that we have.

RS: Yes. I think the nineteenth-century view was typically very species-ist. We could be alive and have minds; in fact, science itself depended on the possession of human consciousness by scientists. But the rest of nature was seen as completely inanimate, devoid of psyche or mind. I would say rather that we have much more in common with the rest of nature, because the rest of nature is alive, as we are; and the principles of memory and habit, which we know from our own experience, I think are general principles that operate throughout the whole of nature.

Whereas the mechanistic reductionists would have liked to reduce all of nature, all of life down to physics, to molecules colliding, physicists have now come to a point where the very basis of physics is in the mind of the observer itself. This suggests that there is something very mindlike underlying all of biology and all of physics.

RS: Yes, I think there is; and the question is to find out how mindlike it is. If we could begin to work out in just what way it was mindlike, we might come to a better understanding of our own minds and the way they are related to our bodies. Right now nobody has the faintest idea how the mind is related to the body. Descartes in the seventeenth century thought that it interacted with the brain in the pineal gland. All that has happened in the three hundred years since then is that it has moved a couple of inches to the cerebral cortex, and most people now think the mind is associated in some way with the cerebral cortex. Some people would say it doesn't do anything; it is just like a kind of phosphoresence around the nerve endings. Others would say it interacts with the cerebral cortex, but they could not say how. Some would say maybe it does it by interfering with quantum processes in the brain. But I think we can see these mental processes as like what I call morphic fields; they are organizing structures or patterns which organize brain activity; and such fields also organize the development of embryos, the development of our bodies, in the first place. They are at work throughout the whole of nature. That which is mindlike in nature becomes easier to relate to our own minds. And the important part, or most of it, is more like our unconscious minds than our conscious ones. It would be a mistake to say that the whole of nature is conscious, because the whole of our own activity isn't conscious. The vast majority of our behavior is not.

One of the stimulating things that your theory has done is to reopen the issue of the inheritance of acquired characteristics, which was a taboo topic until recently. It seems as if your theory would also reopen the notion of magic – that by concentrating on a certain mental image, one can create that; it can become real. Even modern traditions like the power of positive thinking work along these lines, and it would seem to be consistent with your notion of morphic fields.

RS: Well, it is like magic. Morphic resonance, the influence of like upon like, works across time and space, and in that sense it is like magic. But for the last three hundred years, physics and science in general have been domesticating magic, and what was magic yesterday becomes science today. For example,

Newton's idea of gravitation and attraction – that every particle of matter affects every other particle of matter in the universe, through empty space – is a kind of magic.

Action at a distance.

RS: And yet it is the very basis of mechanistic science. Before Newton, the only people who had suggested the influences of distant planets on the earth were the astrologers.

Newton was rather embarrassed by this. He saw it as a big unsolved problem in his own theory.

RS: Yes; and indeed no one really solved it until Einstein came along much later and said it's not action at a distance through empty space, it's action at a distance through fields – gravitational fields. And so fields have now become the medium of interconnection at a distance – the medium of magic, as it were. Nowhere is that more clearly seen than in television. Two hundred years ago it would have been pure magic that people could have seen us on a television screen, far away from where we are talking. This is the kind of thing that's talked about in the ancient books of the Hindus – the idea of seeing things at a distance. And yet today, we don't even think twice about it.

You wrote A NEW SCIENCE OF LIFE while you were living in an ashram in India. You obviously have deep spiritual interests as well as deep scientific interests. Do you see these things converging?

RS: Yes, I do. I think that the gulf between science and religion that we have had in the West for the last three hundred years is largely owing to the mechanistic world view, which led to a complete transformation of our view of nature. Before the seventeenth century, the standard European Christian view was that nature is alive, nature is animate. The Latin word anima, meaning soul, is the basis of our word animal; it means a being with a soul. Animals had souls; plants had souls; the whole earth had a soul; planets had souls or spirits or intelligences. Until the seventeenth century everyone was living in a living universe, and the Christian God was a living God who made a living world. The seventeenth-century revolution turned the world into a great machine; and God, in the view of Protestant theologians especially, became the world-machine-making God; he became the great mechanic of the universe. By the beginning of the nineteenth century, many people were saying we could get rid of this kind of God and just have a mechanical universe without God. The basis of many controversies has really been rooted in this mechanistic world view. If we go back to the idea of nature as a living organism, of all of nature as being alive, and ourselves as living beings within a living world, then we can think about the relation between science and religion in a new light, a different way than has been possible for the last three hundred years. This world view understands nature as composed of organisms at different levels of complexity – a molecule being one kind of organism; a cell, a tissue, an organ, ourselves, and whole societies all being seen as organisms. This is a view in which we can have a proper science, which incorporates the findings of the last three hundred years of mechanistic science, but which also opens up whole new frontiers for experimentation. It's not going to be a matter of blind faith; this new kind of science, if it happens, will simply be a general empirical inquiry that will take us further.

Your perspective may some day help to resolve the current conflict between the religious fundamentalists and the evolutionists. You seem to be agreeing with the fundamentalists that the view of evolution is really incomplete and needs to be expanded – that it needs to incorporate some sense of mind, perhaps even a sense of the divine.

RS: I think that both sides have a point. The materialistic, neo-Darwinian theory of evolution says that evolution is entirely blind and purposeless and governed by blind laws, happening by blind chance, and it is all just a kind of accident. The other view says that there is a purpose, there is a mind behind the whole of nature; but then it ties that to a literal interpretation of the Book of Genesis. Of course many people have rejected both those extremes. The best known in recent years is Teilhard De Chardin, the French Jesuit philosopher, who said that evolution is indeed going on, and evolution is being drawn towards a future goal, the omega point; and so there is both a purpose and a kind of mind behind and within the evolutionary process, and there is evolution. He didn't have to say you either have God or you have evolution. I think there are many people who would like to have a view of evolution that permits both.

I gather you are in substantial agreement with Teilhard.

RS: I am; but one has to ask what kind of God, or what kind of spiritual guiding principle one is thinking of. The kind of God that has become incredible for many people is the machine-making God of the seventeenth century – a God who stands totally outside the universe, thinks up the mathematical laws of nature, and creates the universe like a great machine. That kind of God is, or will be, as obsolete as the mechanistic world picture that went with it. Any new conception of God that we move towards would at the same time be closer to much older conceptions of God, in the Christian and other religious traditions, as a living, creative source of a living, creative world.

In other words, you might draw some inspiration from the Biblical phrase that God created us in his image. As you look deeply into nature, and see these morphic resonances, that must be for you part of your image of God.

RS: Oh, what a difficult question. Well, I think that, if you like, the interplay of habit and creativity, which we see within ourselves, is in a sense an interplay of what is fixed and what is changeable; and in many traditions there have been images of the ultimate which have involved both those principles. In the Christian doctrine of the Trinity, the fixed is the Logos, the second person of the Trinity; the changeable is the spirit, which is free-flowing like the wind. The two together are included within the third, the ground of both, the father.

It is sort of like yin and yang.

RS: Yin and yang are two principles, but it is actually a trinity, because a third principle, the circle that encloses them both, makes the yin and yang, the duality, part of a greater whole. Whenever you have a duality of principles, as we see everywhere in nature – form and energy, positive and negative in electricity, and so on – wherever you have these dualities, and wherever we find them in ourselves, the resolution is usually to be found in some higher unity which contains and includes both. And insofar as one could say that we are made in the image of God, I think it is in that kind of sense that we are made in the image of God – not in a crude sense that God looks like you or me, or actually looks like a person; and I don't think it has ever really been understood that way by serious theologians.

Your concept of the morphic field intrigues me because it is a great mystery to us what fields are at all. It seems as if understanding the mystery of what a morphic resonance is would be comparable to understanding the mystery of God.

RS: I think it would be more comparable to understanding the mystery of creation or the world we live in. The essential feature of morphic resonance is this kind of memory in nature, this kind of habit. Now, it is not clear to what extent memory and habit are inherent in the nature of God; this leads one into very deep theological waters. But throughout the history of theological thought in the West, there have been ideas which would say that within God is the world soul, the *anima mundi*. In modern terms, it would be the universal field, the primal unified field, which modern physicists are talking about all the time. It is the primal field which was there at the beginning of the big bang, which gave rise to the other fields of nature, the ground underlying all of creation. Within that, I think the principles of memory and habit are operative. What one could say is that to find the ground of that ground, which would be God in traditional terms, probably goes beyond any adequate concept we can form. But the ground of this universe, which would be the primal field of the universe, and all the energy inherent within it, and all the creativity latent within it, I think would include this principle of memory or habit which I am talking about.

What we call the laws of the universe, then, which we sometimes believe are inviolable and extend indefinitely and permanently, are in effect memories and habits that have evolved as if the universe itself were an organism.

RS: Exactly, yes. The conventional view would be that the laws of nature are omnipotent, omniscient, universal, and so on. They are derived in fact from the seventeenth-century idea that the laws of nature were made up by God and existed within his mind. When people got rid of the idea of the mind of God in nature, they were left with eternal laws which still had most of the properties of God. Even the most hard-nosed, mechanistic scientist actually believes implicitly in the existence of these universal, timeless laws that are beyond time and space, present everywhere and always; yet there is no reason at all for thinking that is the case.

There's no getting away from God, it would seem.

RS: Well, God has been replaced by laws, but they have most of the same mysterious properties.

SPIRITUALITY AND THE INTELLECT

WITH JACOB NEEDLEMAN

Jacob Needleman is Professor of Philosophy at San Francisco State University and former Director of the Center for the Study of New Religions at Graduate Theological Union. He is the author of THE NEW RELIGIONS, A SENSE OF THE COSMOS, LOST CHRISTIANITY, THE HEART OF PHILOSOPHY, THE WAY OF THE PHYSICIAN, MONEY AND THE MEANING OF LIFE, *and* SORCERERS, *a novel.*

The essential tension between our material and spiritual natures is often forgotten, even by philosophers themselves, as we pursue contemporary concerns. In this interview Professor Needleman points to Socrates as the ideal philosopher who, through the example of his own life, brought people to an appreciation of deeper strata of awareness.

Let's start with Socrates, perhaps the greatest figure in all of philosophy.

JN: Well, Socrates was a philosopher in the original sense of the term, which is a lover of wisdom. Wisdom is not just something in the head; it is a state of the whole human being. A person who is wise not only knows the truth, but can also live it. So the philosopher Socrates was someone who seeks to *be* wisdom, not simply to know facts and propositions and ideas. He was a teacher of wisdom in that sense, a seeker.

Contemporary academic philosophy seems to have deviated a great deal from the path that was set down by the ancient philosophers such as Socrates.

JN: The whole culture has deviated from that. We have all deviated from that. The whole modern culture tempts us and draws us into just one part of ourselves. Socrates, and Plato after him, taught that only the completely integrated being is a true human being. So yes, academic philosophy has deviated from that. But for almost all of our lives, we no longer have that in our hands.

If our culture as a whole has moved away from this sense of being whole people, then I guess we have to look at alternatives to the mainstream culture – to the esoteric or counterculture examples, perhaps, which you have explored extensively – to get a handle on what was once mainstream wisdom.

JN: Yes, we have to look. Many people are looking, and many things are breaking through that we didn't know about or take seriously before – from ancient times, from the East, from God knows where. This seems to be a time when everything is pouring in. We certainly need some new life and new understanding in our culture.

You are a professor of philosophy, but you speak to people in many different communities – to physicians, to students, amongst others. How do you communicate to people this sense of what philosophy is?

JN: It's a very strange thing; and it may even sound sort of obvious, but I don't think it is. I have discovered in my work with groups like you've mentioned – doctors, businesspeople, psychologists, religious educators, young people – that real inquiry is a tremendous moral transforming force. That is what Socrates was doing – inquiring, searching, questioning; he knew how to do that. It's not just looking for a quick answer or an explanation; but the process of inquiry, of questioning, opens something in the human being which has not been touched in our culture. It is really not a question of whether you are in this field or that field. Everybody who is human has in themselves the potential of passionate inquiry after truth, and that is the transforming force. That is what I am doing, no matter where I am; I'm trying.

What you are really talking about is the psyche itself – the ancient term which refers to the soul.

JN: Absolutely. It was never separate. Philosophy and psychology were always together, and it is only a modern thing in our culture that there has been a separation between the search for wisdom and transcendence, and the study of the mind – one's own mind and all its possibilities, not just the pathology. So it's true; the twentieth century is the time when philosophy and psychology got separated off, but it never was that in the past. So I would like to think of myself as trying to be a psychologist, in the ancient sense, as well as a philosopher.

In dealing with the realm of the intellect, you have made an interesting distinction between a concept and an idea.

JN: That's a tough one. It's hard to put it in a quick description. A concept is a kind of mental tool for organizing data and facts; it is like an aspect of a computer or a filing system. But it is part of a rather automatic part of the mind which the human being has, and which is very useful. An idea, on the other hand, is like an expression of a fundamental reality – a force, in a way. Sometimes it takes its expression in words, in an abstract formula; sometimes it is in images; sometimes it is in geometric forms or in art forms. So the verbal expression of ideas is only one way of communicating something that we go beyond just the isolated intellect to understand. Ideas come from a deeper level of the human mind. Concepts are the ordinary mind functioning as it should to organize, cut, dry, put in file cabinets, and do all that.

In other words, normally when we think of the work of the intellect we are thinking about concepts that it deals with. The intellect is also engaged with ideas, but ideas penetrate deeper; they have a greater transformative power.

JN: Absolutely. They are meant to be accepted by the intellect, but they need to penetrate down into the heart and the guts, and concepts don't do that particularly.

An example of a great idea might be the one that was left to us by Socrates: "Man, know thyself."

JN: That is a great idea. The idea of God is an idea, and it points to something that may or may not exist. I think it does, that it is real, but it's an idea. It didn't just appear automatically like a rock or a stone. Somebody had a vision of the idea of God, or the idea of the universe – of oneness, many in one. Among the ancient Chinese, the idea of the yin and the yang, the constant interplay of two forces in the universe, is an idea. The head can figure out the conceptual way of dealing with it, but it can never really understand it, because to understand an idea you have to experience it. You have to be immersed in it with your whole being. There has been a tremendous confusion between ideas and concepts, and therefore the conceptual mind has tried to do all by itself what only the mind of the whole person is able to do. That has been a problem with our whole society, I think.

Let's look at the other side of the equation we're discussing tonight – spirituality. I think of spirituality as somehow a contact with something beyond time and space, something not quite part of this physical realm. Is that a definition that you're comfortable with?

JN: Yes. Of course, it is not part of the physical realm that the conceptual mind grasps, not part of time and space as they are constructed by and understandable by the conceptual mind alone. But there may be other levels of time and space, and there may be another meaning to physical reality. But yes, basically I would agree with you spiritually; it refers to something higher or deeper than we ordinarily can understand and experience.

In your book THE HEART OF PHILOSOPHY you say that true philosophy involves a kind of remembering, having to do with the dual nature of man. Part of us is here in this physical body, in this three-dimensional world, and another part of us partakes of the infinite, of the absolute, of the Platonic or spiritual realms. Having these two parts to us creates an inescapable tension, and real philosophy is in effect grasping that tension and coming to terms with it.

JN: We are creatures in two worlds – the world beyond this one, and this one. Socrates' understanding of philosophy is one of the ways to help us feel the call of something in us that is from a much greater reality. It is what he called remembering, the way of remembering. It helps us to remember that there is something much greater in ourselves. At the same time we live in this world; we are egos, we are people, we are physical. This human condition of being both the high and the low together, both the inner and the outer, of being two things at the same time is what distinguishes human beings from all other creatures. It is our task, as you say, to deal with it – or, at least to face it, to live it.

To agonize over it.

JN: It's a kind of suffering. But it is creative suffering. It can be.

It seems as if the existential philosophers write about this a lot – angst, or nausea.

JN: Yes, but you don't get the sense of great hope with the existentialists, at least some of them. You don't get the sense that there really is a deeper, higher reality. With much of what we call existentialism there is the sense that we as human beings are cast adrift in a meaningless universe and suffering this weird thing called freedom, which brings us this angst and this suffering, and knowing there is no meaning outside ourselves, but still having the guts to stand up and say, that's what I am. That's existentialism of a kind. But that is not what we are speaking about here. We are speaking about a vision of human nature which really says there is great meaning, inside us and outside of us too. The suffering is that we feel it exists, but that we are out of contact with it, and we need to find a way to open to it. It's not exactly existentialism.

Let's contrast existentialism a little bit with what we might call the positive-thinking philosophies – the view that everything is really all bliss, everything is perfect already. Christian Science is one among many spiritual groups who take this attitude towards life. How do you feel about that as a philosopher? Is it too simple-minded?

JN: There is an ancient and deep truth there that can degenerate when it is taken in a simple way, in a stupid way, just as the view that this is a tough universe and everything obeys laws and you have to pay for it, can degenerate into some hard, cynical view. Basically the great traditions have always taught that there is something in us which is godlike, and that there is an inherent joy within us; and that yes, as the Buddhists say, you already are the Buddha; or as the Christians say, Christ has already forgiven you, the kingdom has already appeared. But that doesn't mean we are in touch with it. Those who are have a very deep well-earned joyousness. But those who just take it as an idea, and as something emotionally attractive, may make it look foolish. It can become a very foolish thing, where somebody is saying everything is just fine while the house is burning. Things are not so fine. This is true even in Buddhism; the Buddhist says the house is burning, and you've got to get out of that burning house and realize your inherent Buddha-ness.

So when you ask what I think of it, in its authentic form it is a deep truth. In its perverted forms it can be silly – just as it is a deep truth that you have to work hard and suffer for understanding, but in its perverted form this makes everything impossible, cynical, and tough, as scientism does sometimes – saying there's nothing out there, we are here; we're cast adrift; we're going nowhere. Both views are perverted – what you might call the day-dream view and the nightmare view. They are both fantasies.

Somewhere in the middle, then, there must be a place where it becomes important to develop the intellect to grasp our dual nature – our physical nature and our spiritual nature.

JN: Absolutely. The intellect is a very important function in us. It has been twisted and wrong. It's like an extraordinary tool that is not being used right, or like a computer that is in the hands of a maniac. It is an extraordinary thing, and it is very much part of us. There are many levels of intellect, but even our ordinary level can be used in a different way. For that, we need to have more real experience. The intellect functions well when it feeds on deep, true experiences, and our level of experience is not good. The more we can have real experiences, the more the intellect has reality to work with. As it is, we live on fantasies.

What would be an example of a real experience?

JN: Well, any real impression. Even a philosopher like David Hume, who in many ways is considered to be a cynic, or at least very skeptical, had the idea that impressions are the basis of thought. So we need to have impressions – for example, the impression of sitting here and talking to you. Am I really experiencing you? Am I really experiencing being here? Usually we're not.

As opposed to having some kind of mental chatter going on, which is already interpreting.

JN: Exactly. It's already interpreting. Or the kind of experience you have in emergencies, or shocking situations, or sudden joyous moments – say, when a woman gives birth to a child, this sense of, "This is real. I am here." Experiencing that is a kind of food for the mind, for the whole being.

You seem to be saying that in order to really cultivate our intellect we have to get beyond the habitual interpretive or intellectual responses that we have learned so that we can refresh our thinking process.

JN: Yes. We have to be aware that there is an interpretation, a commentary, going on all the time, and we have to get free of that commentary. That's not something you do just by thinking about doing it.

This commentary, this part of our stream of thought, must have been largely conditioned since childhood. We think in certain ways. We have patterns of looking at the world and understanding it. And I suppose the job of philosophy, or the job of true intellectual development, is to rebuild ourselves as adults.

JN: Yes, and we rebuild ourselves partly by becoming freer from the commentary so that we can take in the nourishment of real experiences, which nourishes what used to be called the soul, but we don't have a name for it now.

Insofar as we expose ourselves to opinions that challenge our own at every level, I suppose this is how we dislodge our habitual patterns.

JN: Yes, if we are willing to accept the suffering that comes from having our opinions challenged. We need to learn to welcome that. But we are very attached to our opinions, and so that is difficult. That's what Socrates taught – to blast yourself free of opinions, so that behind the opinion is the possibility of real vision, real knowing. That's Socratic, I think.

It might be useful to talk a little bit about the life of Socrates and how he dealt with the kind of opposition that he must have engendered.

JN: The life of Socrates is a mystery. It is one of the great spiritual legends. We don't know about his life. We know what Plato wrote about it, and what one or two other people, including Xenophon, wrote about it. It is a life that has become a legend, like the Buddha's life, or even, up to a point, like Jesus' life. We know he stood for this inquiry – the development of the soul, or what we would call the deep self today. According to the legend he was always trying to engage people in this kind of exchange which I am calling real inquiry. That was his life, and that was his only aim. People came to him, and many were shocked and offended because he blasted their opinions away. He made you see you didn't know what you thought you knew. That is the precondition for real learning – to realize that you don't know anything.

Eventually, for one reason or another, he incurred strong political opposition and was put on trial. He was very popular in many ways, but he was put on trial, he was condemned to death, and he was given an opportunity to escape because the people trying him knew that it wouldn't be very good to have Socrates as a martyr. They wanted him to escape; but he wouldn't. He made them choose: "I'm standing for the truth. Will you kill me?" He didn't escape, and he died one of those rare intentional deaths, which I would distinguish from suicide. An intentional death is a death full of meaning, which transmitted something not only to his pupils, but to thousands of years of people. He took poison voluntarily instead of escape, and he stands for somebody for whom the pursuit of wisdom is more important than physical life itself.

There is a sense, as you speak, that somehow the moment of death is the point at which real spirituality and real intellect join – at least in Socrates' life.

JN: I think for some great people that is what happens. But there are little deaths all along in our lives that can become real for us all. But yes, in Socrates, Buddha, Christ, people of that kind, their death becomes the full flowering of their life.

When you talk about little deaths, what comes to mind is sacrifice. When we make sacrifices in the name of pursuing an inner truth, somehow our intellect becomes more aligned with right thinking, with the world of spirit.

JN: Yes, I agree. But we have to be very precise about what we have to sacrifice, because there is lots of wrong sacrifice, which is a form of fantasy or even masochism. But to really sacrifice an attachment, particularly an attachment to a thought, and to feel that brings intelligence, that's a mysterious thing. What do we really have to sacrifice? We have to sacrifice our illusions, our dreams – not necessarily our desires; our desires are probably OK. It is our attachment to the desire that is a problem.

You mentioned earlier that so much of what we hold onto is illusory. We have the term enlightenment. In the eighteenth century it referred to a kind of rationality that was in touch with reality. We also see the term in the spiritual traditions referring to a form of consciousness which is in touch with a higher reality. There seems to be a joining there.

JN: There is a joining; but the Enlightenment ideal has, I think, turned into a kind of promoting of the best functioning of ordinary intellect. Enlightenment came to mean using your ordinary reason. But consciousness is not the same thing as what we call thinking. This has simply in the modern era in the

West never been understood. It is a truth which maybe the originators of the Enlightenment understood; I doubt it, but maybe. But certainly the ancient masters, the spiritual teachers, have always understood that what we call thinking is not the same thing as what you are referring to as consciousness.

Now, that is a revolutionary idea in the modern Western world because we have tended to identify the highest part of the human being as the thinking faculty when it's really operating well. But that is not the highest part of ourselves; far from it. There's something much, much higher. And those higher states of consciousness have with them a quality of thought which is very great. Buddha was a great thinker; Christ, although we don't often think of him that way, was a great thinker, like Socrates. He wasn't just somebody walking around, looking and acting in an extraordinary way. He also thought; he pondered.

But being a great thinker, having thoughts like that, comes from having one's whole being attuned to something greater.

JN: Exactly – attuned to something greater, something finer. That's what the great masters like Socrates, Christ, Buddha, and Moses were. That's what they represent.

I gather from reading your writings in many fields, whether business or medicine or philosophy or psychology, that the ultimate purpose of any discipline is to help bring about that alignment, that attunement of being.

JN: It can be. That is the ultimate purpose of our lives, in my opinion. Of course, it can be a very wide circle we're talking about here. If the ultimate purpose of human life is to become attuned to this greater state we are speaking about, then of course every discipline in one way or another has to contribute to that.

UNDERSTANDING MYTHOLOGY

WITH JOSEPH CAMPBELL

The late Joseph Campbell was one of the world's foremost mythologists and interpreters of myth. Among his books are THE HERO WITH A THOUSAND FACES, THE MASKS OF GOD, HISTORICAL ATLAS OF WORLD MYTHOLOGY, and THE INNER REACHES OF OUTER SPACE.

Arguing against the literal interpretation of ancient myth, Campbell shows how mythology reflects universal human experiences and asserts that modern science provides the raw material for future myths which can serve to unite all of humankind.

You have come to take the view recently that mythology stems from the human body itself – that every mythological story comes from our experiences as human beings in a physical body. That appears quite contrary to the earlier idea that mythology is the product of fantasy or imagination.

JC: Fantasy and imagination are products of the body. The energies that bring forth the fantasies derive from the organs of the body. The organs of the body are the source of our life, and of our intentions for life, and they conflict with each other. Among these organs, of course, is the brain. Then you must think of the various impulses that dominate our life system – the erotic impulse; the impulse to conquer; self-preservation; and then certain thoughts that have to do with ideals and things that are held up before us as aims worth living for, that give life its value. All of these different forces come into conflict within us. The function of mythological imagery is to harmonize them, to coordinate the energies of our body, so that we will live a harmonious and fruitful life in accord with our society and with the new mystery that emerges with every new human being – namely, what are the possibilities of this particular human life? Mythology has to do with guiding us – first, in relation to society and the whole world of nature, which is outside of us but also within us, because the organs of our body are of nature; and then also it guides the individual through the inevitable stages of life, from childhood to maturity, and then on to the last gate. And mythology is concerned with those matters.

So behind every fantasy, behind every mythological story, there is some deeper truth about life.

JC: Well, yes. A mythology is not just the fantasy of this, that, or another person; it is a systematized organization of fantasies in relation to the values of a given social order. Mythologies always derive from specific social environments. And when you realize that every one of the early civilizations was based on a mythology, you can realize the force of this great, great heritage that we have.

In your book THE INNER REACHES OF OUTER SPACE, you point out that we are coming to a time when our society is becoming global — that we can't think of ourselves as a group of competing tribes any longer.

JC: This is a crucial problem today. Every mythology, every religion has grown up within a certain social order, and today these social orders have come into collision with each other. All you have to do is look at what is going on in the Near East now, and it's a horror. The three major monotheistic religions of the world are creating havoc there. I have been in Beirut; it was once a glorious, beautiful, darling little city, and now it is just hell, because each of these units of religion thinks it has all the values on its side, and it doesn't know how to open up and recognize that the others are human beings also.

They think that their particular god is the one god and the only one.

JC: We have given them three names — you have Judaism, Christianity, and Islam there. But they are all right out of the same box and they can't get on together.

What you are suggesting is that a lot of social conflict results from the failure of the leaders of these communities to properly understand the role of their mythologies.

JC: The role of their mythology has been to support their society, and they are hanging onto that. One could say there are two main types of mythology. There are mythologies like that of the Biblical tradition, which have to do with coordinating the individual into a group. He is a member of that group, he is baptized or circumcised or whatnot into that group, and that is his realm of compassion and sympathy, and he projects his aggression outside of that group. There is another kind of religion which grows out of the emotional life of the natural order. We are nature beings, after all, not members of a society primarily. These include such religions as the Dionysian religions of ancient Greece. Hinduism is full of this, and all the religions that have to do with meditation – they are coming over here from the Orient. The main thing for people today are these religions of contemplation and meditation – recognizing within you the powers that are those of the gods. All the gods are simply projections of human potentialities. They're not out there. They're in here: "The kingdom of heaven is within you." And who is in heaven? God is. So where is he? Look in here. You have two kinds of religion – that which is addressed outward like that, and that which is turned inward.

I have been interested all my life in what we might call comparative mythology. You see that what young people are saying in one language, other people are saying in another language, and they are getting mixed up simply because their language is different. If you go into a bakery shop and say you want *pain*, they'll say, "Oh, we don't have that." But you are asking for bread, which is what they have. That's the way it is, across the lines.

I suppose one could say the prime example is the contrasts and affinities of Buddhism and Christianity. The idea of Buddha consciousness is that all beings are Buddha beings, and your whole function in meditation and everything else is to find that Buddha consciousness within and live out of that, instead of the interests of the eyes and ears; these can distract us from our own true, deepest being and purpose. And the goal of meditation is to find that inside, and then let that take control. If you translate that into Christianity, it is finding the Christ in you; it's exactly the same idea. Here they call it Christ consciousness; there they call it Buddha consciousness. Well, the figures that represent the two ideas are quite in contrast in that the Buddhist imagery concentrates on the pacific aspect, you might say, having found peace within; the Christian imagery of Christ crucified concentrates on the heroic attitude of living life which is tearing you apart and finding the one within you in the midst of the turmoil of the world. You have that in

Buddhism also, in the idea of the Bodhisattva – the one who has found the eternal within himself and recognizes it in the world. They have a beautiful term: "joyful participation in the sorrows of the world." You accept the sorrows for yourself and for the world in the realization of what radiance a well-lived life can bring forth out of this. These are the same things – one in the active, you might say tragic, aspect; and the other in the serene, fulfilled aspect.

Paying attention to myths in this sense would really bring out many subtle, deep emotions that we might not otherwise experience.

JC: This hits deep all over the place. I have taught in a college for thirty-eight years, and this is my subject. Students come in with their religions, and then you let them know what the religions are really talking about, and boy, something happens.

In THE INNER REACHES OF OUTER SPACE, you seem to be suggesting that all of our science – astronomy for example – is our modern myth and that this too exists inside of us.

JC: I would say that all of our sciences are the material that has to be mythologized. A mythology gives the spiritual import – what one might call rather the psychological, inward import – of the world of nature as understood today. There is no real conflict between science and religion. Religion is the recognition of the deeper dimensions that the science reveals to us. What is in conflict is the science of 2000 B.C., which is what you have in the Bible, and the science of the twentieth century A.D. You have to disengage the messages of the Bible from its science.

For instance, in the Roman Catholic religion it is dogma to believe that Jesus rose from the dead and ascended bodily to heaven, and that his mother, Mary, in sleep ascended to heaven. Yet you know that going at the speed of light they would not be out of the galaxy yet; and you know what it means for a physical body to go up into the stratosphere. The mythic image does not fit the contemporary mind, so the message can't get into the contemporary body. You've got to translate these things into contemporary life and experience. Mythology is a validation of experience, giving it its spiritual or psychological dimension; and if you have a lot of things that you can't correlate with contemporary nature, you can't handle it.

I suppose one of the first things to go with modern science is the idea that the gods and the heavens are somewhere out there in space.

JC: Of course they're not. You've got hundreds and hundreds of galaxies now, and clusters of galaxies; and every galaxy as great, and some greater than, our whole Milky Way, with our sun on the outskirts of one of these. And God is the one who thought of this whole thing. Of course that's not the god in the Bible at all, because all he thought of was a three-layered birthday cake.

Doesn't it seem that some of the Hindus have anticipated this universe?

JC: Oh, yes, they've got it, they've got it; not only that, but they've got the cycles of the coming into being of stars, and their going out in grandeur. We've got a cosmic cycle of about twelve thousand years. This is ridiculous.

The Hindus seemed to know that there were cycles within cycles, and gods within gods.

JC: God knows how they found it out, but when you read the myths of the Puranas of India, the *Mahabharata,* there is no problem correlating that with modern science.

I have often wondered whether many of the magical powers and siddhis, or psychic powers, that appear in myths aren't evolutionary precursors of what we might become – that the myths are guiding us into our future.

JC: Insofar as they revealed potentialities of the human spirit, they are prophetic, because I think the human spirit is developing. I don't take a negative attitude toward what is happening with the human spirit. I take a very negative attitude with what is happening to our politicians, but that has nothing to do with the human spirit. The chaos in the world today is not a function of the illumination of humanity today; it is a function of the bungling of a bunch of self-interested politicians.

If we are to solve the problems confronting the world today, it seems that we will have to develop a new mythology. The old myths are no longer serving us in some sense.

JC: Two things will have to happen if we are going to have a mythology that is appropriate to man today. One is to take the world of nature as it is known.

I have been hearing recently about some of the things that the physicists and astronomers are finding out, and it is magical and incredible. That's the ground; it's not difficult to turn that into a mystical inspiration. The second thing is to realize that the society with which you are involved is not this group or that group, or this social class or that social class, or this race or that race, but the planet. And we don't have a mythology for recognizing the humanity of a person on the other side of the tennis net. So it will come; but it isn't here yet.

I've often wondered if some of the notions coming out of quantum physics, such as quantum interconnectedness, don't express that.

JC: They do. You find all kinds of suggestions in the modern world of physics. And you can translate them right into Sanskrit without any trouble. The Hindus have the whole thing already.

Yet there seem to be vast sections of our current culture that want to take the old religious myths literally.

JC: Well, this is a disaster, to go back to something that's four thousand years out of date, in every sense – in the sense, in the first place, of realizing what humanity is. They had no historical knowledge of anything but their own little corner of the Near East – no knowledge of the Americas, no knowledge of the Far East at all. And to pull back in that, I think, is criminal.

And yet on the other hand, you pointed out that these myths are based on our bodily experiences, and our bodies haven't changed.

JC: They are, but they have been translated into a local commitment. That's the point, when I speak of comparative mythology; this one sees it this way, this one sees it that way, but they are all talking about bread.

Let's talk a little bit more about some of the underlying unities that occur in myth. For example, what are the common bodily experiences that we have to confront? I suppose part of our existential reality here in the world is the same, regardless of culture.

JC: One existential reality is the mystery of birth. That's more than a biological phenomenon, the mystery of a new being coming in. Next, every culture, everywhere, forever, has had to bring that little nature phenomenon into relationship to a society. That's where the problem comes – into what society are you going to bring this nature phenomenon? The local myths stress that you are coming into our society, our way. That wouldn't be bad if the society didn't think of itself as the only one worth being incorporated in. Every society has had to guide this little biological phenomenon through the inevitabilities of growth, childhood, adolescence, then moving into marriage – and today this is a disaster, because the mythology of marriage has been forgotten. Then you move on to the release of yourself from commitment to the world, and then passing on. That isn't a loss, it's a gain, when you realize that you are gaining an inward life. Death is not loss. All it is losing is simply this passing phenomenon of a body. But the consciousness is becoming more and more of itself. Proper mythology tells you how to die.

Those are the universals. The problem of the relationship of this mortal, passing, phenomenal vehicle of consciousness to the mystery of consciousness, and finding this more enduring aspect of your life in yourself – that's what the religions are talking about. And they personify that mystery; in governing our lives, we have to have thoughts that govern us, certain images that we can target to, and these images then become the end. The Christ idea – you put that before you, and it helps you to move to this thing which transcends the Christ idea. The myth is this side of the truth, but it leads you to it. And think what else it does socially – namely, the Christ image that is your life is the life of everyone else too. And so this relieves you of your sense of special ego privilege.

I suppose when they really understand the myth, Jews or Arabs or Hindus can also appreciate that Christ essence within themselves.

JC: Yes, they have the counterparts in their own religions, and it's a shame that that aspect is not accented. What is accented is the local value, not the universal value of the image that happens to be in the religious tradition.

Another trend within our culture is that individuals who see the horror of religious wars would have us do away with myths completely.

JC: Well, that has been the result. The word myth has come to mean lie. It is a lie to say that somebody has ascended to heaven; he hasn't. Mythology is a compendium of metaphors. But when you interpret the metaphor in terms of the denotation instead of the connotation, you have lost the message.

That's like going into a restaurant and reading the menu and deciding what you are going to eat, and you eat that part of the menu. The menu is a reference to something that transcends that piece of paper.

As with a fine meal at a restaurant, when one really understands the connotations, one's life becomes far richer. There are so many flavors and tastes.

JC: When you know what to order. You have been taught the message of this mythology, you might say, this set of metaphors, and you know what to order.

Your study of world mythology seems to have led you to become in many ways a mystic.

JC: Well, I'm not a mystic, in that I don't practice any austerities, and I have never had a mystical experience. I am a scholar, and that's all. I remember when Alan Watts asked me, "Joe, what yoga do you practice?" I said, "I underline sentences." That's all I'm doing. I have just had the great good fortune to find this golden world of myth, and I was also well trained in how to write a book. All I have done is gather what has excited me into my books, and by God, it works for other people just as well as it worked for me.

What would you want to tell young people today, who are coming into this world, in a different phase of life – you who are now into your eighties and who have gone through so much?

JC: How do you find the divine power in yourself? The word enthusiasm means "filled with a god." So, what makes you enthusiastic? Follow it. That has been my advice to young people who ask me, "What shall I do?" I taught once in a boys' prep school. That's the moment for young boys – or it used to be – when they had to decide their life courses; you know, where are they going? They are caught with excitement. This one wants to study art, this one poetry, this one anthropology. But Dad says to study law; that's where the money is. That is the decision. You know what my answer would be – go where your enthusiasm is. Follow your bliss. The bliss is the message of God to yourself. That is where your life is.

THE PRIMORDIAL TRADITION

WITH HUSTON SMITH, PH.D.

Huston Smith is Visiting Professor of Religious Studies at the University of California, Berkeley, and a former Professor of Philosophy at M.I.T. His books include THE RELIGIONS OF MAN (revised and reissued as THE WORLD'S RELIGIONS), FORGOTTEN TRUTH: THE PRIMORDIAL TRADITION, and BEYOND THE POST-MODERN MIND. He has produced award-winning documentary films on Hinduism, Tibetan Buddhism, and Sufism.

The modern Western world view is dominated by the materialism of science. According to Dr. Smith, this withdrawal of emphasis from human values has led to alienation and social discontent. In this interview, he suggests how we can assign science its proper place and allow room for other realms of experience that give life its meaning and beauty.

The term primordial tradition implies something that goes back beyond recorded history to the most ancient roots of humanity.

HS: That's true. It does have the ring of being timeless – and, I would add, spaceless as well, because it was not only always, but everywhere. So the easy way to think of primordial is no matter where or when.

From your perspective, our modern scientific outlook might be properly seen as embedded within this larger primordial tradition.

HS: That's exactly right. With the advent of modern science, I think we have discovered a near-perfect method for learning about the physical reaches of reality. The danger is that our excitement at what we are discovering and what we can do there will divert our attention from other regions of reality which continue to exist whether we attend to them or not.

Throughout history we have had religious wars and conflicts among religious groups. I think it's marvelous that you are able to see the common thread that unites them all.

HS: It was really while writing the book *Religions of Man*, in which I endeavor to paint portraits, you might say, of the major enduring religious traditions, that I became more and more struck by recurrent themes that seemed to surface time and again like echoes. That led on to the later book, *Forgotten Truth*, in which I tried, so to speak, to run a sieve through the great religious traditions and see what emerged by way of common denominators that ran through them all.

You point out that in the scientific frame of mind we see ourselves as in the middle world between the vast reaches of space and the microscopic world of atoms, cells, and molecules; and yet in the primordial tradition we are in a different middle world.

HS: That's true. The middle world that science places us in is sometimes called the macro world, which is in between the micro world of the incredibly small and the mega world of the incredibly large. But all of those, once one thinks about it, are distinctions of space; they are quantitative. The primordial tradition also sees us as situated in a middle world, but there the order of measure is quality. We're in the middle of a world which is a middle world, but also in a way a middling world. It's fifty percent happiness, fifty percent sorrow; fifty percent knowledge, fifty percent being in the dark about things. It is again situated midway between what in the traditional cosmologies are shown as the heavens, which are incomparably better, and the hells, which are, alas, incomparably worse. But the interesting point is the difference in quality, whereas science gives us almost the same structure, but in quantitative rather than qualitative terms.

In our modern scientific culture we often tend to dismiss the religious worlds — the heavens, the hells, the worlds of demons and spirits – as being, well, we can't test them, we can't measure them, and therefore they are irrelevant and nonscientific. Yet it may be that the methods of science simply have nothing to say. That doesn't mean that these aren't important for us.

HS: Well, I think you're exactly right. Just because the science of acoustics can't handle the notion of beauty, it doesn't follow that Brahms isn't beautiful. Much the same is going on there. Science everywhere can pick up quantitative distinctions; but qualitative ones, like beauty and spirit, slip through its nets as the sea slips through the nets of fishermen.

Ultimately it seems as if the human mind is intimately linked to these spiritual worlds.

HS: That is wherein we live and move and have our being, really. The quantitative world is there; but the world that we live out our lives in is the world of ups and downs and joys and sorrows and disappointment. So it is really in the qualitative world that our lives are lived.

The issue of the soul is an important one.

HS: You're starting to sound like Plato. Good; let's talk about the soul.

We've done away with the soul in modern culture. It's kind of a quaint, archaic notion; it's unnecessary now, and we're much better off without it.

HS: That makes me think of the last time I saw His Holiness the Dalai Lama. He was at a conference in Bombay on science and religion, and there were a couple of Nobel science winners there. The Dalai Lama gave the opening address, and he was commending the scientists for what they have done for humanity. But then he said, "In addition to the physical, material world, there is the invisible world. That might be awkward for you scientists, but never mind, it's there anyway." I liked the direct way in which he came on. And that applies to the soul. Certainly the soul will not show up on any brain scan, and it won't show up on any diagnostic tool that the psychologists have, but that doesn't mean that it doesn't exist. It's just that there are different regions of reality, and certain instruments are splendid for picking up certain dimensions. Radio and television are a perfect example. Just because certain waves are not picked up on a given frequency finder doesn't mean that those waves are not there. This room is filled with waves that simply are not visible at this moment.

You have described the attempt to examine the soul as akin to trying to see one's own eyes by stepping backwards. And yet, just as we earlier described the mind as swimming in a sea of spiritual activity, the soul yearns for something closer to the divine.

HS: To the divine and the infinite. On the other hand, the soul is the final locus of our individuality. It is what makes you, Jeffrey Mishlove, unlike any other person who ever has been or will be, and yet is constant with you throughout your career. But the soul also has a tropism, a kind of dynamism in it, in which it is forever reaching beyond anything you have ever attained thus far, and it will never stop that reaching until, we are told, it finally loses its individuality by merging with the infinite.

In a sense, then, all of our yearning, all of our desires are ultimately the yearnings of the soul. We may seek to satisfy ourselves through career advancement or through the attainment of material wealth, but ultimately these things are only poor substitutes for what the soul really desires.

HS: That is what we think we want. But the fact that when we get it, no matter how wonderful it is, it still cannot satisfy us completely, is evidence that it is ultimately not what we really wanted. You might say it is the symbol of what we really wanted.

This must be why many religious traditions talk about the need to let go of desire; desires interfere with the real spiritual path.

HS: That is a very complex and tricky subject, desires. They can be evidence of greed and clinging and grasping; but Buddhism and Hinduism, which really are the most severe in talking about desires, nevertheless both acknowledge that some desires are wonderful – the desire to help other people, the desire to grow and become more than one has achieved. So we have to winnow when we come to desires, and separate those that are helpful from those that hold us back.

In your book FORGOTTEN TRUTH you have a marvelous quote from the Sufi poet Jelaluddin Rumi. It describes how a lover has an ardent desire to kiss. But what is being kissed is just like clay. Some other beautiful quality which exists independently of the clay in which it's embodied is what we are really searching for.

HS: I wish I could bring back those lines from memory. The beloved is saying something like, "'Tis that" – namely, the ultimate – "that you were seeking and were reaching for when you touched my lips, not these lips of clay." Beautiful poem. In a way, with every desire that we seek, it is that ultimate that we are really seeking. It shows itself to us in fragments through the concrete object that we think we are reaching for; we are reaching really for what is beyond that, but that is all of it that we see at the moment.

And yet there is a paradox, in that the seeker who is driven by these yearnings to achieve that closeness to God, somehow can never really attain it.

HS: That is probably true in this life, but all of the traditions point to a continuity which is shrouded in mystery, and which probably the very nature of our minds makes it impossible for us to imagine. But if we do not stop the picture with physical death, then there is a completion. In the West it is called the beatific vision. It may be a dualistic image, implying that there is something that one is enthralled by, but the viewer is separate from it. But other statements use images like, "The dewdrop merges into the shining sea" – at which point the dewdrop loses its separate identity, and there is absolute oneness with the ultimate. So I think it is not true that this yearning goes on forever. I think there is a time when it phases beyond time, and is ultimately and totally fulfilled.

SCIENCE AND RELIGION

WITH WILLIS HARMAN, PH.D.

Willis Harman is President of the Institute of Noetic Sciences in Sausalito, California. He previously conducted futures research at SRI International, and is a professor emeritus of Engineering-Economic Systems at Stanford University. He is the author of numerous books including AN INCOMPLETE GUIDE TO THE FUTURE *and* GLOBAL MIND CHANGE, *and coauthor with Howard Rheingold of* HIGHER CREATIVITY.

In this interview, Dr. Harman suggests that a new set of values emphasizing the inner life of the mind is emerging spontaneously among many social strata and in different parts of the world. He points out that these inner disciplines have their own procedures for investigation and verification, which are just as valid in their realm as is the scientific method in the realm of modern science.

S*cience and religion have historically been thought of as antagonistic. Even today the debate over evolution and creationism still seems to be raging. Yet you seem to be pointing out that there is another, opposite trend, which is the convergence of science and religion, the unification of these two seemingly vastly different disciplines.*

WH: I think both trends are happening at the same time, and that is typical when a society is going through a major change; you have the old trend still continuing, and you have a new one starting. Now, the religion that is part of the old trend is not the same as the religion that is part of the new trend, and the science of the old trend is not the same as the science of the new trend.

Let's start by distinguishing between what you might think of as the old-trend religion and the new-trend religion.

WH: There are a lot of differences. In the first place, there were a lot of religions, and I think what is emerging is one spirituality. Some of the religions, at least, tended to put a lot of stress on what you believed and to emphasize sin and guilt. What is emerging seems to look upon sin and guilt more as pathologies to be outgrown, and it tends to put emphasis not so much on what you believe as on your experience, and to encourage experiencing the divine within. That's another difference – that some of the old religious forms put the emphasis on God out there somewhere, as contrasted with discovering the divine nature of ourselves.

Do you feel comfortable with the concept of new age religions to describe this new trend?

WH: New age has so many meanings that it is not a terribly useful term. New thought religions is a bit more precise — I think that's the Church of Religious Science, Unity, and things of that sort. That has gotten to be a fairly precisely defined term.

I suppose that the ecumenical movement, the attempt to find the common ground that all religions share in common, is a movement more and more in the direction of these new thought religions.

WH: Well, either that, or back to the esoteric, timeless core of all the spiritual traditions, which is essentially the same thing. The reason it has not been so obvious to us is because it has been esoteric for a number of reasons, one being that heresy could be hazardous to your health in certain eras.

What is the distinction between the old scientific viewpoint, which was somehow antagonistic to religion, and the new scientific approach, which is not?

WH: Well, I think that's a little harder, especially since the new science isn't really here yet to the same extent that the new thought churches are here. Of course the new science includes the old; it's really an expanded science. If you think back, we have always had controversies within science, quite apart from the science-versus-religion controversy – determinism versus free will; vitalism in the life sciences; various explanations as to how we come to be here, such as evolution versus creationism; and so on.

How do you deal with consciousness or with action at a distance? There have always been paradoxes and mysteries in science.

WH: There are two new principles that help us get started here – actually they're not new, but understanding their implications is new. One is the principle of complementarity, which emerged first in physics. You can think of light as having a wavelike nature, or as having a particle nature. Those are not contradictory positions; they are complementary. Now, if you apply the same principle in science, there would seem to be a contradiction between a science which is deterministic and a science which includes the concept of human consciousness as a causal factor in the universe. But then we come to recognize that they are rather complementary.

The other principle is that the whole is greater than the sum of its parts, which is to say that when you consider whole human beings, or a whole universe, you may run into things that you can't really explain in a reductionistic science which is focused on studies of the parts.

For example, if determinism and free will are really complementary in this larger view of science, there would be a deterministic level, and then another level of human affairs, for example, where free will is part and parcel of that level.

WH: I think you have to have at least four levels in the extended science. One level is the physical sciences, more or less as we know them. Those are objectivist – that is, you can study them from the outside more or less. They are reductionistic and positivistic – that is, what you study is what you can physically measure. A second level on top of that is the life sciences, and there you have to introduce new concepts, teleological concepts. You have to be able to think in terms of a stomach as not being just something with a certain shape and a certain chemical composition, but also as having the function of digesting food. So you bring in something new, a sense of function, that doesn't exist in the physical sciences.

At a third level you come into the human sciences, and you have to introduce something new still, which is that human consciousness causes things to happen. There is no place for that in the deterministic physical sciences. Then there is a fourth level, which I would call the spiritual sciences. We don't have very good representations of that yet, although some of the Tibetan Buddhist psychological work would certainly qualify as part of it, as would elements of the Gnostic tradition of Christianity and of transpersonal psychology.

If one searches the great spiritual literatures of the world, one would find some very precise and rigorous philosophies, such as the yoga sutras, that deal with the laws of this realm.

WH: They certainly do. Of course the way you verify things in that area is different from the way you verify things in the physical sciences. One of the problems is that there has not been widespread understanding of how to validate knowledge. Another problem has been that these things were essentially in different languages in different cultures – and I don't mean just language as we ordinarily consider it, but out of totally different traditions, with different pictures of reality. So they were hard to compare, and it was hard for anybody to say that underneath all of that, there seems to be one growing body of knowledge that accumulates just as knowledge in the sciences does. And yet, if you look back over the centuries, that would seem to be so. There were even research laboratories, recognized as such; only we didn't recognize it for a while because they were called monasteries. Their particular field of study happened to be the world of inner experience rather than the outer. But they went about it in very much the same way a scientist goes about the matter of science. You build knowledge on knowledge on knowledge, out of cumulative experience.

In the nineteenth century, Wilhelm Wundt, the father of modern experimental psychology, began using a method called introspection to deal with direct experience. This has been largely discarded by psychologists today, who felt that inner experience wouldn't conform to the positivistic standards of a science. You are saying that people are now reexamining that.

WH: I'm glad you said people, because it is not just scientists that we are examining. There is a great heresy abroad, and it is ordinary, reasonably well-educated people who are doing something quite parallel to what happened in the seventeenth century with the scientific heresy. In the seventeenth century you had a widening group of people who were saying, first quietly to one another and then finally out loud, "You know, there's something wrong with the picture of reality that the church authorities have been giving us. It doesn't correspond to our total experience." So then they leapt on things like the new theories of Copernicus and the observations of Galileo, and this spread very rapidly, among non-scientists as well as scientists. We call this the scientific revolution; it marked the end of the Middle Ages and the beginning of modern times. It changed everything.

At about the same time there was a sort of division of territory between the scientists and the church. The scientists would look at the measurable outer world, and the church would keep the soul and the spirit. And so we developed certain biases that entered into the scientific inquiry – the objectivist one, the positivist one, the reductionist one – and science took on a particular character. If science had developed in India first, it would have taken on a different character. But it didn't; it developed in Western Europe.

Getting back to science and religion, there is one other important point worth mentioning; you develop a science, or you create a religion, or you get involved with one or the other, because you want to understand things, you want to explain things. If you think of the hierarchy of physical sciences, life sciences, human sciences, and spiritual sciences, part of science's prejudice was that explanations that are scientific are downward-looking explanations. They are explanations in terms of how those atoms and molecules are moving around in the electromagnetic field, or what kind of chemical juices are causing your behavior.

In other words, we explain psychology by resorting to biology, we explain biology by resorting to chemistry, and we explain chemistry by resorting to physics.

WH: Exactly. That is the downward, reductionistic kind of explanation. That gradually came to be thought of as the only valid kind of explanation, certainly in academic scientific circles. In the religions, on the other hand, you had the other kind of explanation, the upward-looking explanation; if I want to really understand you, I need to understand your spirit, I need to understand you in a God-permeated universe. And so I am always looking in the other direction.

In the extended science I think you will have both of these things. In one case I am explaining in terms of a downward-looking cause – what is the chemistry and physics that is bringing about my behavior, say? In the other case, I'm looking upward for the understanding; I want to explain in terms of perhaps the level of human causation, conscious and unconscious processes; or perhaps the level of spiritual causation. Both kinds of explanation can go at the same time. They are complementary; they are both true at the same time. What we are dealing with is a giant leap, and the important thing is that it is coming not primarily from the scholars themselves, but from a shift in the culture – people insisting that they have to validate their own experience, regardless of what the authorities say. That's why it is another heresy, in a sense. Whereas the scientific heresy was people saying that the world is not like what the church authorities told us, and we have a new way of looking at it – we eventually call it empirical science – this heresy is saying the world isn't like what the secular authorities told us either. Reality is not like what any authorities tell us; reality comes out of our own experience. But if we are then going to represent that as best we can with some conceptual framework, we need some broader frameworks than the ones in conventional science.

So this synthesis of science and religion is a personal search that probably thousands of people are all engaged in simultaneously now; it's a groundswell of activity.

WH: Don't underestimate it. I'm sure that five to ten percent of the population, at any rate, have already shifted over to a totally different metaphysic. That's not a majority by any means, but it is an influential and spreading minority. There are a lot of other indications, too, that this thing is moving very rapidly.

Didn't some of the research you were involved in at SRI International indicate that there is an elite group of people – the inner-directed people – who are the leaders, the movers and shakers, who are really asking these searching questions and developing these new metaphysics?

WH: That's true. The early survey data that indicated this shift included some by Daniel Yankelovich, and some that was done at SRI, the so-called VALS study, Values and Life Styles; and there were various other sources. It all seemed to indicate that sometime between about the mid-seventies and the early eighties, there suddenly came into being a group which was maybe as large as twenty percent of the adult population in the country, that were living their lives on the basis of more inner-directed values and less on the basis of outer-directed, esteem-related values such as economic or social position – more inner-directed, ecological, humanistic, spiritual kinds of values. Now, I don't by any means think that all of those people were really seeing reality differently, with a different set of metaphysical assumptions. But some fraction of them certainly are – not just in this country, but in any country I go to.

Earlier you mentioned the notion of verification in the so-called spiritual sciences, and establishing a consensus view of what reality is. How does that work?

WH: Interestingly, the spiritual traditions have had a tradition of validating data in various ways, just as the sciences have. Because it's a different kind of data, describing a different kind of experience, the validation procedures had to be different. You can't very well do a controlled experiment with spiritual experience; it doesn't work that way. There were at least three tests that have traditionally been used. That is, the person who wanted to do his own explorations, or move up in the priesthood, had to keep in mind that just as you don't believe everything you see, because there are optical illusions, you also don't believe everything you see inwardly; you don't believe everything that seems to be a vision or an inner voice.

There needs to be a test or a method of discernment.

WH: One of the tests was, how does this check with what other people have experienced down through the ages? In other words, how does this check with tradition – not really how does it check with church dogma in some rigid sort of way, but how does it test out with regard to other people who have made similar explorations and reported them? And then a second test is, how would the world be if everyone behaved in accordance with this great insight you've got? If you got an insight that says, "God says I should do so and so," how would it be if everybody in the world followed that sort of precept? Then the third test is, does it still feel noetically true? Does it feel as though intuitively you know it's so, even though you can't demonstrate it? Does it still feel that way? If it does now, does it feel that way tomorrow, or next week, or next month?

So there is a tradition of testing, of cumulative knowledge, and now we are finally getting to the point where we can open up the concept of science to include all of that. Not very many years ago, that was sort of a taboo thing to try to do.

There is a big difference between qualifying to be an expert on the level of the spiritual sciences and on the level of the physical sciences. It's fairly cut and dried how you become qualified as an expert in physics. It's a little bit less so in an area like systematic biology, because there is a lot of connoisseurship that comes in there – how can you tell whether this plant is really a new species or not? You use a lot of intuition, a lot of pattern recognition. It's another ball game. In the human sciences it is even more so – how do I recognize a personality trait? But in the spiritual sciences, there is not only more connoisseurship involved, but also you have to allow yourself to be changed internally. You have to undergo change in order to understand the concepts at that level. In the physical sciences you may undergo change of a sort, but it is more intellectual change. This is a more total character change.

Do you see us moving to a point in history where the so-called spiritual sciences will be integrated with mainstream science – maybe even acknowledged by the American Academy or the Association for the Advancement of Science?

WH: Well, those things always take a generation, for obvious reasons. Yes, I think we are definitely moving that way, because the power is coming from a cultural shift. I'm not sure that given the structure of universities, divided up into departments, that there is very much force coming from the universities toward this sort of unification. There is a lot of force coming from ordinary people changing and saying, "Look, it's one world, one experience. It doesn't feel right to have it all carved up in little bits."

So there is this groundswell, and it keeps growing and pushing us in that direction.

WH: Yes, and my reason for feeling so certain of that is that first of all, I've been tracking it professionally and personally for about twenty years. We were not at all sure of this when we first began to talk about it at SRI around 1969. Then the farther we went with it, and the more things we watched, the clearer the pattern seemed to become. And then, in the last few years, there have been indications all over the map. If you go back twenty years, who was talking about near-death experiences? Who was talking about channeling? Who was talking about karma? Not only were they not being talked about, but there wasn't any sense that there was anything there to talk about.

There is permission now to talk about a lot of things that there didn't used to be. But underneath that, the most revolutionary thing of all is our new view of consciousness. Yes, the evolutionary picture looks OK; there was material evolution of stars and planets and life forms and human beings; but consciousness/mind/spirit/universal mind was there all along. It didn't wait for neuronal cells to develop in the human brain; and furthermore, each of us in the depths of ourselves taps into that whole thing.

CONSCIOUSNESS AND HYPERSPACE

WITH SAUL-PAUL SIRAG

Saul-Paul Sirag is a theoretical physicist who has papers on unified field theory and cosmology in NATURE *and the* INTERNATIONAL JOURNAL OF THEORETICAL PHYSICS. *He is the author of the forthcoming book* HYPERSPACE CRYSTALLOGRAPHY.

Nineteenth-century theologians developed the idea of multiple dimensions to explain God in scientific language. In this interview, Saul-Paul Sirag discusses current theories of multiple dimensions, which have been fabricated to account for subatomic interactions, and the implications of these theories for the psychology and technology of the twenty-first century.

I remember when I was in college maybe twenty years ago, people talked about maybe there were more than three dimensions, but then they kind of laughed it off. Now physicists take the notion of hyperspace, or multiple dimensions of reality, as being matter-of-fact.

SS: Perhaps it's not quite matter-of-fact yet, but they are taking it very seriously, and from my point of view it is practically a matter of fact. The modern idea of hyperspace really goes back to the nineteenth-century mathematician Hilton, who talked about a four-dimensional space. That was superseded by Einstein's idea of space-time. Einstein showed that space and time were connected together in a four-dimensional system, and so people kind of pooh-poohed the earlier ideas of a four-dimensional space, because they said the fourth dimension really isn't space at all, it's time.

More recently, we have discovered in physics that what we were for a long time calling the internal spaces of subatomic particles are really spaces as much as space-time is. In fact, the picture that has emerged now is that really there is a much higher dimensional system than just one extra dimension or two extra dimensions. There are many extra dimensions, and depending on how you count dimensions and how your theory works, you might have ten dimensions, twenty-six dimensions, or many more dimensions than that.

These are considered literal, factual dimensions of space.

SS: The physicists working on these theories consider them that way, yes. The idea really is that space-time, the four-dimensional system of Einstein, is really just a subspace of this much higher dimensional space; and so the three-dimensional space of our ordinary experience is very much an illusion. It reminds me of Plato's allegory of the shadow world inside the cave. Plato said that the people chained in this cave in such a way that they could not move their heads or their limbs would identify themselves with the two-dimensional shadows. Plato was trying to say that we are more than three-dimensional beings, but we tend to identify ourselves with our three-dimensional shadows, namely our bodies. Of course geometry wasn't very highly developed then; it was just starting, and so he didn't have the language to talk about hyperspace the way we do today, but I think he intuitively had the idea.

We have the more modern notion now of the Flatlanders.

SS: The Flatlander notion was invented in the nineteenth century by a minister, Abbott, to try to make the notion of the spiritual realm more understandable. One of the old ideas, going back to Plato and even earlier, is that there is a spiritual realm which in our modern terminology is a hyperspace realm. In this hyperspace realm the ordinary realm is only a partial view of reality; the spiritual realm is a much greater and richer realm and this ordinary realm depends on that realm for its very existence. This is very much the way unified field theory views the world today. There are many different versions of unified field theory today, but each theory in a sense implies a different type of hyperspace with different dimensions and different structures in that space.

So what they are disagreeing about is the nature of the higher dimensions of space, not whether or not higher dimensions exist.

SS: Yes; each dimension corresponds, in the old way of thinking, to a different type of subatomic particle; so the way we test these theories is to find evidence for the existence of these subatomic particles. These subatomic particles aren't like little BBs at all; they are very different from that, and that is why they can correspond to dimensions of hyperspace.

Human consciousness, too, normally seems to have strange dimensions of time and space. We close our eyes and we have dreams, fantasies, and mental imagery of various kinds. With the speed of thought we can go from Egypt to Athens to San Francisco. Is there some sense in which inner space, as we experience it, might be describable in the same language that you are using for hyperspace?

SS: That is really what I believe. I believe that from the full hyperspace, however many dimensions that is – and in some sense it's probably infinite-dimensional – there are many projections, subprojections you might say, down from an infinite-dimensional space, say, to a 192-dimensional space, to a 96-dimensional space, to a 48-dimensional space, and then down to a twelve-dimensional space, and then down to a four-dimensional space-time. And each of these projections entails different things being left out, so to speak.

Is this string theory we're talking about now, or fiber-bundle theory?

SS: Well, fiber-bundle theory is the mathematics behind this. String theory is a term being used in unified particle physics now, and virtually everybody working on unified field theory today is essentially working on some version of a fiber bundle theory, mathematically speaking.

With these various dimensions stepping down, or projecting from one to the other, as you've just said.

SS: Yes.

What is unified field theory? Why is it so important?

SS: The whole history of physics has really been the pursuit of unifying forces of nature. Newton, for instance, unified what we call celestial gravity with terrestrial gravity. In other words, he unified celestial gravity, the force that makes the earth go around the sun and the moon go around the earth, with the force that makes rocks fall, all into one beautiful scheme. That's Newtonian mechanics. Later on, in the nineteenth century, James Clerk Maxwell unified electricity, magnetism, and light, three very different things, into electromagnetism; so light is an electromagnetic wave. Very recently, we have been able to unify electromagnetism with what we call the weak nuclear force

– the force that controls, for instance, radioactive decay. So now we say radioactive decay is just an aspect of the electro-weak force. There is another nuclear force that we call the strong force, which actually holds the nucleus of the atom together against electrical repulsion, and we are attempting to unify that with the other forces. The biggest problem of all is unifying gravity with all these other forces, and also finding out whether there are any forces that we have left out of the picture – some new force lurking in the experimental data. For instance, I and other people have reason to believe that there is another force, sometimes called the fifth force or the feeble force, that needs to be in there and unified with these forces.

The reason for doing this is that we are always seeking a more all-embracing, a simpler, view of reality. The irony is that in order to achieve this simpler view of reality something has to give, and what gives is that the dimensionality of the system becomes much more complicated in a sense, but also very beautiful.

So the ultimate unified theory would be one in which consciousness also fits into the picture.

SS: Well, more than fits into the picture. What I really think is that in some cosmic sense there really is only one consciousness, and that is really the whole thing – in other words, that hyperspace itself is consciousness acting on itself, and space-time is just kind of a studio space for it to act out various things in. Of course this is an old, old idea in many different spiritual traditions.

But you are saying that by using the tools of modern physics you can come to that conclusion.

SS: Yes. Essentially what we are in the process of doing is describing that realm. You might say that we are describing the spiritual realm, if one takes this point of view. Obviously most physicists don't take this point of view yet, but I think they will in another couple of decades.

Actually, the structure that we discover in physics is the ultimate structure of our own minds. I didn't make this idea up; I got it from other physicists such as Eddington, who held it very strongly. Eddington was ridiculed for it actually, but the idea makes much more sense in the context of what we are doing now in physics. It's too bad that Eddington isn't around now to see what is going on, because he was very interested in unified field theory.

So unified field theory carries with it these notions of hyperspace of multiple dimensions, and somehow we are looking at the structure not only of the physical universe, but of the human mind itself.

SS: Yes, but the human mind is just a part. Just as space-time is just a part of hyperspace, the human mind is just a small part of a much greater mind – cosmic mind, if you like; we don't have good words for it yet.

In philosophy there is something called the mind-body problem; namely, that if the physical world out there seems so different from the world we experience internally, then how do these two things have anything to do with each other? So some people attempt to solve the problem by saying, it's all mind; that's the idealist solution. Then there is the materialist solution, which is to say that it's all matter, and mental phenomenon are essentially epiphenomenon, a byproduct of matter. Our way of looking at things is a little bit of a different way of solving it than either one of those. It may lean more toward an idealistic position, but actually one could also consider it a materialistic solution, because there is now developing a physics of this hyperspace.

You're saying that matter isn't what we used to think it was.

SS: That's right. Matter has for a long time been taking on more and more of the mindlike qualities. On the other hand, people who have been studying the mind through the techniques of biology, neuroscience, neuropharmacology, and so on, find more and more material kinds of explanations for what we would traditionally consider mental phenomena. The two have crossed over each other somehow at this point in history, and I think that the solution for the mind-body problem will be found in this hyperspace picture of things.

The old spiritual idea was that the mind is not in the body; if the mind is in the body, then you definitely have a mind-body problem. The new view is that the body is in the mind – the cosmic mind being this hyperspace. The body is just a shadow that is projected, so to speak, from hyperspace, and so there is no problem, because our internal experience is not just connected to the hyperspace, it is an intimate piece of the hyperspace. Our own minds are projections from a much greater mind.

What might be some practical consequences of this view? How would it change my life to understand that?

SS: Well, there might be ethical kinds of considerations, like if I'm projected from a greater mind and so are you, and we're together in superspace –

These bodies may be like little puppets with the same pupper master.

SS: And of course people who have psychic experiences claim to experience this sort of thing directly – a kind of mental link with another person. In the dream realm we also possibly experience a different kind of oneness than we ordinarily experience. Physicists have never taken seriously the dream world – or worlds; there are many, probably. It's a state very much like a physical state, because to a certain extent things make sense in a dream world and to a certain extent they don't make sense. But suppose in the dream realm one were to do physics experiments; one would come up with a different physics, so to speak. It would be a different space-time projection, as we experience it; in the dream realm, for instance, your identity can change very quickly. I could have a dream in which you appear and suddenly I am you and you are me, or somebody else; and that can change very quickly. We don't experience reality that way, but that doesn't mean that realm isn't real. This sort of thing makes more sense if reality is truly a hyperspace and there are all sorts of projections going on. Perhaps even things like reincarnation could be reinterpreted in such a model.

As I understand your theory, the entire physical universe as we experience it is in some sense predicated upon the mathematics of the fine structure constant in physics, the number 137; everything else sort of emerges from that. Other levels of hyperspace –parallel universes, or other dimensions – might be predicated on other mathematical constants in the same way. Is that basically correct?

SS: Yes. We are very impressed by certain constants in physics that play a very fundamental role. Earlier when I was describing the unification of the forces, I could have said that this means that all the forces have the same strength at some hyperspace level. The fine structure constant is a measure of the strength of the electrical force; essentially our idea is that all the forces have that same strength at the unification level, the hyperspace level. If that strength were ever so slightly different, say one percent different, then a world totally different from ours would occur. This may be precisely what dream worlds are like; they are simply a kind of physics with a different fine structure constant.

So using the mathematics that you have developed, you could predict what other realities ought to look like, at least how the physical laws would operate.

SS: In principle one could try to do that, but we are talking about a very long-term program here. We are really talking about what physics is going to look like in the twenty-first century. You see, Maxwell's equations were written down in the nineteenth century, early in 1865; and yet all of these marvelous electrical phenomena that are our high technology today really grew out of that one set of equations. The twentieth century has mainly been, technologically speaking, the exploration of that beautiful unification of forces that took place over a hundred years ago. In the next century probably a vastly different technology, much more detailed than even electromagnetism technology, will evolve, and consciousness will be very intimately involved with those technological developments, I believe, due to the unification of all the forces such as we know them today. It will be a very exciting thing. I am not saying physics is coming to any kind of end by this unification; it's more like a true beginning – a true beginning to a new technology, even.

What are some of the things you would envision?

SS: I can guess some things, but let me remind you that one of the last things in the world that Maxwell would have predicted would have been television coming out of his equations. From Maxwell's equations one found out that besides visible light there had to be invisible light; but how vast that invisible light was nobody really knew. Then radio waves were discovered as one kind and X-rays as another kind, for instance; Maxwell didn't predict any of these things specifically. So it is very hard to predict, if you are just a physicist writing down a few equations.

The main thing that I have already predicted follows from what I said earlier – that from the hyperspace we project space-time. I think that what we might be learning how to do technologically is actually to work in the hyperspace realm. In other words, if we are living in a 3-D movie now, what we are going to learn is how to make our own movies, so to speak, rather than just acting in somebody else's movie. We are going to play a higher role in the production of the movies that we then act in. Basically that is just a way of saying that we are going to play the whole game more consciously.

It sounds as if you are saying we will become like gods, or what we imagine gods to be today.

SS: Of course this will just be a minute step up into the hyperspace; there will be many dimensions beyond us, and we would perhaps talk about godlike beings beyond us then, who are higher in the hierarchy of consciousness, and so on. A whole new vocabulary would evolve that would be much more precise. The mathematics for thinking about this is already developed, as far as I am concerned. Mathematicians are way ahead of this in the sense that they don't have to test their theorems by experiments. The only test of a mathematical theorem is a logical proof, and so new ideas in mathematics go very quickly. Fiber-bundle theory started to be worked out in the thirties, and developed very rapidly in the fifties, and we are only now really beginning to apply it in a big way in physics. The mathematicians are ahead of us. Those of us who do new things get our cues from the mathematicians.

When I was a child I was told that only twelve people on the planet would really understand Einstein, because it takes a while for brilliant, new ideas to filter down to the masses of society. Now I suspect there are more than twelve people who understand Einstein. You're talking about the leading-edge theories. I wouldn't be surprised if there were only twelve people on the planet today who understand your work.

SS: Well, that's not really true. The mathematicians I talk to generally understand it very well, especially if they know an area of mathematics called group theory; and if they know fiber-bundle theory then they really understand it. Both of these are very big areas in mathematics. Physicists generally find it more difficult to follow. I presented this theory to a special colloquium session of the physics department and the math department at Georgetown University. The physicists by and large were just out of it, so far as understanding went, but the mathematicians followed very well.

If physicists are having a hard time now following your work, it may take a hundred years before it will really affect the masses of people.

SS: No, no, not a hundred years. Things move a bit faster than they did in

Maxwell's days, and technology also moves much faster now than it used to. The hyperspace idea will definitely appeal to the younger generation of physicists, and they will get into it right away, I think, just as they are getting into superstring theory right now.

EXPLORING THE PSYCHE

THE HUMAN DILEMMA

WITH ROLLO MAY, PH.D.

Psychotherapist Rollo May is a recipient of the Distinguished Career Award of the American Psychological Association and a founding sponsor of the Association for Humanistic Psychology. He is author of numerous classic works including LOVE AND WILL, PSYCHOLOGY AND THE HUMAN DILEMMA, FREEDOM AND DESTINY, DREAMS AND SYMBOLS, THE MEANING OF ANXIETY, *and* MAN'S SEARCH FOR HIMSELF.

Existential psychology, a discipline pioneered by Rollo May, emphasizes philosophical rather than psychopathological aspects of the human condition. In this interview, Dr. May proposes that genuine growth comes from confronting the pain of existence rather than escaping into banal pleasures or shallow positive thinking and that genuine joy can emerge from a recognition of despair.

You are best known as a pioneer in establishing existential psychology as an independent clinical discipline. Unlike most forms of clinical psychology that rely on a medical or a behavioral model, existential psychology relies more on a philosophical model.

RM: Yes. In 1956 or 1957, a publisher called me up and asked if I would edit a book on European existential psychotherapy. I was delighted to hear there was such a book. I hadn't known a thing about the existential movement there, but I knew that in this country I believed in it very firmly, because existentialists are the ones who emphasize anxiety, the individual, courage, and guilt feeling – that it has to be taken into consideration at least – and they see human beings as struggling, sometimes successfully, sometimes not successfully. This was exactly the model that we needed for psychotherapy. The medical model had turned out to be a dead end, and I welcomed the chance to edit this book of existential chapters from Europe. It met my own needs and my own heart.

When you speak of anxiety, I assume that you don't think of it as a symptom to be removed, but rather as a gateway for exploration into the meaning of life.

RM: That's exactly right. I think anxiety is associated with creativity. When you are in a situation of anxiety, you can of course run away from it, and that is certainly not constructive; or you can take a few pills to get you over it, or cocaine, or whatever else you may take.

Or you could meditate.

RM: But I think none of those things – including meditation, which I happen to believe in – none of those paths lead you to creative activity. What does anxiety mean? It's as though the world is knocking at your door, and you need to create, you need to make something, you need to do something. For people who have found their own heart and their own souls, anxiety is a stimulus toward creativity and courage. It is what makes us human beings.

I suppose much of our anxiety comes from the basic human dilemma of being mortal, of ultimately having to confront our own demise.

RM: We are conscious of our own selves, our own tasks, and also we know we are going to die. Man is the only creature – men, women, and even children sometimes – who can be aware of his death, and out of that comes normal anxiety. When I let myself feel that, then I apply myself to new ideas, I write books, I communicate with my fellows. In other words, the creative interchange of human personality rests upon the fact that we know we are going to die; of that, the animals, the grass, and so on know nothing. Our knowledge of our death is what gives us a normal anxiety that says to us, "Make the most of these years you are alive." And that is what I have tried to do.

Another source of anxiety that you have described in your writing is our very freedom – our ability to make choices, and having to confront the consequences of those choices.

RM: That's right. Freedom is also the mother of anxiety. If you had no freedom, you would have no anxiety. That's why the slaves in the films have no expression on their faces; they have no freedom. Those of us who do have freedom are alert and alive. We are aware that what we do matters, and that we only have about seventy or eighty or ninety years in which to do it; so why not do it and get joy out of it, rather than running away from it? That's a little capsule of the meaning of anxiety.

Isn't there a bit of a conflict between allowing oneself to be open to that feeling of anxiety, and then also seeking joy?

RM: Oh no. There is a conflict between that and what is generally called happiness – the flat, meaningless forms of feeling good. I am not against anybody feeling good or having happy hours, but joy is something different from that. Joy is the zest that you get out of using your talents, your understanding, the totality of your being, for great aims. Composers, Mozart and Beethoven and the rest of them, always showed considerable anxiety, because they were in the process of loving beauty, of feeling joy, when they heard a beautiful combination of notes. That is the kind of feeling that goes with creativity. That's why I say the courage to create. Creation does not come out of simply what you are born with. That must be united with your courage; both cause anxiety, but also great joy.

Much of our modern culture seems to be an attempt to cope with this fundamental anxiety by diversions and what you have called banal pleasures.

RM: Well, you have just put your finger on the most significant aspect of modern society. We try to avoid anxiety by getting rich, by making a hundred thousand dollars when we are twenty-one years of age, by becoming millionaires. Now, none of those things lead to the joy, the creativity that I am talking about. One can own the world and still be without the inner sense of pleasure, of joy, of courage, of creation. I think our society is in the midst of a vast change. The society that began at the Renaissance is now ending, and we are seeing the results of this ending of a social period in the fact that psychotherapy has grown with such great zest. Almost every other person in California is a psychotherapist. This always happens when an age is dying. The Greeks began their great age in the seventh and sixth centuries B.C.; then they talked of beauty and goodness and truth, all the great things that the philosophers talked about. But by the second or first century B.C. that had all been forgotten. The philosophers now talked about security, and they tried to help people get along with as little pain as possible, and they made mottoes for human beings. Beauty and truth and goodness had been lost. Our Renaissance began the modern age, and at the beginning of an age there are no psychotherapists. This is taken care of by religion and by beauty, by art and music. But at the end of an age – every age down through history has been the same – every other person becomes a therapist, because there are no ways of ministering to people in need, and they form long lines to the psychotherapist's office. I think it is a sign of the decadence of the age, rather than a sign of our great intelligence.

In your book LOVE AND WILL you refer to the great poem by T.S. Eliot, THE WASTE LAND, and the way so many people seemed to relate to it when it was first written early in this century. It seemed to characterize the emptiness of modern society.

RM: Yes, the king in *The Waste Land*, remember, was impotent. The wheat and the grass did not grow. Therefore it was a waste land. And he goes on in marvelous detail. Now, just about that time, in the 1920s, in the Jazz Age, there was written another prophetic book, *The Great Gatsby* by F. Scott Fitzgerald. It's a small book. It is a marvelous picture of how our age is disintegrating. Gatsby ultimately dies, and dies a completely lonely man; there is nobody at the funeral, and it is a tragedy. Fitzgerald saw that this was happening, not in the Jazz Age – everybody was earning lots of money then and trying out new styles, just like nowadays – but he knew what was going to happen, and therefore *The Great Gatsby*. We are now in the age when those things, *The Waste Land* and *The Great Gatsby*, are coming to fruition. That is why I believe that if our world survives the nuclear threat – and I believe it will – if it survives, we will move into a new age, when the emphasis will not be on making piles and piles of money and being scared to death the stock market is going to drop tomorrow; rather the emphasis will be on truth, on joy, on understanding, on beauty – these things that to my mind make life really worth living.

You have characterized our present age as one in which modern man seems to be robbed of his own free will; through Freudian psychology and other scientific movements we see the human being as influenced by deterministic forces. It seems that there is nothing that we can do, and there is a feeling of helplessness and alienation. And yet you suggest that through philosophical and existential exploration we can enter into another state of consciousness, where we reconnect with our will at a deeper level.

RM: Yes, this is why I wrote *Love and Will*, because you cannot love unless you also can will. I think, and I thought when I wrote that book, that a new way of love would come about. People would learn to be intimate again. They would write letters. There would be a feeling of friendship among people. This is the new age that is coming, and I don't think it is chiefly a matter of philosophy. Nowadays there are no philosophers; the last philosopher in this country was Paul Tillich. People now have given up; they now call philosophy the kibitzing on science – a way of simply looking over the scientist's shoulder, and seeing how they can help science put things together. That is not philosophy. Philosophy is a deep search for a truth by which I can fulfill myself, by which I can create. Philosophy is the basis of freedom. It is the basis of goodness, too, which seems not to trouble many modern people, but I think that is a great mistake because of all of our lack of ethics and morality. We need goodness, and we need beauty. All of those are philosophical terms.

You see, I am really a psychotherapist, after saying all these nasty things about psychotherapy. It is the way we have at the end of the twentieth century of helping many people to find themselves and a way of life that will be satisfying and that will give them the joy that human beings certainly have a right to have. I am not ashamed at all that I am a psychotherapist. I became a therapist because I saw that is where people unburden themselves and that is where people will show what they have in their hearts. They don't show that in philosophy, and in most religions these days they also don't show it. This is why so many people in California join the cults. Now, I happen to believe in meditation; I do it myself. We have learned a lot of things from India and Japan; but we cannot be Indians or Japanese, and we must find a form of religious experience that will fit us as pioneers of the twenty-first century.

A few moments ago you referred to a new age; of course new age is a popular term these days for a wide scope of activities. I gather from your work that you are critical of a good deal of this as glossing over basic human pain.

RM: Exactly. I don't like the new age movement; I think it is oversimplified. It makes everybody feel temporarily happy, but they avoid the real problems. The new age can come only as we face anxiety, as we face guilt feeling for our misapprehension of what is the purpose of life, as we face death as a new adventure. None of these things does the new age talk about. It talks about only being gleeful, and everybody singing songs.

But you know, I sense another paradox here. In your book FREEDOM AND DESTINY *you have a section on mysticism, and you refer to the great Western mystics Jacob Boehme and Meister Eckhart and their search for the divine fire within themselves. You seem to see that almost as a model of deep existential probing.*

RM: Oh yes; I am very much a believer and follower of these mystics in our tradition. I am not a believer and follower of Rajneesh, or Maharishi. Muktananda I found the most companionable of these leaders; but most of them that come from India build up cults and get into all kinds of trouble, and they are sued for millions of dollars, and the cult then collapses. Or take Jim Jones, who took nine hundred people to the jungle, where they were going to set up a perfect community, and they all committed suicide, 919 of them.

But your criticism goes much deeper than just the scandals themselves. My sense is that you are saying that in this retreat to a mystical lotus land, or perhaps even to beliefs such as spiritualism and reincarnation, people are losing touch with the basic issues of their very existence.

RM: Oh, absolutely; you said it beautifully. I am very critical of these movements that soft-pedal our problems, and that indicate that we should forget them. I think the mystics that we were talking about back in our tradition – Jacob Boehme, who was burned at the stake, and the other Christian mystics, the mystics of Mohammedanism, and so on – are very important. Although the Church at the time opposed them, they neverthe-less left great books full of knowledge that we can read, understand, and learn from.

Some of the existentialist philosophers, such as Camus and Sartre and perhaps even Genet, made quite a bit out of the idea of rebelling against the conventional mores of society. You seem to be saying that genuine mysticism has to also involve this kind of cutting-edge rebellion against the herd instinct.

RM: Yes, it does. It is a rebellion against the herd instinct. Sartre was very important in this movement of the rebel. Camus wrote the book *The Rebel.* And Paul Tillich was my dear and very close friend for some thirty years; he and other existentialists understood that joy and freedom come only from the facing of life, the confronting of the difficulties. Sartre, when France was overrun by the Nazis, wrote a drama called *The Flies*. This is a retelling of the ancient Greek story of Orestes; the little bit of it that I want to quote is that Zeus tries to get Orestes not to go back to his home town and kill his mother, which he was ordered to do to revenge his father. Zeus says, "I made you, so you must obey me." And Orestes says, "You made me, but you blundered. You made me free." And then Zeus gets quite angry, and he has the stars and the planets zooming around to show how powerful he is, and he says, "But do you realize how much despair lies ahead of you if you follow your course?" Orestes says, "Human life begins on the far side of despair." Now, I happen to believe that. It's like alcoholics. They cannot get over the alcoholism except as they get into despair, and then AA can take them and free them from alcoholism. That is why I think despair has a constructive side, as well as anxiety having a constructive effect.

You mentioned earlier the great artistic achievements of Mozart and Beethoven. We have the expression, "tears of joy"; it seems that when one experiences deep joy, it is because it somehow incorporates the wholeness of human life. We see the joy bubbling up, emerging through the despair itself. And that is real joy.

RM: Yes, you have understood it very well.

And yet it is almost intimidating. Many of us, as we live our lives and go through our routines, are afraid to really drink deeply of the fullness of that.

RM: Well, if it were easy, it wouldn't be effective. It is not easy. Life is difficult, and I believe it has many conflicts in it, many challenges. But it seems to me that without those life wouldn't be interesting. I am reminded of the end of Beethoven's Ninth Symphony: "Joyful, joyful, we adore thee." That "Joyful, joyful" comes only after the agony that is shown in the first part of that symphony. Now, I believe in life, and I believe in the joy of human existence; but these things cannot be experienced except as we also face the despair and the anxiety that every human being has to face if he lives with any creativity at all.

BOUNDARIES OF THE SOUL

WITH JUNE SINGER, PH.D.

June Singer is a Jungian analyst, a member of the C.G. Jung Institute of San Francisco, and a founder of the C.G. Jung Institute of Chicago. Her classic work BOUNDARIES OF THE SOUL *introduced many people to the psychology of C. G. Jung. She is also author of* SEEING THROUGH THE VISIBLE WORLD: JUNG, GNOSIS AND CHAOS; A GNOSTIC BOOK OF HOURS; LOVE'S ENERGIES; ANDROGYNY; and* THE UNHOLY BIBLE.

Jungian analysis focuses on unconscious archetypes that operate beneath our cultural conditioning. Transformation, says Dr. Singer, must emerge from within, apart from any preconceptions of the analyst. In this interview she explores Jung's unique view of the unconscious as a boundless source of creative energy and growth.

I*n* BOUNDARIES OF THE SOUL *you write about your final examination at the Jung Institute. You were asked to describe the process of individuation, which is the goal of Jungian therapy, as if you were talking to a street sweeper while you were waiting for a bus. Could you repeat that definition for us?*

JS: Yes, and that was a shocker of a question, I might add, because I had studied all the parallels of the individuation process, from the alchemists down to the present day. When this question came to me – to describe this process while you are waiting for the bus and talking to a street sweeper – I looked out at the Lake of Zurich, and I thought, well, it's something like being in a sailing boat on the lake and utilizing the wind, understanding that the wind is something that you don't make and you can't control. You need to understand how to live your life in the same way that you understand how you would sail a boat, taking the power of the wind and going with it and allowing your own knowledge and understanding of it to help you go in the direction that you need to be headed. And so in Jungian analysis you learn how to deal with your own power, or rather the power that comes through you, and live your life in such a way that it is harmonious with that power which is above and beyond and all around.

It's as if the forces within our psyche are like the winds that might blow us about, and as we learn how to work with the winds we can direct ourselves through our lives.

JS: And we don't change them. In Jungian analysis we don't try to make somebody different from who they are. What we try to do is guide people to recognize themselves, discover themselves, and find out what was always there but hasn't been recognized or lived out.

You have pointed out that in modern culture people tend to sacrifice their individuality for the sake of security. The price that they often pay, I suppose, is that they lose their soul in a sense. It's almost as if Jungian psychology is a rediscovery of the soul.

JS: Yes, it is very much like that, in a certain way. There is an old Jewish legend about God calling an angel to bring a soul down to a mother who is about to give birth to a child. This soul, during the pregnancy, is taken on various trips to find out what his or her life will be like. At the moment of birth the angel hits the infant on the head, and at that moment the child forgets all that it knows about the soul and all its adventures, and then has to spend its whole life recovering bits and pieces and putting together that essence of who he really is. It is a beautiful story, because it suggests that we are born not as a *tabula rasa*, not as a blank tablet with society and the environment writing experience upon it and shaping the individual, but we come with some very definite tendencies, and while what happens to us certainly influences what we are going to become, it never really changes it totally.

There is really a striking contrast between Freudian psychology and Jungian psychology in this regard. The great influence of the Freudians in our society was to look at the religious impulses and the religious traditions and reduce them down to sexual instincts and their expression. Jung took almost the opposite view; he looked at sexuality and saw it as a symbol of our spiritual strivings.

JS: He certainly did. In fact he is often quoted as saying that when somebody comes to him with a sexual problem he is quite sure that at base it is spiritual, and when they come with a spiritual problem he has a pretty good idea that it may be based in sexuality. Jung saw the totality of the person, a kind of wholeness, in which you look at many, many levels of experience. When you look, for example, at sexuality, you are not only looking at the relationship between a man and a woman, but you are also looking at what each person brings of their concepts from their parents, the relationship of the parents to each other, and more than that, the parental belief system, the guiding principles that were prevalent in the household. And that fits into spiritual issues as well – was sexuality an expression of the divine creative spirit, or was it a kind of falling into the material and sensual and leaving the creativity of the spirit? So the two are not in any way separated.

You described a dream that Jung himself had when he was a young child that conditioned his whole outlook in this area. Could we go into that a bit?

JS: That was a famous dream. When he was about three or four years old, he dreamed that he was going down into an underground chamber. He went down and down and down, and he came to a huge room, and at the far end of the room there was a golden throne, and on the throne was an object that was nothing less than a golden phallus. He looked at it wonderstruck; it was radiant, and he felt that he had found something miraculous and amazing.

It was about the size of a tree, as I recall.

JS: Something like that, yes. Then he heard his mother calling, "That's the man-eater." And he shuddered and was frightened. He had what so many of us have – a tremendous spiritual attraction to sexuality, and a fear of its awesome power. It's never simple; it is always the tension of the opposites. Jung had much to say about the tension of the opposites. One of the things he is quoted as saying is that whenever something you find out is true, the opposite is equally true.

This gets us into the way that Jung dealt with the conflicts that he encountered in the Vienna Circle, the early psychoanalysts in the Freudian movement. When he would hear Freud arguing with Alfred Adler, for example, about the structure of the psyche – about whether it was based on the sexual instinct or the drive for power – Jung would say, "Well, there must be a sense in which both of these are expressing a single dynamic."

JS: Actually, Jung was very concerned about this, because his own view was different from that of both Freud and Adler, and the difference was one of the things that led Jung to leave the Vienna Circle. After he left it, Jung began to wonder how it could be that every time a case came up and the psychoanalysts were sitting around discussing it, Freud would always say that it came from the influence of the parents or some childhood trauma, and Adler would always say that it was something else, the will to power. Out of that Jung came to a discovery that was quite amazing at that time – that it wasn't the situation that was debatable, but that each person brought to it something of his own personality typology, and that no matter what the issue, the psychological makeup of the person would determine his perspective on it.

This is a very important part of Jung's work, as I see it, because if we believe that there is a right way to look at something, and that something is as it appears to be, then there is really no negotiating, no arguing, no chance to harmonize when people of different types come together. If you can recognize that if people are of different types, they each bring something novel to the discussion that the other person doesn't see, then you can welcome the opposite perspective. If Russia and the United States, for example, could recognize that they come out of different typologies — to expand this to an international perspective — we could learn much from each other.

In this context Jung introduced the terms introvert and extrovert which are so common now in our culture.

JS: Yes indeed. Freud was for Jung the example of the extrovert, because the extrovert gets his energy, his reason for being, from the external world; there is where the meaning is, and there is where you have to be effective. The introvert is more concerned with what the external world does to him or her – how that influences the individual psyche. These are two very different perspectives.

I gather that Freud was a strong personality; he dominated this group of very powerful intellectuals in the Vienna Circle. Adler, who broke away from him, seems to have been described as a much milder, meeker fellow.

JS: Adler is a typical introvert who doesn't really want to get out and fight, doesn't want to make demands. He is not trying to change the world. He is only interested in changing the self. When you have somebody who wants to change everybody else in conflict with somebody who doesn't want to, the person who doesn't want to tends to withdraw. In our American society, the extrovert tends to be more successful, in the business world for example. At least an extroverted persona is more successful – that is, a capacity to behave like an extrovert even if you aren't one, if you are a secret, closet introvert.

I suppose Jung's really major contribution to psychology, and where he really broke off from Freud, was his introduction of the concept of the collective unconscious.

JS: Yes. Jung's and Freud's concepts of the unconscious are very, very different. For Freud the unconscious was primarily an offshoot of the ego. Whatever the ego rejected or repressed – and by the ego I mean a person's self-concept – whatever I can't accept into my self-concept goes into the unconscious. I don't want to deal with it; I don't want to know about it. But for Jung, it was the unconscious that was basic. Everything was in the unconscious originally, and consciousness emerges out of the unconscious like an island out of the ocean; and then the effort is to expand that consciousness, to let it grow. There is no idea in Jungian psychology of gathering up the whole unconscious and making it the province of the ego, because the unconscious is like the universe, and you can't scoop up the universe in a teacup.

In other words, Freud seemed to suggest that at one time very early in human history there was no unconscious because we didn't need to repress; we were animals; and it was only with the veneer of civilization that we got the notion that our aggressive instincts and our sexual instincts were forbidden and couldn't be expressed. So we repressed them, and thereby created the unconscious.

JS: Exactly. And with Jung it was quite the opposite. He believed that at one time there was nothing but unconsciousness. We lived in a kind of world where we didn't think much about things – we didn't organize, didn't plan; we were very much an integral part of nature. And consciousness only grew gradually, and is still growing, and becomes more and more complex and defined. So Jung had a very different perspective, because with a Freudian perspective there is a necessity to recover what has been repressed. With Jungian psychology, certainly the concept of repression is there; I think Jung built on Freud, and accepted much of what he said with regard to repression. But what also is there is a tremendous source of creative energy; all that we can possibly become is already there in the unconscious, and we have only to learn how to find it.

You mentioned earlier that Jungian analysis isn't designed necessarily to correct a problem or to change a person, but it is more a path of self-discovery. I imagine many people come with symptoms, but you are not all that concerned about whether they leave after many years with or without their symptoms.

JS: Generally the symptom is not what it appears to be. It is something that precipitates a process that is long overdue. I know in my own experience, when I got into analysis I went because I thought that there was something valuable to be learned there; I didn't recognize that I personally had a lot of serious problems. It took quite a bit of analysis to find out why I really was there, but it was the idea that I wanted to be educated and understand more that precipitated the process.

To show you how unintellectual my initiation into Jungian analysis was, I'll tell you my first dream. Jungians put a lot of stock on initial dreams; we call them the first dream that you have in analysis. I was going to go the next day to my analyst, and I dreamed that I was laid out on a butcher's block. My hands and feet were tied, and someone was standing over me with a butcher knife, ready to plunge it in and open me up. I realized that I was really frightened about being seen, being revealed, and of course it came out in the analytic work, little by little, that I had held so much back and been so unwilling to look at what was there. Of course that's typical; almost everybody has that experience in some way or another. They know there is a lot there; they're curious, they have intimations. Dreams often give us intimations; we sense in strange ways that there is something that we know and yet don't know, and we want to know.

Jung seems to suggest that we often find the very opposite of what we manifest consciously when we go into the unconscious.

JS: Yes, and dreams can point the way to this, because all of the defenses that we have during the day keep us from recognizing all the demons and monsters and strange creatures of the night that we don't look at during the day. We don't allow them to exist. But when our forbiddings are taken away from us and we are vulnerable in sleep, they come sneaking out of the corners and show themselves, and we see then what it is that we have been hiding from ourselves. It is really wonderful, if you have the courage to face it, to be able to look at those and see what they mean.

So that after five or six years of Jungian analysis, it's not as if those demons are gone, it's just that we recognize the terrain and we are able to sail our boat a little better.

JS: We can make friends of them also. We have a very interesting process in Jungian analysis called active imagination, where we encounter the figures of our dreams, the figures of our imagination, and have a dialogue between our conscious ego and that creature – whatever person or manifestation it might be.

It could be any dream image.

JS: It could even be a rock or a castle or a plant or whatever. We would pose a question, for example, "Why are you here? What do you want of me? Why are you pestering me all the time?" And then we don't try to visualize or make anything happen, but we withdraw from it. We go deep into ourselves and allow the thing to come up of itself, and give it space, and listen to what comes. People often say, "How do you know that you are not just making this up, that it doesn't really come from the unconscious?" The way that I know is that when I am making it up it sounds kind of like what I expected. When I am really surprised, then I know it comes from down there – when it comes with something so amazing and so unexpected.

Your book BOUNDARIES OF THE SOUL opens with a quote, I think from Heraclitus: "No matter how long you probe and how far you look, you'll never encounter the boundaries of the soul."

JS: Yes. That sense of vastness is an integral part of Jungian work – the idea that the psyche is not only my psyche or your psyche, but that at some level it is collective, that we as individuals are part of our families, and our families are part of a community, and our community is part of a culture, and the culture is part of the whole human race. Each level has not only its conscious beliefs and behaviors, but also its unconscious aspects, so that at bottom we are on the foundation of the collective unconscious that is shared by everybody. The collective unconscious has characteristics which are not limited by time or space, but are universal and have existed ever since we knew anything about the psyche. Those characteristics, or those areas, so to speak, in the collective unconscious are called archetypes. This is a very difficult term to understand, because archetypes are unconscious. How can we explain what is unconscious? We can only talk in analogies.

So while we can't really define the limits or the boundaries of the soul, the archetypes constitute the structures within the soul – the energy constellations, the things that we organize our lives around.

JS: Yes, or they organize our lives for us, I would prefer to say, because we don't have too much to say about that process. They make us who we are.

A GUIDE TO RATIONAL LIVING

WITH ALBERT ELLIS, PH.D.

Albert Ellis is one of the most influential figures in the history of psychology. He is author of more than 600 academic papers and more than 50 books including A GUIDE TO RATIONAL LIVING, HOW TO LIVE WITH A NEUROTIC, HUMANISTIC PSYCHOTHERAPY, THE ART AND SCIENCE OF LOVE, and SEX WITHOUT GUILT. Considered the grandfather of cognitive behavioral therapy, Dr. Ellis is the founder of Rational-Emotive Therapy (RET) and one of the architects of the sexual revolution.

Working to change your personal philosophy is a valid therapeutic technique which can lead to genuine growth. According to Dr. Ellis, behavior, emotion, and cognition are all interrelated. In this interview he tells us how to recognize irrational belief patterns based on "musts" and "shoulds," and describes his methods for self-analysis and therapy.

ou are probably most widely noted for introducing into the field of psychotherapy an idea that seems almost self-evident – that our behavior is affected by what we think.

AE: Right, and conversely, many years ago, when I first formed RET, Rational-Emotive Therapy, I introduced the idea that our thinking is also affected by our behavior and our feelings.

So in effect it's all one system.

AE: That's right, it is interactional.

That system can therefore be affected by dealing with any part of it, I would assume – behavior, emotions, or thoughts.

AE: That's right; but if you profoundly change your philosophy, your thinking, then you are more likely to profoundly change your feeling and your behavior, and especially your disturbed feeling and your disturbed behavior.

You drew on the ancient philosophers, and came to the notion that philosophy itself could be a form of psychotherapy. At that point you broke away from psychoanalysis and developed a form of cognitive therapy.

AE: Yes, I practiced as a psychoanalyst for a while, but then I discovered that it didn't work – I have a gene for efficiency, while poor Sigmund Freud had a gene for inefficiency. So I went back to my hobby since the age of sixteen, philosophy, the philosophy of the ancients largely – of Epictetus and Marcus Aurelius; and in the East, of Confucius and Lao Tzu and Buddha – and I amalgamated it with behavior therapy, which I had used on myself at the age of nineteen to get over my phobia of public speaking and of approaching young females.

The kernel of your thought is basically that whatever happens to us in life is not totally responsible for our emotions.

AE: Right, although it contributes to it. A, activating events, contribute to C, consequences in our gut. But it is B, our belief system, our philosophy, which mainly, or certainly in great part, makes us feel and think the way we do and behave the way we do, especially in a disturbed manner. We disturb ourselves.

Typically, I suppose, when people are very angry or very depressed, they almost always think that it's something outside that is causing that.

AE: Right. We normally tend to think that because C, consequences – say, my anger – immediately follows your treating me unfairly, that you made me angry; instead of, "You made me feel sorry and regretful to some degree, but my anger I added by commanding and demanding that you not do what you indubitably did."

You broke with Freud in suggesting that the parents aren't responsible, early upbringing isn't responsible – that we teach ourselves these kinds of neurotic behaviors.

AE: Right. We are born gullible to our parents, influenceable, teachable, in the first place; therefore we stupidly listen to our parents. But then we invent many musts, shoulds, oughts, demands, and commands, in addition to the standards, the values, that we adopt from our parents. But the standards don't upset us; we mainly upset ourselves with those Jehovan commands.

You've coined a term – "musterbation."

AE: Yes. "Masturbation is good and delicious, but musterbation is evil and pernicious," is one of my sayings. The three main musts we tell ourselves are, "I must do well or I'm no good"; "You, you louse, must treat me well or you're worthless and deserve to roast in hell"; and "The world must give me precisely what I want, or it's a horrible, awful place." If you didn't musterbate, then you wouldn't awfulize, terribilize, catastrophize, say "I can't stand it," and put yourself down. If you only stuck with, "I'd like very much to do well, but I never have to," then you wouldn't disturb yourself.

So the technique that you engage in with your clients is one of disputing their musts, their ideas, and showing them that logically, scientifically, things are not that way – that nothing must be, if it isn't.

AE: The technique is a scientific method. We say – and we are the only cognitive behavioral therapy that does say – that when you think antiscientifically, piously, dogmatically, which is inflexible and antiscientific, then you disturb yourself. We therefore use the flexible scientific method to get you philosophically and otherwise to undisturb yourself.

Many therapists, particularly the Freudian school, would suggest that simply being told by your therapist that you are thinking things wrong isn't going to make a bit of difference – that you will continue with the same old behaviors anyway.

AE: We would agree; being told it, or told where you got it – namely, that you didn't get it from your sacred mother and father – won't help you. But the insight that I made myself disturbed, that I foolishly listened to my mother and father and took them too seriously, and I am still doing it, and that now I require work and practice, work and practice, to give up my biological and sociological tendency to disturb myself – that will help you. The belief that I disturbed myself and that I don't have to, will help, but not that much.

The idea that if you can simply change your philosophy your whole behavior will change, seems to go against the behaviorist or materialist notion that the mind doesn't really influence matter. You are saying that the mind does influence.

AE: Very significantly; but we also say that since you practiced, since you worked at this foolish philosophy, engrained it in yourself, and conditioned yourself, that therefore it requires work and practice to give it up, and it requires feeling against it. So we always use cognitive thinking and emotive, dramatic, evocative, and behavioral techniques to get people comprehensively to change and to stay changed.

In effect, every emotional state has its concomitant belief system.

AE: Right. Even sorrow and regret, which would be appropriate emotions when you are not getting what you want, have the belief system, "It's too bad. Isn't it unfortunate?" Horror and depression are, "It's awful; it must not be this way; I can't bear it." So each of the negative, self-defeating states such as depression or anxiety or despair or rage has some individual difference in what you tell yourself, what you believe philosophically.

So the heart of your philosophical approach is to distinguish between what we might call appropriate philosophies, appropriate emotions, and inappropriate ones.

AE: And oddly enough, I discovered after years of doing Rational-Emotive Therapy, RET, that there only are a few differences. One main difference, and it is crucial, is taking a preference, a desire, a goal, a value, practically all of which are legitimate, and escalating it, transmuting it into a demand, a should, an ought, a must, an absolute.

In other words, the most terrible thing could happen to me – perhaps I have leprosy, or some kind of fatal disease; or maybe somebody is slowly torturing me to death. That doesn't necessarily justify my going into a state of depression.

AE: Or a state of horror. But it does justify your saying, "I don't like this. I wish it weren't so. What am I going to do about it?" You won't do that if you're horrified; you'll freeze and make yourself worse. So you control largely, though not completely, your emotional and behavioral destiny, and if you change your basic philosophy of life, then you can change it. You have the power to do so, but you sit on your rump and don't use that power.

How would you distinguish your approach, say, from Norman Vincent Peale's Power of Positive Thinking?

AE: Well, that is good in a limited way. Instead of saying, "I can't do well," it says, "I can hit the tennis ball better," and it helps you perform better. But underlying this philosophy is, "and I have to, and if I don't hit that damn tennis ball well, there is something rotten about me as a tennis player and a person." So we undermine the negative thinking and don't just cover it up with positive and often Pollyannaish thinking: "Day by day in every way, I'm getting better and better and better." That was Coué's formula. But he went out of business because people fell on their face and didn't get better day by day.

What you are saying is that things may or may not get better; they may even get worse. But they don't have to get awful.

AE: Right. One of the techniques in RET is to show you that you can do better, which is positive thinking; but if you don't, you don't. We sometimes implode what you may do or what may happen to you at the worst, to show you that you don't have to be miserable. My new book for the public is called *How to Stubbornly Refuse to Make Yourself Miserable about Anything – Yes, Anything.*

That's quite a title. You just used a technical term, implode. Can you elaborate on that?

AE: Implode means really get into your feeling or your behavior, and do it many times forcefully, vigorously – feel the worst, feel very upset – and then change it to appropriate negative feelings. We are not against feelings, we are just against inappropriate, self-defeating feelings such as sorrow and regret and frustration and annoyance – which will drive you back to A, activating events, bad events in life, to change them. So we want you to feel; we don't want you to have no feeling, indifference, nirvana, desirelessness, or anything like that, but real feeling.

It would seem that when people awfulize, when they make things awful, they are using that as a screen to keep from getting in touch with their genuine feelings of disappointment.

AE: That's right. Their very genuine feeling, their good negative feeling, would be disappointment: "I don't like this. What can I do to change it? How bad, how unfortunate." They miss that with, "How awful, how horrible, how terrible." And they then get bad results and sit on their rumps again and do nothing, instead of forcing themselves to go back to the grind and change what they can change and accept what they cannot.

It sounds like good old-fashioned American philosophy, in a way.

AE: Well, Emerson had some of it, and Thoreau, and some of the other American philosophers. I got it mainly from the original philosophers, and also from their derivatives – from John Dewey, who had a good deal of it; Bertrand Russell, the English philosopher; Karl Popper, the great philosopher of science; and other modern philosophers.

In your work as a therapist you don't just sit back and calmly philosophize. You try to use philosophical approaches that really get inside a person to their inner thoughts, and work with them to change those inner thoughts, what they tell themselves.

AE: Right; and we teach them to do it. We have cognitive and behavioral homework, so that as homework they can do most of it themselves. That's why Rational-Emotive Therapy is an intrinsically briefer therapy than almost all the others; that's the way it usually is, but not always.

Most people are irrational much of the time. Not only do we feel that we have to be a certain way, and that we must do this, but we also feel bad if we don't. That is, if I'm a little bit upset, then I feel I must not be, and I make it even worse.

AE: Yes, the secondary disturbance is worse than the primary. The primary is, "I must do well and I'm no good if I don't," or, "You must love me and you're no good if you don't." But the secondary one is, "My God, I feel anxious, I feel depressed, I feel angry, as I must not, as I should not, as I ought not to be." You get anxious about your anxiety, depressed about your depression, guilty about your anger, and then you are not able to really correct the primary. In RET we first get you over your self-downing about your disturbance, then we go back to the original disturbance, showing how you largely created it, and how you have the power within you to think differently, act differently, and feel differently, and undo it.

A good deal of this, I suppose, has to do with the labels that a person applies to himself: "I am a horrible person."

AE: Right, and we quote general semantics – Alfred Korzybski, a genius, not a therapist, who said, "When we overgeneralize we render ourselves unsane." So we are against overgeneralized thinking, which is one of the cores of human disturbance.

So if a person thinks that he is a horrible person, you would say, "Well, maybe you did a horrible thing, but that doesn't mean that you're always a horrible person."

AE: Right, and that you're never a good person. If you do a good deed – for example, save a child from drowning at the risk of your own life – that's a good deed. But ten minutes later you might kill somebody, or steal, or lie. So you are a person who does good, valuable, self-helping, and bad, unfortunate, self-defeating things. You are not ratable; we teach people how not to rate themselves. They are only what they do – their performances, their deeds, their acts.

Consequently, when they are angry at someone else, you teach them not to damn the other person, no matter what they do.

AE: Right. One of the main derivatives of the musts is, "You must do well as I think you must, and if you haven't done what you must, you are a totally rotten individual, and you deserve never to get any joy on earth and roast in hell for eternity." So we are against damnation of you, of other people, and the universe.

This must involve an unconditional acceptance of whoever might walk into your office, no matter what they may have done in their lives.

AE: Right. We and the late Carl Rogers had unconditional positive regard or acceptance for people. But we also teach them, which I'm afraid Carl did not, how to positively regard themselves – how to teach themselves always, under all conditions at all times, no matter how badly they act, no matter who doesn't adore them, to accept themselves, just because they are human, just because they are alive. Period.

That aspect of your work has caused many people to label you profoundly humanistic.

AE: Oh yes, I am. One of my best and most popular books, published by McGraw-Hill, is called *Humanistic Psychotherapy: The Rational-Emotive Approach*, which is a little different from some other so-called humanistic approaches.

When a person is really all worked up, in a state of panic, do you find that disputing with them is effective when they are in that aroused state? Or are there other techniques that are more appropriate at such a time?

AE: We have many emotive, evocative techniques. One of them is accepting them ourselves, which is emotive. We have Rational-Emotive imagery, where we get people to imagine the worst and then feel terrible, and then work on their feeling. We have my famous shame-attacking exercise, because shame is the essence of much disturbance, where we get you to go out and do something asinine, ridiculous, foolish, and not feel ashamed. Now don't get in trouble; don't walk naked in the streets or anything like that. But yell out the subway stops, if you are civilized enough in your city to have a subway. Or stop somebody on the street and say, "I just got out of the loony bin. What month is it?" and not feel ashamed when they look in horror at you and think you're off your rocker; but you're really not – you are being very much saner than they are.

In other words, it's almost the opposite of positive thinking. You have people confront their greatest fear; and then in the middle of what they thought would be the most awful thing that could ever happen to them, they learn that at least it's not totally awful.

AE: Right. I got this partly because at the age of nineteen I was scared witless of public speaking and approaching young females. I made myself speak, alive, uncomfortably, in public; so I got over my fear, and now you can't keep me away from the public speaking platform. And I approached a hundred females, and got only one date, and she didn't show up; but I saw cognitively that nothing terrible happened, and I got over my fear of approaching women. So we get people to act against their nutty philosophies.

When a person thinks that things are hopeless, if you can use your approach to show them one tiny little ray of light, that's an improvement for them.

AE: That's right. When you say, "I can't stand it," you mean, "I'll die of it," which you won't; or, "I can't be happy at all if you reject me, or if I fail an examination." We show you that you can often be very happy, despite the failure, despite the rejection, and therefore nothing is really that hopeless.

One of the techniques in your work that strikes me as interesting is the use of sarcasm.

AE: Right; we use humor. We are sarcastic about your ideas if you are upset, because when you are unhumorous you take things too seriously, and we reduce your ideas to absurdity. But we never laugh at you, only at the way you think and act and feel; and we show you how to laugh at yourself and not to take yourself too seriously, which is what emotional disturbance is.

You've even written a whole series of little songs that you teach people to sing, to sort of sarcastically laugh at their own ideas.

AE: Right – rational, humorous songs, to show them that they can look at themselves and what they do and laugh at it, and not upset themselves about it, even when they fail.

Psychotherapy in general is controversial today; scientists question whether any form of therapy works. But there is quite a bit of research that suggests that the approaches that you have developed are effective with specific problems.

AE: We have about 250 studies of our therapy, mainly RET, but also what is called cognitive therapy, or cognitive behavioral therapy, that show that when you get people to basically change their irrational thinking, they become significantly improved in about 80 or 90 percent of those 250 cases. We have another 250 studies concerning what I call irrational ideas, such as, "You must do well, and it's terrible when you don't." We believe that when you endorse more of those, you are more disturbed; and the people who are psychologically and psychiatrically disturbed do endorse more of them, so it looks as if they are valid. These are experiments. They are not clinical studies, which are always prejudiced by the therapist, but these are objective studies.

Some of the reports go rather far – for example, helping a person get rid of a physiological addiction, like cocaine or alcohol, by working through their cognitive processes.

AE: Yes, working cognitively and behaviorally. We have a new book on the

Rational-Emotive treatment of alcoholism and substance abuse, by myself and some of my collaborators, and we show people that they don't have to get themselves anxious, and when they are anxious they don't have to run for the bottle or the coke or the methadone or whatever they use when they are anxious, and they don't have to put themselves down for being alcoholics or drug addicts. We show them that if they change their basic attitude and then push themselves not to take the substances, then they can overcome it, and they do overcome. The two main things that upset people are, one, "I have to do well and be approved, and I'm no good"; but, two, "Things must be easy, and my anxiety or my despair or my depression must not exist. I can't stand it, so I'll cop out by taking the alcohol or the drugs." We show them they can stay with the anxiety, define it as a pain in the neck and not as awful, as horrible, and then work using RET to give it up.

But when a person's belief system is that they have to have the drug – when they say, "Physiologically it's a disease; I know I'm addicted" – how do you logically dispute that?

AE: Well, some alcoholics, for example, do have a gene for alcoholism, so they find it most difficult to drink one drink and not finish the bottle. But they don't have to drink even one drink, and when they are anxious or depressed, they can say, "Too bad, tough; that's the way I am. I don't have to cover it up or drink to feel better. I'm going to get better by facing my pain and then working through it" – which again RET specializes in telling them how to do.

It seems to be very much influenced by the Stoic philosophers, in showing people how to lump life.

AE: Right, and by St. Francis' philosophy, and by Reinhold Neibuhr, and Alcoholics Anonymous – "Give me the courage to change what I can change, the serenity to accept what I cannot change, and the wisdom to know the difference between the two." That is one of the precepts of RET, which we got mainly from the ancient philosophers.

Is there any final thought you'd like to leave us with?

AE: The main thing is to accept responsibility for what you do – you do it, it doesn't do itself – but never to damn yourself or other human beings, no matter how abominable or stupid or incompetent your behavior. In a sense, you can like yourself and dislike what you do, and acknowledge what you do and work to change it. But even if you never change, you are you. You are neither good nor bad. You are a person who does good and bad, self-helping and self-defeating things. Now, how do you stop it and change?

COMMUNICATION AND CONGRUENCE

WITH VIRGINIA SATIR

The late Virginia Satir was one of the most influential psychologists of the twentieth century. She was a founder of family therapy and the author of many influential books, including CONJOINT FAMILY THERAPY, PEOPLEMAKING, SELF ESTEEM, *and* SATIR STEP BY STEP.

In this interview Ms. Satir points out that our fear of communicating our true feelings can lead to conflict and misunderstanding. She shows how internalized rules for social behavior limit our communication, and demonstrates the effects of a variety of communication styles.

You make the point about communication that we often fail to express what we are feeling inside.

VS: That's true; and if that happens, do you know how often we can be misunderstood?

All the time.

VS: So you don't understand me, and you make me up. When we aren't really understanding each other, we hallucinate each other, and then we behave as though our hallucinations are fact. All over the world, the same problems are present. One is that people are expected to know what somebody else means. If you love me and you don't read my mind, that must mean you don't love me. I encounter that a lot.

Without your ever having to tell me what you need, I should just be there for you.

VS: And you know, when we talk about that right now, it sounds so ridiculous. And yet, this is how a lot of people function. I think it came from when we were little kids. I often use this example: Mother was at the top of the stairs, and we were putting our hand in the cookie jar. She said, "Take your hand out of the cookie jar," and we got the idea that people could read our minds. Or we were very unhappy at a moment in time, and Mother came in just at that time and patted us, or something of that sort; and so people could read our minds.

There is a difference between being able to connect with somebody else, and acting on that information without checking. If we didn't have this thing called rapport between people, we wouldn't be able to even make connections. But the idea that I read your mind, and then I do what fits for me in relation to you, without ever checking with you – that becomes a terrible thing.

I say to people that we haven't developed a science of ESP that well; so let us not go on the basis of thinking that we can do this. Let's check things out. If I have a sense about something with you, instead of acting on that I'll ask you, "Is this so?" That to me is loving, it is considerate; it opens up a chance for me to learn something about you, and also a chance for us to commit in a deep way.

That's a normal part of healthy communication, checking with a person; very often we can misunderstand what a person means.

VS: Oh yes, it happens all the time. In fact, I think that I can demonstrate the relationship between communication on the one hand, and health and illness, intimacy and distancing, competency and incompetency, making sense and not making sense, on the other. And it all comes within the frame of how we handle communication. Let me tell you something that came out clearly after I worked with many, many people. There are two dialogues that go on. One is the dialogue of the words, and the other is the dialogue of hearing; and many times those are different. I'll give you a little illustration. Ask me how I am.

How are you?

VS: I'm fine, Jeff.

Hmm.

VS: Now, when I said that, tell me what happened to you.

Well, you had a very cold tone to your voice, so I thought you were trying to distance.

VS: But didn't you hear the words – that I was fine? You see, this is typical. Ask me again if I like something, whatever it is.

OK. Do you enjoy being here on TV today, Virginia?

VS: Oh, I think that it's just wonderful.

(Laughter).

VS: Now I am doing something else. I am sending out another message about the words that disclaim what I am doing. Now, just like in the first illustration, those two levels of the dialogue come from two different places in the person. They are not an attempt to cause trouble for other people. They are totally unconscious.

I think you call one level the metacommunication level. In other words, every time we communicate we have a message, and we are also communicating a message about our message.

VS: That's right, exactly. When people give what we call double-level messages, which is where my body and voice say one thing, and it is different from my words, they think that this is deliberately done. It isn't. The words come from the left brain – what you should do. The other part comes from the right brain. Now, suppose I have a rule that says that I should never complain to you. Let's suppose I am in terrible pain and you ask me how I am, and I say, "Fine." What am I doing? One side says I've got a rule that I should never complain; the other side says I have pain. But I am giving the message of what I should do, which is I should never complain.

So underneath any conversation, no matter I suppose how abstract or intellectual, there is always a human being under there with emotions, often needing to be validated.

VS: That is of course one of the things I try to teach people. Let me tell you something. I go to lectures, and I listen, and all of a sudden, they may be talking about all this erudition, but underneath I hear, "I'm hurting. I feel disappointed. I would love for you to help me." And it comes out in these very erudite terms. Now, if I were to go to one of those people and say, "I'd like to help you," chances are that they would say, "How did you know I needed help? What makes you think I need help?"

They might even deny it.

VS: Sure, because usually people like that have rules that they shouldn't ask for help – not that they don't need it. This goes on with people all the time. Most of our emotional rules have to be broken, like: "I should never get angry at somebody I love." You realize what a difficult thing that is. Or, "I should always be perfect." How about that one? Or, "I must never show fear." You know that one?

Oh, I share all of those.

VS: Those rules have to be broken, because they are inhuman rules that can never be lived up to. Whatever rule you are following, if it doesn't fit the harmony of your body and the harmony of the universe, it is going to give you trouble.

In our culture, I suppose one of the very common rules is never to reveal what you really feel, especially the vulnerable parts.

VS: That's absolutely true. If you think about it, people's feelings about what is vulnerable are their really deep feelings. Most people give themselves "credit" for only having bad things inside, not good things. I have even found people who felt that they couldn't talk about love feelings because somebody else will be jealous. As a result, we don't communicate the thing that is really what human beings are about. You can put people on a computer, and they can talk back and forth to each other, but they have no arms, nothing else. We behave a lot of times as though that is what human communication is, and I know better than that.

You have developed caricatures of the stances that people characteristically take, like the blamer or the placater, when they are trying to cover up what they really feel inside.

VS: This is a way that people have of protecting themselves. Why do we have to be so worried about protecting ourselves? We think, "I must never get myself into a position where I might have to protect myself, so I lie all the time; I say yes when I feel no, and I say no when I feel yes." It's kind of like I am on tenterhooks all the time, worrying about what is going to be found out, or who is going to criticize me. And so we can't use the very things that would make it possible for you and me to connect, because we can't be truthful. I'm talking now about truth in the emotional sense – just saying how I feel.

It's hard to imagine how we are going to be able to run our governments and deal with each other in politics and business and nations when we have this problem in our families.

VS: I have said that we can't even begin to heal the world until we learn how to heal the family. We are beginning to learn how to heal the family. One way we don't heal the family is by taking sides; and yet, that has been one of the ways that people have traditionally done it.

One of the things I have found out when I work with families is that I have to work at making an emotionally nurturing triad for people, where nobody wins over anybody else, and nobody has to lose, and everybody contributes A triad is the basic family unit – Ma, Pa, and the kid. There isn't anything else. Do you realize that three is all there is in the world? Everything is a multiple of three. Think about the trinity; that's a religious symbol. Buckminster Fuller was always one of my heroes; for him the triad was the basis of the most sturdy building that there is. The triad is a complete unit; and it is composed of three complete units. If I grow up, and I have not come to a place of feeling an equal part of a triad, then I always have to feel either guilty or rageful when I leave.

This is something that we all go through in dealing with our own parents.

VS: Yes, if that is the way we were brought up. And you know how to do that, if you were brought up by parents who have a submissive-dominant role relationship. It can either be mean or benevolent; but it is still a discrepancy between the two of them. That's the big thing that we have to take a look at now, so that we can have relationships that are equal. Equality between people results in good family relations and ultimately is the key to peace.

The relationship of a government to its people is like the relationship of the parents to the children; it can be healthy or unhealthy. Young children are told, for example, that they must obey because the father says so; and it is the same way with the government. It's as if a model for a healthy government would also be a model for a healthy family.

VS: Exactly. If you are brought up to conform and obey, you are never brought up to become an independent choice maker. At this point in time, the ones who really are willing to stick their necks out and say, "This is what I believe," and at the same time are not putting other people down, will eventually rise to the top.

In a healthy family, at some point the triad evolves to the point where it is no longer parents and children, but three equals.

VS: That's right, equal in value. One of the other important things about this equality is that each one is unique; equality means really revealing and considering and respecting our uniqueness.

We were talking earlier about people not communicating what they really feel. Isn't it often because they are trying to cover up low self-esteem?

VS: Sure. And you know, when anybody tells me that they just want to be good, I get an awful sinking feeling inside, because I hear them say, "I want to fit in, and I don't want to rock the boat." Self-esteem for me is the willingness to say where you are. And if that rocks the boat, I am not going to blame you for it, and I am not going to be unhappy that the boat is rocked. I read something the other day that said if we love our country, we have to be free to criticize it.

We have to be free to rock the boat.

VS: Once we are willing and able to give out criticism in a real way, without blame, we can also love in a real way.

A lot of people have the attitude that they don't want any criticism, that any criticism is really an attempt to put them down.

VS: You see, I can do that. I know four ways to criticize you in which you'll feel like a worm. Just for fun, let's take something that has no effect at all. First, let me say that you have a wonderful tie; that's what I really feel, for me. Now I'm going to make believe that you could have a better choice for a tie, OK? I start out by saying, "Jeff, I have something to tell you. I don't know if I should tell you or not, but it's really quite . . . well, maybe I won't tell you."

Oh, you can tell me.

VS: That tie you're wearing. I wish you wouldn't be doing that. But then, who am I to say anything about your tie? I don't dress that way.

Oh no, your opinion is important.

VS: Are you ready to feel what's going on inside of me?
   My God, you're coming out with that tie again. I don't know why you wear that thing all the time, just because your mother gave it to you.

That one really gets to me. I don't know how to come back on that.

VS: What do you want to do? What's the feeling inside?

Well, I wouldn't mind punching you. But of course I wouldn't ever say that.

VS: Exactly – the point is, because we don't say the feelings doesn't mean that they're not there. You tighten them in your teeth, and maybe one day you put a knife in me; or you dream about bad things for yourself.

Or if I live with you, I get an ulcer.

VS: Exactly. Or I could say to you, "Jeff, I just took this article out from *Esquire*. It has to do with the choice men make of ties. I just thought that you might want to have this. It has in detail what you need." How do you feel about that one?

Well, it's a little easier. I can sort of put it off on an intellectual plane and not take it personally; it's in Esquire *magazine.*

VS: Do you feel very good about it?

Not great.

VS: But at least it's a little less.

It is more my style.

VS: Or I could say to somebody in your presence, "Did you get a load of that? Just imagine, here he is, a fantastic guy, but look at that tie! Can you imagine?" How do you feel about that?

Not too good.

VS: Or I can say, "Jeff, I have something I'd like to share with you. Are you willing to listen?"

Yes.

VS: I just was looking at your tie, and I thought, "You've got better ties than that." How do you feel about my telling you that?

That's . . . all right. It's not so bad.

VS: You see, criticism is never pleasant, but it can be without blame.

I think you were demonstrating here the different personality styles you have enumerated – the placating, the blaming, the intellectual type, the silly type. The last one seemed a bit more real.

VS: Well, it's between two people who value each other. What did I do? I asked you if I could share with you and you said yes; I didn't come in and do what I did before. And then I shared with you. Now, that doesn't mean you have to do anything about it, but at least it's clear. We both have the freedom to comment, and you know that on some level.

In other words, when people are really connecting at this level of being real with each other, then criticism can be constructive; it can be healthy and normal. But when people come at each other trying to hide what they really feel – maybe their own low self-esteem – then they may be taking out on the other person some of the bad feelings they have for themselves.

VS: We have a term for it. What I won't accept in myself which is there, I can project on you. I project on you what I will not accept for myself. So this is a very important piece. At the beginning of our talk together, I said that communication from me can be related to the difficulties in intimacy, in health, in making sense, and in being competent. I was at a conference not so long ago where they talked about some new ideas about choosing people to work for corporations. One of them is Gore-Tex, which does a wonderful thing. Do you know what their criteria are for choosing people? To be kind, fun to be around, and competent – all three. Now, so I always ask myself, what stands between myself, or anyone else, and being kind, fun to be around, and competent? Why are we busting our necks to do something that simple? One of the things I am interested in now is a vision of a new consciousness about people, where we can say and do, we can be kind, fun to be around, and competent. There is no reason why we can't.

No matter what kind of families we came from.

VS: Exactly; I have spent a lifetime demonstrating that. People oftentimes think this is so simple-minded; but maybe it is the simple things that are going to make a difference.

HUMANISTIC PSYCHOTHERAPY

WITH JAMES BUGENTAL, PH.D.

James Bugental, a noted psychotherapist, was the first president of the Association for Humanistic Psychology. He is the author of numerous professional papers and several books, including THE ART OF PSYCHOTHERAPY, PSYCHOTHERAPY AND PROCESS, THE SEARCH FOR AUTHENTICITY, *and* THE SEARCH FOR EXISTENTIAL IDENTITY, *and editor of* CHALLENGES OF HUMANISTIC PSYCHOLOGY.

In this interview, Dr. Bugental places modern humanistic psychology in its historical and theoretical perspective and describes the goals and strategies of his own discipline of existential-humanistic psychotherapy. The goal of this therapy, he says, is not necessarily to alleviate symptoms, but rather to open the client to a larger sense of who he or she is.

Humanistic psychology has often been referred to as a third force in psychology. Can you elaborate on what the term third force means?

JB: Surely. It grew up because in the twenties, thirties, and forties, the humanistic trend that is concerned with the human experience was subordinated by the rise of psychoanalysis and behavioristic psychology.

Those would be the first and second forces.

JB: Those are the first two forces, yes. All along there have been humanistic psychologies; it didn't just start in the sixties. But in the sixties there was a feeling that we needed to represent that kind of psychology which was more concerned with the human experience, treated as uniquely human; and that often meant concerned with what is subjective, what goes on inside a person – not just treating a person from the outside like a white rat or a pigeon or a computer. Abraham Maslow, Carl Rogers, George Kelly, and Rollo May were some of the people instrumental in bringing together a group to develop and enunciate a humanistic perspective.

I understand from what you're saying how humanistic psychology would be distinguished from behaviorism, which looks strictly at the externals of behavior. Behavioristic psychology is based a lot on experiments with rats.

JB: We know more about the white rat, the pigeon, and the college sophomore than we do about human beings.

How do you distinguish humanistic psychology, then, from the psychoanalytic tradition?

JB: Well, it's not a complete separation, since many psychoanalysts are also humanistic, and many humanistic psychotherapists also practice some phase of psychoanalysis. But in the concept of the person, psychoanalytic psychology tends to be deterministic. Freud really had the model of nineteenth-century science – the scientist in the white smock, standing removed, watching, introducing things to affect the object, the patient.

And as I gather, probably the biggest difference in your writings and the writings of other existential-humanistic therapists is the enormous respect you have for the process that the client is going through – an enormous faith that each person can solve their own problems with a little facilitation.

JB: Let me enlarge on that just a little bit, because it is sometimes misunderstood when we say that each person can solve his or her own problem. That's true, but very often our job is to make space for that power that is resident in the person to come out. I very often think of it as like weeding a garden. You can't make a plant grow by pulling on it, but what you can do is clear away the weeds, be sure it gets nutrients, sunlight, and water, and then the inward growth process will have a chance to operate. Well, it is the same with human beings. We have weeds – we have habits of thinking, ways of seeing things, ways of defending ourselves, of trying to push ourselves to be something that maybe we are not. These things are the weeds that keep that healthful growth process from having a chance to operate. Now here is where psychoanalysis and at least my kind of psychotherapy have a lot of overlap, because we are concerned with weeding, with getting rid of what are called the resistances to the growth process.

Even though there is this natural urge within people towards wholeness and towards growth, many people may live their whole lives without experiencing the fullness of what it is to be a human being.

JB: I would almost say everybody lives without experiencing the fullness. It is beyond us. It always stretches to a horizon that moves ahead as we move and grow. But that is encouraging. We don't have to do it all. We can keep growing, we can keep opening up new possibilities, and know that there is still always more.

You describe the psychotherapy work that you do, as opposed to analyzing and providing intellectual insights for your clients, as more a kind of gentle prodding – gently nudging your clients to be in touch with their own deep experience.

JB: Not always so gentle; but yes, to be more in touch with the subjective experience.

It seems as if there is a tendency to get caught up in looking at one's life intellectually, not really feeling things fully.

JB: A lot of things in our life experience teach us to make ourselves into objects, and to lose the subjective center that is really where we live. To be alive physically but in a coma is not to be very much alive, psychologically at least, and most of us would not regard that as very much vitality. And all of us to some extent reduce our vital awareness to preserve a stable world and a stable self-definition.

You suggest that most of us develop self-images that are not really accurate. One is the idealized self-image, where we tend to think of ourselves as a little more perfect than we really are; and then concomitant with that is the despised self-image – we hate ourselves at some level. In order to maintain these we often live away from the here and now, away from our real experience.

JB: We blame ourselves for not being that idealized self. We fear and hate ourselves sometimes because we feel we are close to the despised image. That was Karen Horney's division, and a very useful one. Many times it is not conscious in those extremes, and it is only as one works with a particular patient that one may find that he never can be content with himself;

although he succeeds reasonably well in his work and he has a feeling of accomplishment, it soon fades because it is not the perfect accomplishment. Another person, no matter what the kinds of rewards or recognitions from the outside, may never feel these are really deserved, may never feel really clean, because that despised image is hidden back there.

How do you deal with that as a therapist?

JB: That is where helping the person to become more aware of that internal life is so important – to get past making oneself into an object. Let me take a step back from your question to try to illustrate. A new person comes in for the first time, and I say, in effect, "What bothers you? Why are you here?" The person starts to tell me, let's say, of a tragic incident in his life, but he tells it with a laugh. He has objectified his own experience; he doesn't let the pain of the tragedy come in. Instead he stands apart, dismisses it, makes it impersonal. Now when that happens, he can't really find all that is going on inside himself. He has built an artificial wall between his awareness and his genuine experience. So the first job is to help him really let that experience through – to discard the need to distance from the pain and let the pain come through. He may say, "Well, if I ever let that through, I'll never get out of it; it will be too much." That is where the therapist can say, "Hang in; we'll find our way through it. It's not all you are." It is having someone who can really stay with you and go through the pain, go through the fear, and then emerge on the other side. In *The Flies* Sartre has Orestes say, "Human life begins on the far side of despair." Only by going through the despair do we get to that opening of awareness, that creative possibility of life.

There is an enormous risk in going through the pain, not just for the client but for the therapist as well. Each client brings a new kind of pain, and it is always unknown territory.

JB: Exactly so.

Can you talk about how that has affected you personally in your years of practice?

JB: Well, I think cumulatively it has changed my life immensely. What I think of first when you ask the question is how in earlier years I was trying to be what I thought I should be as a therapist, a psychologist, whatever, but not trusting; it was always as if I had to hammer myself into the shape I should be. But as I was trying to help the people who consulted me to be more genuinely in themselves, in their own lives, it was holding up an unrelenting mirror to me, with the result that I went into classical analysis, and later into psychotherapy, group therapy, and individual therapy. I have done a lot of that sort of thing, because this work continually says, "And what about you?"

People sometimes say, "How can you stand to listen to so much unhappiness and pain?" The answer is that isn't all I hear. I also hear courage and joy and growth. So there are both sides to it.

One can't really quite get to the joy without going through a lot of the pain.

JB: That's very true. So long as we are denying our experience, happy or sad, the other part is being denied too; so that we laugh without the full laugh, we weep without the full tears. And to help someone else get more in touch with their genuine experience is to call on oneself to be there too. You can't do it as you would to a rat or to a college sophomore.

You have written about therapy as a long-term process. You are not a therapist who sort of patches up things, or gives people short-term counseling, but you really help people to go through the many layers of the onion, to reach deeper and deeper into themselves, and in that process discover a larger and larger sense of themselves. As we get deep inside the self, beyond some of the superficial resistance, you find within some people an enormous loathing and self-hatred.

JB: That despised self, yes.

You described it so elegantly in one of your books as the kind of thing that if not handled therapeutically, may lead a person to run amok. And it happens from time to time.

JB: Indeed so. Let me back up a little bit to comment on what you are saying. We have to create a self, a definition of who I am. We create a definition of what the world is. Different people create different world definitions and self-definitions. That's not as surprising today as it was at one time, because television and other sources help us see how different it would be if we were born in Hong Kong or in Uganda or something. We know there are different world views and ways of constructing who and what I am and who and what this world is. But the work of depth therapy inevitably leads us to question the way we have constructed the world and defined who we are. As that questioning comes, it is very much like feeling the ground shaking under you, and it is a very frightening experience. In the spiritual traditions it is often referred to as the leap of faith or the dark night of the soul. In our work we think of it as the existential crisis, the crisis of existence. When we come to realize how arbitrary is the way we have defined our own identities and our world, then comes that period of panic sometimes, of fright. If there is not a therapeutic container, and someone gets to that point, there is a feeling of desperation, of impotence. Sartre describes it as nausea – that nausea of finding the arbitrariness of things. That is when some people, feeling helpless to change that, helpless to find something that will rescue them from that nausea, can run amok.

When you describe this as an existential crisis, you seem to be suggesting that this is somehow latent in all people, not only those who go to psychotherapy. We all are confronted with an existential dilemma, even if we choose not to look at it.

JB: It is always latent. I think that possibility is there, and if life is reasonably congenial, and the established ways of doing things work out well, we may never have to confront that crisis. In the latter part of the nineteenth century and early part of the twentieth, the world was a pretty stable place. You knew your place in it. You knew who you were. In the latter part of the twentieth century, all of our world definitions are in question. Our idea of what is the good and the true is debated now; it is not taken for granted. So we are much more apt to come up against that nausea, that feeling of world-sickness, and I think it is one of the reasons that such a great number of people have been seeking therapeutic help now, as compared to the past – this feeling that there must be some truth, some anchoring point, to make things steady down, because they are too wavery.

As a psychotherapist, do you seek to comfort people who are going through this search and this nausea, or rather just to help them move through their own journey without any advance expectation as to where it will lead?

JB: Absolutely the latter. It would not be helpful to promise there is a rosy outcome if you will only hang in. But when you stand steady with someone going through it, and portray, less in words of reassurance and more in attitude, that you know that they can find their own way through it, you come out in very different places. That is a support, a container, which makes it possible for people to go through. But not everyone needs to; I don't want to sound as if this is a uniform prescription. For some people it is the only way to get to a real sense of their own strength and potential. For others, other shorter-term things are appropriate. I don't want to put those down; they serve an important role. I tend to work in one part of a very broad dimension.

Some therapists will see clients for five or six times, others for twelve to twenty, others for three years or six years. How do you know when you are really involved in psychotherapy, and how do you know when it's over?

JB: That's a good question. The trouble with the word psychotherapy is part of the answer to your question. It's sort of like saying, "What's a good form of transportation?" Well, where are you going, and what's your time schedule? You have to answer a lot of questions to know which means of transportation we are speaking about. And so it is with psychotherapy. When Carl Rogers was first writing, he published at least one case, or one of his students did, that was a successful single-interview therapy case. Of course for many of us, the number of hours went up into the hundreds. I had a classical analysis, five hundred and some hours – five times a week for three years, I think it was.

That's an enormous investment.

JB: Yes it is, and I don't think it is necessary for everyone. It depends what one seeks to accomplish. For some people the opportunity to take a very long, tough, full look at their lives, to decide, "Is this the way I want my life to go?" is an engagement of tremendous pull. They are drawn to it – sometimes by the pain of the way their lives are going, sometimes by a kind of seeking for the more that they sense is sleeping within them. For that kind of person, once a week is really very difficult to carry off, as far as I can see. Twice is minimal. Before inflation made it so hard, I liked to work three and four times a week.

This is vastly different from what behaviorists do when they look at symptom change. The behaviorists would advise any client going into psychotherapy to develop concrete, specific objectives that they want to get out of the therapy. You are suggesting that therapy is going to result not necessarily in a symptom change, but in an existential shift which might even be metaphysical in nature, not measurable really.

JB: You're right on; yes. I don't want to put down what the behavioral therapists can do for dealing with certain phobias, with habit patterns that are intrusive. It can be very valuable; it is just a different task. Our kind of work doesn't seek to change symptoms. The symptoms may or may not exist when we are through.

In other words, a person could spend three years coming three times a week, and still be as phobic or anxious or neurotic as when they came in?

JB: No – the word "as" is the trick. But they could still have that pattern. I don't think we change basic patterns. Think of it this way. In one of my books I describe working with a lady who, whatever she was doing, that was the thing that should be. At one point she was into carrots for eyesight, and nothing would do but she had to tell everybody she knew they must have lots of carrots. Moreover when she was feeling well, she thought, "Well, it's going to be this way from now on," and she didn't see why she ever had to feel bad again. When she came to me, it was like an iron mask was fastened on her. Everything she saw was in terms of this extreme; it was distorted by this. Our work gradually moved that mask out. It was still there, but she could see other possibilities around it. It wasn't dominant; it didn't control her life.

I went to see her one time some years after we finished our work, and at that time it was shiatsu massage; nothing would do but I must have shiatsu massage. She would find out who was the best shiatsu person in my home town, and so forth. Then suddenly in the midst of it she stopped and laughed and said, "I'm doing it again!" See, it had moved out here; it wasn't controlling everything. Earlier, not only would she have insisted no matter what, had no perspective on it, not been able to see it in relation to the rest, but if I didn't do it she would feel her worth was gone. Now she could laugh, and when I say, "Well, maybe I'll do it and maybe not," she could say, "Well, you ought to do it." It didn't control her.

When our work goes well the person feels life is bigger – there are more opportunities, more possibilities: "I have more power; and those patterns that have been part of me are probably still there, but I'm not in their control, I have more choice about them."

When one looks at this kind of outcome in existential-humanistic psychotherapy, we then begin to move into the transpersonal possibilities of life.

JB: Indeed so – particularly as we look at the ways we have defined our own identities, and look at the way we have defined the world, and begin to see that it doesn't just have to be that way. Then for some people – but not for everyone – there is a sense of greater fluidity of being. Krishnamurti says at one point, "You have to have an ego to get to the bus." We've got to have a self-definition to get around in the world. We can't just strip and run around naked without a self. But we don't have to be its creature; it can be our creation. And knowing it as our creation, then we have much more choice.

So at this point a person might open up to mystical or peak experiences.

JB: All of these sorts of experience – and there is a tremendous range of them – are potential. Some of the people that I have worked with have moved to realms of experience that I only partially understand. There's an old saying, "You can't take anybody anyplace you haven't been yourself." That's not so; they have taken me places I haven't been. I have seen them make trips I haven't.

THE TOTAL SELF

WITH HAL STONE, PH.D.

*Hal Stone is a psychologist, therapist, and teacher.
He is author of* EMBRACING HEAVEN AND EARTH, *and coauthor with his wife Sidra of* EMBRACING
OUR SELVES *and* EMBRACING EACH OTHER. *Hal
and Sidra Stone are the originators of the Voice
Dialogue technique for contacting
subpersonalities.*

*In this interview, Dr. Stone proposes that we
are not unitary beings, but that we consist of
many autonomous subpersonalities, including
both primary and disowned selves. He discusses
how to recognize our disowned selves, and the
importance of embracing all our inner selves if we
are to be fully conscious and free.*

When I was an undergraduate psychology student, the diagnosis of
multiple personalities, as in THE THREE FACES OF EVE, was thought
of as a very rare, fascinating, and obscure condition. Today, it seems
as if we are developing a whole new view of the multiplicity of
personalities within us.

HS: Technically speaking, the multiple personality is still thought of in
psychiatry as a condition of abnormality. But it is also a reality of the psyche.
The psyche is made up of very, very different personalities. They are called
different names by different people; some call them subpersonalities, or subs;
Jung used to call them complexes; Gurdjieff called them the different I's of
the personality. My wife and I refer to them as selves, or as energy patterns,
because they are that also.

The question is, what is the difference between the abnormality of multiple
personalities and what we have discovered to be the reality, which is that we
are all multiple personalities? What makes it abnormal? It becomes abnormal
when there is no one around to say, "Oh, that's an interesting part of me." So
if some part of me takes over in a certain moment and says something, I have

a reflecting capability; I can say, "That was interesting. Where did that come from?" But the true multiple personality doesn't have that part of him, that reflecting agent that can say that is a part. For example, a therapist friend tells of a woman who called her three different times in one evening with three different voices, and the woman had no connection at all to the fact that she had done that. Literally, the three took over; that is the abnormal condition.

In the classical abnormal multiple-personality condition, one personality often has no idea what the others are doing, and sort of goes unconscious.

HS: Absolutely. Well, that is not very much unlike what happens to us adults. Most of us have a fantasy that we are very much in charge of our lives, making free choices and exercising free will. When you begin to work with these subpersonalities, you begin to discover that that isn't the case at all. The reality as we see it is that we are all identified with certain selves. Now, in a way that is inevitable. You grow up in the world; you can't be everything. So if you grow up in a family where the family is rational, then you either are going to identify with being a rational person, or you are going to push off and go to the other side and be an irrational person, or an imaginative or an intuitive person; that can happen also. We are going to identify with certain parts, and we are also going to push off on other parts.

If I grow up in a family where I identify with my rationality, automatically that means that I am going to disown certain other parts. I am going to disown my intuition; I am going to disown my imagination. If I grow up identified with being a powerful person because that is what my father wants, then I am going to disown my vulnerability. I won't be able to show weakness; I won't be able to show neediness in my relationships. For every part that we identify with, we have on the other side a system of selves that we call disowned selves; every one of us, then, is in this condition of being identified with primary selves and disowning other parts.

Typically, I suppose, we identify with those parts of ourselves that are consistent with what we admire in ourselves. I would identify, for example, with being likable and competent.

HS: Because those are the values of the prevailing culture. If you grow up in a culture in which fighting and beating people up are valued, then that becomes the primary self, and being nice becomes a disowned self. So it depends on the family, the culture, the historical time. And even in one's life these selves can change. For example, in the consciousness movement, many people start out as quite conservative, identifying with contracted values, and then in the course of their psychological and spiritual work they change their primary selves, and pretty soon the primary self is the one that says, "You should be more expanded, you should be more expressive, you should be more sexual, you should meditate more." Expansion becomes the primary self rather than contraction. In one's life it can shift many different times.

I gather that typically we tend to disown parts of ourselves that are not valued by the culture – what we might think of as ugly or horrible, extremely aggressive, or dishonest.

HS: Well, the selves that are disowned are the selves that the primary system doesn't want around. For men in our culture, vulnerability is a very, very big one. Another system that is disowned a great deal is the instinctual energies, which we call demonic energies. Among women, until the women's movement, power was disowned. Women were trained to be loving daughters and mothers, essentially to please the man; and they have begun to embrace their power side, as they move out of that particular system of selves that they were identified with.

You have used two words here – embrace and disowned. Could you amplify those a bit?

HS: The way we think about the evolution of personality is that first we have to discover that these selves exist inside of us; they are very real, very autonomous.

As if they were spirits or energies of their own.

HS: If we lived in the Middle Ages, we would have language that is much more accurate. In the Middle Ages they talked about spirit possession. When these subpersonalities take over, we are literally in a spirit possession, but we are too sophisticated these days to talk about it.

The thesis of our work is very simple: we have to become aware of all the selves, and we have to learn to embrace all the selves. That doesn't mean becoming them; it means embracing them. For example, suppose I am identified with being a nice guy; he's sitting over here next to me, let's say, and that is my prevailing way of operating in life – I'm a nice guy, I like people, I want to please you, I want the audience to enjoy what I am saying, and I don't want you to be unhappy with me. On the other side is a very different person, somebody who says, "I don't care what people think. If they like you, they like you; if they don't, they don't. If Jeff likes you, he likes you. What's the difference? Just be yourself. Say it like it is." The nice guy says, "Hey, wait a minute. If I say everything like it is, and I share every reaction I have, I can end up with all enemies. Who needs that?" The other guy says, "If you don't say it like it is, and you don't express yourself, you'll end up with a heart attack." These characters are at war in us. It's like a car that is being driven by twenty different people; the primary selves are always fighting to be in charge of driving the car. So if being a nice guy is primary, that part of you always wants to be in charge; it is afraid of your not being a nice guy.

So embracing the selves means that you have to find out what are your primary selves. If you are raised as a nice guy, how do you know that? How do you know that that is a primary self? How do you know that you are disowning your not-nice guy? Well, there is a very simple way to find out. Who can't you stand? What kind of people push your buttons? What kind of people irritate you? What kind of people do you judge? There you have the direct picture of your own disowned selves. It is literally that simple.

Typically, though, a person might say, "Well, that's not me. I mean, I can't stand that. How could that possibly be me?"

HS: That lets you know what a good disowned self it is. See, this is a normal condition. Everyone has selves. Everyone has to be identified with primary selves; there is no way not to be. And consciousness means separating from that and learning what is disowned.

Let's say a woman, for example, has three children, so she is identified with being a mother. On her other side is a part of her that hates mothering, but she knows nothing about it. The kind of woman that makes her the most uncomfortable is a woman who is very uncaring, a woman who is very cold, like a businesswoman. Whenever she meets a businesswoman she gets very irritated with that person. Why does she get irritated? Why does she have to judge that kind of person? Because her unloving self is disowned. The part of her that doesn't really enjoy children, that never wanted to have them in the first place, is disowned. Automatically what happens is that life brings you whatever it is that you disown.

What about the case of a great saint? Mother Teresa spends her whole life caring for the sick and the dying. Do you think that inside of her there is somebody who hates it, who would really just as soon go and murder people herself?

HS: Well, I don't know what's going on in Mother Teresa, but I would be willing to give fairly heavy odds that she has a considerable system of naughties operating in her. It may be that in this particular incarnation, in this particular life process that she is in, her particular task is to live exactly what she is living. I don't judge it in any way, but I am no longer naive enough to believe that she doesn't have the other side in her. I have spent thirty years working with people, and I don't have a lot of naiveté left about these things. I don't happen to judge that. The fact that I have in me a lot of unconscious selves doesn't disturb me. I just know that they are there, and my task in life is to discover as many of them as I can.

You see, the reason that it is very important to discover these opposites is that only then do I have real choice. For example, if I am writing a book, and I have only my rational, linear mind available to me, that doesn't give me a lot of choice about what I write or the ideas that come to me. If you make me aware of my intuition and my fantasy life, and I can separate from my mind, now I have a wonderful situation. I have my mind over here on one side, and on the other side I have my intuition and my fantasy life. I now am able to embrace both of these without being identified with either one.

This makes life more uncomfortable, you see. If I am the woman with the three children, I now separate from the mother, and I now have an ego that is aware. I embrace the part of me that loves children, and I also embrace the part of me that doesn't like children, that never wanted children. What this results in is sweat, and my personal fantasy about God is that God loves sweat. God loves people who are able to embrace opposites. It makes life more difficult; it makes life more complicated. Decisions aren't so easy, but at least they come from a place in us that is born of knowing opposites.

In this multiplicity of opposites that is the psyche, where is the you? Where is the self?

HS: Well, I can tell you how we think about that, because everybody has their own way of looking at that. We think about consciousness as operating on three different levels. Awareness gives me the ability to witness whatever is going on. It is a wonderful gift, as you well know. If I have awareness, I don't have to be identified with anything I am saying. Even as I communicate these ideas to you, my awareness witnesses, and a part of me doesn't have to be identified with what I am saying. Awareness gives me the gift of not being attached to what I am saying. It is a wonderful thing.

But awareness isn't enough, because if you are just aware then you never experience anything. So the second level of the definition is experience – the experience of all of this multiplicity. We are an unbelievable array of energies; it's awesome what is inside of us. So the second part of consciousness is experiencing these different parts. I may not be able to do all of it this time around, but I do the best I can, and that is the journey that all of us are sharing, because every kind of consciousness work, at some level, is learning and experiencing these different energies. If you are a Jungian, you learn it the symbolic way. If you are gestalt, you learn it the emotional way. If you are transpersonal, you learn it that way. If you are a Reichian or a bodyworker, you learn it that way. But it is all dealing with all these different energies.

So there is awareness and experience; but we need one more thing. Who is going to put it together? Who is going to figure out how to act? Who is going to make choices? The ego. But that's a little complicated, because what we discover in this work is that what we think is our ego is really our primary selves. If I have been trained as a rational man, and you say to me, "Who are you?" I would say I am a rational man, until you help me separate from that.

So I am all three of these things. I am an aware ego that is taking advantage of this pure awareness and taking advantage of the experience, and I am not identified with any. I am an orchestra conductor who is trying to learn how to handle this amazing array of energy around me. I am a gardener who learns how to take care of all these plants and feed the animals that are inside of me and that inhabit my nature.

And if we use these metaphors, to really be the fullest person that you can be, you want a garden that has a great variety of plants growing, or an orchestra that plays every tone of music for you to conduct.

HS: Well, it makes life very interesting, and I can't imagine anything worse than a boring life. But some people are aware of some of these different things inside, and some people are aware of a great many of them, and I believe that we are living in a time when more and more people on our planet are becoming more and more aware of this fantastic garden and zoo living inside of us.

The classical fairy tales of Western culture often tell the story of the innocent young prince who goes out on a quest into the world and encounters dragons that have to be slain, and it is the slaying of the dragon that transforms this innocent being into a hero. What does that mean to you?

HS: Every disowned self means that the primary self is sitting on top of another part. A woman has a dream that she is trying to stuff a fifty-foot snake into a box, and she is exhausting herself doing it. That is a beautiful example of the primary self, her rational mind, trying to keep control over the snake. The snake is her instinctuality, and she is exhausting herself. Every disowned self means there is a sum of energy that is not available to us. Every disowned self becomes a dragon in our life, because whatever we disown, the universe brings back to us. If you are a powerful business person and you disown vulnerability, your oldest son will be vulnerable, or you will marry a woman who is ultimately vulnerable, or your German police dog will be totally vulnerable. If you disown power in your life and you identify with love and relationship, then if you are a woman you will bring into your life a man of immense power and immense authority. If a woman can't stand bitchy women, her boss at work will be a bitchy person. The law of the psyche is that whatever we disown, life brings us.

If we can step back and see the dragon for what it is, we realize that the dragon is really our disowned self – that person out there who is causing us all this stress and all this difficulty is really a teacher for us. The longer that we allow disowned selves to remain there, the more heads they grow, exactly like in the fairy tale. They start out with one, and they end up with twelve or more. By the time we are older, these get to be very serious conditions.

We need consciousness today; that is our most precious commodity. We need to learn about these selves and what it is that moves people, because if we don't get enough consciousness we pay a big price.

But how can we embrace our disowned selves when we truly find them disgusting?

HS: Well, you are asking the sixty-four-dollar question. I don't expect somebody to embrace their disowned selves in one hour. But it really is very much like Greek mythology. The lesson that the early Greek had to learn was that all the gods and goddesses needed to be worshiped. Say you were a worshiper of Apollo, and he was your primary god; he had to do with the mind and clarity and so forth. It was OK for you to worship Apollo and for him to be your favorite god. But in mythology, if you did not worship Dionysius at all, if you kept him out of the picture, he was the one that punished you. The disowned god or goddess in mythology is the one that kills you; that's the principle. That means that you have to build a shrine to every god and goddess. You can have your favorites, but you can't leave anyone out. From our perspective, we say that you have to learn to value every self that is in us. That doesn't mean that these disowned selves have to take you over; it just means they have to be valued. You have to build a shrine to them.

You're not implying permissiveness, though.

HS: Oh no, no; as a matter of fact, I think that one of the major problems of the consciousness movement is that it has been too permissive. It has moved people from contraction to expansion. It has moved people from being more conservative to being identified with being more liberal. We have to step back from both those conditions into a condition of awareness. With an aware ego we embrace the conservative part of ourselves, and we embrace the liberal part of ourselves; and if we can hold the tension of those two parts, then we have a much better opportunity to make real choices for ourselves.

If I locked you in a dungeon and shut the door, and then opened it eight years later, you would bite me, and I would deserve it, because I have locked you away. These disowned selves are just little pieces of energy. As far as I am concerned, all energy is God, and all I am doing is locking away a piece of God, putting it into some kind of purgatory; so when it comes out it is vicious, and we say, "Oh, that's a terrible part." But it is terrible because we locked it away. You see, I am not talking about becoming these parts, but when you allow them out in a safe setting and begin to pay attention to them, they change.

In dealing with the disowned parts of ourselves, we might want to strengthen the primary part, so that it is large enough to incorporate the parts we formerly thought of as disgusting.

HS: The way we approach it is that we always work with people through the primary selves. For example, let's say that you have a disowned energy that has to do with being a very selfish, self-aggrandizing person; that is a self that is in everybody. But you are identified with being a proper, nice person; the other one is disowned. So we would spend a lot of time working with your nice person, until you as an aware ego could separate from it. Once you are separate as an aware ego, and you recognize that you really appreciate this part and what he has done for you, now we go to the other side. But you are there as an aware ego, and you are able to appreciate and love both of them.

You know, we live in a time when love has become very important. I have no objection to love as a principle; it feels very good. I like when it comes to me, and I like to give it. But if you are going to be loving, you have to do the whole shot. You can't just love the primary selves; you also have to love the disowned selves. To love and embrace the disowned selves takes great courage; but you can't be selective about it. The danger is that you can build a love temple on top of a garbage dump. That kind of loving does not support the evolution of consciousness in the world. We have to deal with the dump also. We have to pick up all these disowned selves and begin to bring them into the light of day and see what they are about.

SPIRITUALITY AND PSYCHOLOGY

WITH FRANCES VAUGHAN, PH.D.

Frances Vaughan is a psychologist and author of AWAKENING INTUITION *and* THE INWARD ARC: HEALING AND WHOLENESS IN PSYCHOTHERAPY AND SPIRITUALITY. *She is a former president of the Association for Transpersonal Psychology and the Association for Humanistic Psychology.*

True psychology is incomplete without an understanding of the spiritual yearnings of human beings. In this interview, Dr. Vaughan discusses the role of transpersonal psychologists in helping clients transcend the limited self and explore their connections to society, the environment, and the realm of the spirit.

You write extensively about spirituality in your work, and as a transpersonal psychotherapist, you have a professional interest in the interface between spirituality and psychology. What is the role of psychology, as opposed to the role of religion, in helping people to develop spiritually?

FV: Traditional psychology tends to take a very dim view of spirituality, because psychology tends to see many people trying to avoid issues of personal confrontation by turning to spirituality. Psychologists often see spirituality as a kind of escapism from the existential realities of our mortality, our aloneness, and the human condition – something that people believe in to make themselves feel better.

Conversely, it seems that a lot of religions describe psychology in those same terms. The Fundamentalists feel that psychology is sort of a fantasy and that it is avoiding the real issues.

FV: Exactly; they tend to take an oppositional stance. Traditional spiritual teachers or traditional religions often see psychology as simply concerned with the ego, as selfishness, and they fail to see the value of that in terms of personal growth or healthy personal development. So I think a lot of education needs to happen on both sides, because in fact I see them as complementary aspects of human development, both of which are necessary for wholeness and for real healing in our lives. There needs to be a lot of bridging work between the two, so that people don't feel that they have to choose either a psychological discipline or a spiritual discipline, but can recognize that in fact both are important.

In your work, you have drawn from many traditions. You have looked at the Christian spiritual path, at Zen Buddhism, yoga, and a number of others in your writings. You seem to be saying that they all point in the same direction.

FV: I like the analogy of truth as a mountain, with all the different religious paths as different approaches to climbing the mountain. You see many different paths up the mountain, and when you are down on the lower slopes, you may argue about the shape of the mountain. But the more you work on it, and the further up you go, the more you see that there is a convergence – that there are certain values, for example, that tend to be common to all the different traditions. And even though different paths provide different experiences along the way, I feel very strongly that there is a universal experience of self- transcendence that is possible, and this can be very healing for people. It can have a very positive effect in terms of their psychological development, if such an experience is appropriately integrated.

A universal quality of self-transcendence – how does that translate to a therapy practice when you are working with someone?

FV: In my practice I find that sometimes people seek me out because they know I have a transpersonal orientation, particularly if they have had some kind of experience that has opened up some spiritual issues for them. Or perhaps they have been practicing meditation, and want to talk things over with someone who has an understanding of the practice and what those experiences might be like. Or they may have had some kind of spontaneous opening, an experience of self-transcendence, that they want to make sense out of and integrate in some way.

What if a person came to you who was having marital problems or some other type of conventional psychological problem, and they didn't have a thought about spiritual experience? Is there any application there?

FV: My experience is that it depends on how deeply people want to do inner work. Often people come into therapy seeking relief for some kind of interpersonal stress. Relationship issues are very common, for example – either a marital problem or the breakup of a relationship. But sooner or later I think everyone has to confront themselves. Very often in relationships we tend to think, "Well, if only the other person were different, then everything would be all right." But ultimately I think we have to take a look at what we are contributing, and how we can make a difference in the quality of the relationships we have in our lives. And then we start to look at how our state of being or our state of consciousness affects the relationships that we tend to bring into our lives, and patterns that we find ourselves repeating.

Can you give me an example of this?

FV: Yes. For example, recently I have been working with a woman who is in her second marriage. She separated from her first husband because he had a problem with alcohol, and she felt that it was all his problem. Well, she found that she was recreating similar patterns in her second marriage, and the second time around she didn't want to just leave. She wanted to stay in the relationship and work through some of her own issues.

In other words, she had thought she could get rid of the problem by getting rid of the first husband.

FV: Exactly; and of course it never works, because as soon as you get rid of a relationship you find that you either recreate a similar relationship, or you have to deal with the same issues in yourself.

It's like Pogo when he said, "We have found the enemy and he is us."

FV: Yes, and that is one place where spirituality and psychology converge, because we recognize that we are all mirrors for each other in some way. I see, for example, that in some way all of my clients reflect aspects of myself. I can empathize with them, because I know how it feels to be in the kinds of situations that they describe. This is something that is really available to all of us. The more we are willing to look at ourselves and understand the dynamics of the way the mind works, the more we realize that these are really universal patterns, and that people everywhere have to deal with issues of love and fear and anxiety about loss and facing death. Often it is just at these times, when people feel some kind of crisis in their lives – maybe facing their own mortality, or the death of someone that they are close to – that spiritual issues become really meaningful and important.

In the case of this particular woman, how did she begin to look at spiritual issues?

FV: Basically it was a question of values in her life: what were the things that really were most important to her? What she came to see was that in order to really love the person she was with, she also had to take herself into account. This is often true – that it is not a matter of either loving oneself or loving someone else, but it seems to be both. Both are necessary. I sometimes think of spiritual disciplines as teaching us to forgive others, and psychotherapy as a way of learning to forgive ourselves.

That's a very interesting distinction. In your work you describe the self as if it were an onion, with different layers. Could we go through the onion a little bit, and see it from your eyes?

FV: All right. I like to use the image of concentric circles, because I think that as we become more conscious and more aware of the nature of the self, the sense of self expands, and when we are afraid, or when we are unwilling to be in touch with the world around us, our sense of self gets constricted. First of all, I see it in a developmental framework. We are usually primarily identified with the body, the physical self. Then we also become aware of our feelings; we get a sense of the emotional self and the mental self, our thoughts about feelings. We even start to think about thinking.

So the first three layers would be physical, emotional, and mental.

FV: Right, and those have been mapped by Western psychology very thoroughly. The areas that haven't been mapped so clearly are the ones that go beyond ego. That is, the ego is generally referred to as what we think we are, the ideas about our identity in terms of roles and relationships. Then the existential self is what we generally get in touch with when we become concerned about authenticity – when it's not enough to have a good image or to play a role, but it really matters if you have a sense of integrity, a sense of choice, a sense of having your inner experience match your outer expression, so that there isn't that split between the two. This would be a sense of a healthy existential self.

I have great appreciation for the contribution of the existential psychologists, such as Rollo May, James Bugental, and others, who have pointed out the importance of coming to terms with the existential issues of value, meaning, and purpose in our lives. Then there is another area, though, because with the existential view we are only isolated, individual, separate entities in the world, existing usually in a state of alienation.

The sense one gets from existential writers like Camus, Sartre, and Genet is that when you really get in touch with life as it is, it will make you sick.

FV: Because the ultimate reality here is the idea that we are separated and alone. However, it seems to me that there is another side to experience which is just as valid, which is that we are all connected, and that yes, we all have the experience of being separate and alone; but we also have the experience of being connected – to each other and to the environment – and we are not just independent, we're also interdependent. As soon as we start recognizing how we all exist in this intricate network of mutually interdependent relationships, then I think that we wake up to the possibility of another kind of awareness that transcends the existential separateness.

So we are moving beyond the existential here. I would think of this as sort of a systems approach, where we're beginning to look at networking.

FV: Yes, exactly.

Human beings would be analogous to cells of the body, and the social structure could be thought of as a body, in that sense. But it's also transpersonal.

FV: It is, and it is what Ken Wilber has called vision logic, which is looking not only at ideas and how beliefs affect experience, but also at networks of ideas and how we become more creative in terms of the way we view ourselves and the planet as a whole. It's a more global view, if you will, which takes into account not only the individual in isolation, but also in relationship to the larger whole – to society, and to the environment.

Frances, you're an expert on intuition. Let's move beyond the agony and the loneliness of the existential self, and talk about the creative process. We hear about so many artists who struggle, who experience this alienation, and then they have a breakthrough, and what comes out of it is the music of Mozart or of Wagner, this great creativity. That's not the same as what we have described as this networking phenomenon. That's a different level also, isn't it?

FV: It is a different level, and I think that intuition is often associated with inspiration and insight. Again, it is a kind of self-transcendence, in that something seems to come through us, rather than being a product of something that the ego invents. This is where we can learn something from some of the Eastern disciplines, because learning to quiet the mind opens up all kinds of creative possibilities. That is something that I think psychology needs to investigate in more depth; and also, that what we believe to be true about this process tends to become true in our experience. We create our own inner experience by our beliefs about it. So I think that it is an appropriate task for psychology to investigate these experiences, and to understand more the role of beliefs in generating our experience, and what that means for psychological health.

How do you define the term transpersonal? We have discussed intuition, creativity, and the sense that there is a larger part of us that is not totally separate, that we are connected with other people. Am I missing something?

FV: Well, literally transpersonal means beyond the personal. But I think it also refers to the transcendental, as expressed in and through the personal, so that it is the link between the personal and that which is transcendent. It is a psychological view of spiritual development, rather than a religious point of view; so that transpersonal psychology doesn't espouse any particular religious orientation, but it tries to understand the universal human experience that leads to different paths of exploration.

Transpersonal psychologists have been accused – for example, by the existentialists such as Rollo May – of being advocates of religion, and not practicing psychology at all. How do you respond to that?

FV: Well, that's not my experience at all, and I have had the opportunity to talk to a lot of transpersonal psychologists all over the world. They are indeed psychologists; and some of them have a particular religious affiliation, and some do not. But I don't know that any of them would try to convert anybody or impose their beliefs on their clients. Functioning as a psychologist means maintaining a certain objectivity, or at least putting the client's interests ahead of your own, whatever your beliefs may be.

There is an enormous movement in modern psychology that says psychologists must be scientific, and that they should never go beyond the bounds of what the experiments say. And yet as I read your writing and the writing of other transpersonal psychologists, it seems that the science that you are looking to is not experimental science, it is the accumulated wisdom of people who have practiced meditation and spiritual disciplines and have reported phenomenologically on that.

FV: Well, I think that we do need more investigation. I think that more research would be an excellent contribution to the field; there is a lot of work to be done yet. But in fact there is considerable data to say that there are methods of training awareness, of training the mind, that have worked very well in other cultures, and that we could learn something from.

I would like to describe you in a way as a psychologist's psychologist – for people who have mastered the Western scientific traditions, and who are now looking for something more in their lives. They begin to wonder about the spiritual dimension, and yet for many people in the modern world, religion is unpalatable to them. Do you serve as a sort of substitute priest in that sense?

FV: In a sense perhaps that's so, because it's too bad if a person doesn't feel comfortable with conventional religion and doesn't have the opportunity to do the inner work and find out for themselves their own connections to that inner source of wisdom, that sense of relatedness. It may or may not be a sense of connection to God; it depends. Some religious traditions, such as the Zen Buddhist, for example, are not theistic at all. Nevertheless they have a lot to contribute to spiritual development and to values in one's life.

In your work you have had a chance to study the phenomenological, autobiographical reports of mystics of many different religions, and you have come to realize similar patterns, I think.

FV: Yes, I think there are certainly universal experiences. In looking for the transcendental unity of religions, from a psychological perspective I tend to take the psychological viewing frame; we can't avoid taking some type of viewing frame if we are going to say anything at all. We need to speak in a particular language, and as soon as we say anything we are already taking a position. It seems to me that psychological language offers a way of exploration and investigation that is not already predetermined by a long tradition of particular religious views.

One of the most intriguing areas in the interface between spirituality and psychology is the notion of KUNDALINI – that perhaps some people whom we would define in our traditional Western sense as having a nervous breakdown or a psychotic break, from another perspective may be experiencing a spiritual awakening. Is this part of what you deal with in your practice?

FV: I think the real issue here is to ask, what happens when you have an experience that you can't account for in terms of ordinary psychology? I think there are two possible hazards here. One is to pathologize experiences that might in fact be an opportunity for a larger, expanded sense of self. But on the other side, there is the hazard of romanticizing all experiences that in some way involve the dissolution of ego boundaries as being breakthroughs or transpersonal. I think there are both kinds. There are breakdowns and there are breakthroughs; and as psychologists we need to know the difference.

How do you do that?

FV: There are definitely certain characteristics that are typical, say, of prepersonal experiences and characteristics typical of transpersonal experiences. The prepersonal are generally regressive, and they generally have a lot of fear associated with them, and there is the sense that the reality that is perceived at the moment seems to be the only possible reality. There is a sort of constriction of consciousness.

What do you mean by prepersonal?

FV: Well, when we take a developmental frame, we talk about prepersonal development; that's before you have become fully self-aware of your own ego identity. We talk about personal, and then transpersonal. I think there is a confusion between the pre and the trans; that is a very important area that needs further documentation and investigation so that it can be clarified. But I think that we are really on the way to doing that.

In the transpersonal area, I should think it would sometimes be hard to tell. I read

*a book by the Eastern guru, Meher Baba, in which he talks about the mad Musts,
or God-intoxicated people, who can't tie their shoelaces, they can't dress themselves,
and their disciples come and feed them. The disciples somehow recognize these
people are very holy; their consciousness is lost in God. But to another person they
might seem to be severely retarded.*

FV: Well, of course we need to take the cultural differences into account here.
But when we talk about a developmental approach, we are talking about
expanding consciousness into higher states. We need to differentiate higher
states from altered states, because altered states are simply states other than
our ordinary waking state, and that might include this God-intoxication that
you are talking about. Higher states include all of the faculties of the ordinary
waking state, plus additional faculties, so that they have a noetic quality; that
means that there is a sense of deeper knowing and understanding. Usually
the affect is one of loving- kindness, and the motivation that comes out of
these experiences tends to be one of service in the world.

*You seem to be saying that people who are experiencing these higher states have
integrated the transpersonal level into their lives. They are more than just average
or normal; they are able to inspire other people and share with them a sense of
enthusiasm.*

FV: Yes, I think that's true, but I also think that it is available to all of us, and
that we all have moments, if not days and times, when we tap into these
states. That is what we need to remember – that we all have access to that
source of transcendent wisdom within ourselves, if we are willing to take the
time and give it the attention that it deserves.

GROWTH AND ACHIEVEMENT

TRANSCENDING LIMITATIONS

WITH JAMES FADIMAN, PH.D.

James Fadiman, a distinguished humanistic psychologist, is the author of UNLIMIT YOUR LIFE: SETTING AND GETTING GOALS and BE ALL THAT YOU ARE. He is President of The Fadiman Corporation, a consulting firm, and an Adjunct Professor at the Institute of Transpersonal Psychology. He has served as a consultant to many large corporations and is a former Director of the Institute of Noetic Sciences.

We all limit ourselves by attachment to old attitudes and outworn ideas. In this interview, Dr. Fadiman offers techniques for recognizing and discarding such atittudes and setting goals for the changes we desire.

L*et's begin by talking for a moment about human potential, about what is possible. Why would we even think it was possible to transcend our limitations?*

JF: We use so little of what we have in almost every area you can imagine, that transcending limitations is the obvious thing to do on any given day. We have all said to ourselves, "I can't do this," and then the situation changes, and we do it. Every parent knows that they can't possibly raise children, but they do. Every author knows they can't possibly complete a book whey they are in the middle of it, and they do. Most students will tell you again and again if you try to teach them anything, "I can't possibly learn this," and they do.

You are almost making it sound easy, as if all we have to do is carry on. A lot of times people blow it – a lot of children are not properly raised; a lot of books never do get written.

JF: The part that interests me is working on those few small obstacles that are critical. If there is only one door between you and perfection and you never open the door, it doesn't matter if there are a hundred doors.

So what you are suggesting is that we could all be doing a lot more than we are.

JF: Well, the data is fairly clear – that any child or adult, given a more supportive environment, eliminating some of the psychological drawbacks, given a little better educational opportunity, does very well. It looks as if we could all be doing better without any massive changes in the culture.

What is the key to how we hold ourselves back?

JF: The key is our own image of ourselves, our own self-concept, the way we rate ourselves against other people: "I'm not as good as; I'm only as good as; I'm better than." The way we maintain our opinion of our abilities is the major stumbling block towards doing better than our abilities.

A lot of people would say, "I am who I am, and I can't change my self-concept because I would be lying. I have these limitations; they are real."

JF: Well, people know who they were. For instance, if you ask a crowd of normal people, "Who here is terrible in math?" you'll get a few hands. Then you ask, "What's your evidence?" I am amazed that many people – they may be forty-six years old now – will say the evidence is what they were in their junior year in high school. They got a C minus back then, and therefore they have this scar deep inside their soul called "terrible in math." So you simply get them to grasp the possibility that they are not stuck in high school. You say, "Did you change anything else since high school? Are you a little more mature in other ways?" And everyone says, "Of course. High school was dreadful." Then they can begin to see that if everything else has changed, maybe, without their noticing it, their ability to do reasoning and mathematics has also changed. I have had case after case of people sending me letters that end by saying, "I did go back to school. I'm in an accounting class," or "I'm in a computer programming class, and I just got an A on the final. Yours sincerely, I-Used-to-Be-Bad-in-Math, Jane."

So one way we can transform our self-concept is, rather than saying, "I am bad at math," or "I am a bad parent," to say, "I used to be."

JF: As soon as you say, "I used to be," you are telling the truth. You have evidence that you used to be this and that; but that doesn't mean that you have to be in the future.

To what extent are we the product of our past experiences? Can we just break away from the past?

JF: We can't break away from the past, but we can slowly pull ourselves away from the past into the future, if we wish to. Example: if you go to a foreign country, you are going to start by speaking English, because you have an enormous past history of speaking English effectively and correctly and in all situations. Well, when you do that in Paris, people look at you hard. They would rather you speak French, and you therefore will begin to develop some new behaviors, and after a while, when someone walks up to you, you will speak in French – a little bit at first, and then a little bit more. You haven't lost your English. You haven't given up your past. You haven't become a new human being. When you visit the United States, you will find your ability to speak English is unimpaired.

Now, that's a tough one. I understand what you are saying, but you've hit me at a sore point, because I kind of don't believe I could learn French.

JF: Because you used to not speak French.

Right. All my life I used to not speak French.

JF: From when you were very small. Did you speak anything when you were born?

No. I babbled.

JF: You babbled, and not too well at that perhaps. But you learned English. Are you less capable of learning now than when you were two years old?

I suspect I am, yes. Languages have been hard for me, so maybe it's a good example to talk about.

JF: So when you were two years old, you were able to learn a language. Of course you were taught in a much more healthy and sane environment than you were in school, because you had people who loved you, and you had lots of practice, and they didn't push you beyond whatever you could do in a given day, and you had lots of rewards. Well, it turns out that if you try teaching a language that way to adults – with running around and playing and singing and play-acting, and lots of things with food – people learn a language in one-fifth, one-sixth, or one-eighth the time that our conventional educational system says it takes.

You know, now that you mention it, that's true. It's called accelerated learning, or superlearning. In fact I even attended a seminar and learned how to speak quite a bit of Spanish in a few hours that way; but I forgot.

JF: Because you had a belief system that says, "Since I'm not good at languages, even though I learned a lot of Spanish in a few hours, that didn't count."

So my own attitude towards what I am capable of doing is probably the biggest limitation that I have.

JF: It looks like it. Now yes, there are social limitations; yes, there are economic limitations; yes, there are physical limitations. But if we look at a hundred disadvantaged people and come back twenty years later, some of them have done magnificently. What happened? Why did those few do differently? When we ask them, they say, "Well, my attitude was different than the other people."

People around them will say it was just luck.

JF: That's the people who are still there. I have a definition of luck. It's cute, but it is useful to me. Luck is Laboring Under Correct Knowledge, which is why some people have more of it. Why do some people tend to make better decisions much of the time? If you ask them they say, "I don't know. I just pay attention and do the best I can." But it is the paying attention that turns out to be critical, and that gets back to their attitude about themselves.

If we have an attitude about ourselves that limits us, you might call that incorrect knowledge.

JF: Right. "I used to be bad at math" is correct knowledge. "I don't know what will happen in the future" is correct knowledge. But "I am bad at math and don't you try and teach me anything" – is incorrect knowledge.

Or "I am a bad spouse," or "I am not a good parent" – any attitude in any area of life.

JF: Or "I am an overweight person," which is the polite term; or, "I can't control my —" whatever it is, drinking, smoking, cocaine.

If we want to play generations, there was the Me Generation and the Narcissistic Generation, the Human Potential Generation. Someone has suggested that our generation is the Anonymous Generation, because there are so many groups of Alcoholics Anonymous, Overeaters Anonymous, Narcotics Anonymous. When you visit them, they are full of people with transformed attitudes, people who used to have the attitude of addiction, and now they have the attitude of power, pride, self-control, and remarkable development. They are among the most impressive people that I have been meeting.

How do we all become so ignorant about our potential that we allow these attitudes to become so deeply engrained?

JF: Well, if you go to a kindergarten, and you ask the teacher, "What percentage of the kids in this class can learn to play a musical instrument?" the answer from any kindergarten teacher is one hundred percent. If you go to a sixth-grade class, and you say to the teacher, "What percentage of the children can learn to play a musical instrument?" the answer is about forty percent. What has happened? It looks as if a combination of parents and the school system have snuffed out not the ability, but the willingness to have the ability. If you turn it around and get one of those kids who think, "I can't play a musical instrument; I have no talent; I hate to practice; and I'm tone deaf" – the ultimate safety from learning any music – if you get that child, or even an adult, to simply let go of the attitudes, they can learn to play a musical instrument, not as quickly as a kindergartner, but almost. It is that kind of letting go and taking up a new attitude that I find very exciting.

In other words, it doesn't matter how we got the attitude. No matter what happened to us – our parents may have beaten it into us, for example – it's possible to change the attitude anyhow.

JF: If it's possible to learn a new language by living somewhere else, if it's possible to learn to drive a stick shift if you have only driven an automatic, if it's possible to learn a computer, clearly we are capable of learning new things. If we look back at the things we have decided we can't learn, we see they are just attitudes.

It sounds a little too easy to me, Jim. Learning a skill is something that most people can do, but sometimes changing your attitudes is more than just simple learning. You may have to let go of something that you have a very strong emotion about.

JF: Right – if you want to be that way; or if you would disappoint your parents by being better. I know that sounds paradoxical, but if you are brought up in a family with a couple of kids, in most families one of the kids is nicer, and everyone in the family knows who that is. One of the kids is smarter; everyone knows who that is. And after a while, if you are the not-nice one, or the nice one, you don't get out of line. You don't disappoint your parents by being different than they expect you to be. Take kids with reading. Children don't start out as bad readers, because they all start out as non-readers. Then they get into school, and some of them decide, "I'm not a good reader," for various reasons – parenting, education, who knows? But then they can maintain it, usually with the school system's support. They then are moved into a special group. You know: "Which reading group are you in?" "I'm in the Turtles." "What are the Turtles?" "That's the dumb kids. We're the bad readers." Then those children begin to think of themselves as bad readers, as kids who are not as bright, and each year it is reinforced and redeveloped. If you take an adult who says, "I'm illiterate," the first thing you have to do in a literacy class is convince them that they are now going to stop being illiterate. That is why they came to the class. Otherwise they will maintain illiteracy through all the reading training, and go out saying, "Well, I went to a literacy class, and I'm still illiterate," because they have hung on to the attitude. So unless you change the attitude first, a lot of what we call learning experiences are thrown away.

Can a person who has an attitude like this, to which they may have a strong emotional attachment, simply change it because someone else persuades them? Is it through logic?

JF: No, it is through desire. It is through greed, in the sense that if you aim for people's greed and lust, you will find they are very, very interested. If you aim for their higher spiritual development, some are interested, some are not. So for instance, say someone wishes to stop smoking. Smoking feels terrific; that's why it is popular. Not smoking doesn't feel terrific to a smoker; that's why it is less popular. But if someone genuinely wants to stop smoking, they can, even though they are addicted and it's terrible, and so forth and so on. At some point people will say, "Something in me is capable of making a massive change in a habit, an attitude, an addiction," and they literally take a cigarette and put it out and never pick up another.

But there must be other techniques as well. Let's suppose I fervently desire to change my habit – say, my belief that I can't learn a language. But I feel blocked, I'm uncomfortable, I'm afraid, and changing my attitude creates a whole new set of problems for me.

JF: There has to be information. You can't learn a language by sitting on the edge of your bed and saying, "I love French. French is so good. I'm now speaking French." Unless you have some French training, it is not going to work. There is a human-potential attitude that if you shut your eyes and wish real hard, good things will fall out of the sky on you. It turns out that if you shut your eyes and wish real hard, when you open your eyes the first thing that comes into your mind is the first thing you need to do towards the goal that you have just wished for.

That's interesting. I think you just said something important.

JF: Right, because what you have done is say to yourself, "I genuinely want this," and the part of you that lives in the world and notices things says, "Well, if you're serious, if you really want this, there are some things you might look for."

The answer is somehow within us.

JF: There is a saying that the hungry man sees only bread. When you are motivated you become a little homing device. I have a cat at home, and I watch my cat. I'll open a can of something and the cat is thirty-five feet away, and I'll watch my cat's nose start to go into radar mode. It starts to search, and as soon as it homes in on the direction of food, it knows exactly what to do next. It doesn't take any attitude change or training. It takes desire plus practice, plus the information that opening a can is probably worth sniffing around for. Just the sound of a can opening begins the procedure.

Let's take a hard example now. You mentioned smoking earlier, and I know the research indicates that there aren't any really good methods for helping people to give up smoking. Almost every method has more failures than successes. And yet there are successes; people do succeed. What's the difference?

JF: Well, two things. The first thing is, they used to be a smoker, meaning up until the last cigarette. When I talk to groups of adults, and I ask, "How many of you have given up smoking?" usually a rather large percentage have given up smoking. Then I ask, "How many of you simply stopped cold turkey – no methods, no techniques, no schools, no cigarettes with ever-diminishing filters, no crummy cigarettes that taste lousy – just stopped?" About half. So there is a magnificent method out there, which is believing in oneself enough, believing that one has enough capacity to actually do what one decides to do. And at that moment, not smoking is simply a difficult thing to do. I have also investigated some of the research on methods, and it was amazing that they didn't work very well. They don't work very well because the people who go to these things say, "Nothing is going to help, but I'll try this mechanical outside system that won't bother my attitudes."

There's a wonderful story in the alcohol world. One of the ways that people try to cure alcoholics is what is called aversion therapy, where they give them Antabuse, a drug which is neutral, but if you add alcohol, people get nauseous and feel horrible. Well, some people at a local VA Hospital were all on Antabuse therapy, and they decided that they were very depressed by that, because they really would prefer to drink. They decided to support each other. They fled the hospital, went to the local bar and ordered liquor, took it and threw up, took some more and threw up. They basically supported each other and encouraged each other, until they were able to overcome the effects of the drug and drink.

The power of transcending one's limits, right?

JF: So it works either way.

That's fascinating. What do you see in terms of some of the higher realms? We have role models in our culture of outstanding athletes, scholars, mathematical geniuses. I am interested in psychic phenomena, which many people say is impossible. Do you think it's likely that in the far distant future the kind of human behavior that we think of as exceptional would be considered normal, because people will have learned that they don't have to limit themselves?

JF: If you look at athletics, it is happening all the time. When I grew up, it was assumed that people in their sixties, seventies, and eighties didn't do much exercise and certainly didn't do it well, or for very long. Now there are marathons, and a man in San Francisco used to win in the eighty-plus age group in every marathon; he was the only person running. Now he is ranked fourth nationally, and in any marathon he runs there is competition. Now, if people in their eighties can run marathons, what is normal behavior?

Runners are wonderful people to talk to, because they all have their stories. Most of them, particularly middle-aged runners or older, will say at some point, "I ran for the bus, thirty-two yards, and I panted and I sweated and thought I'd die, and I was ashamed, so I started running." A friend of mine is very typical. The first time he ran he made about a hundred yards on a clear day, dressed properly, and a year later he did his first marathon. How did that happen? He is not a great athlete; his athlete friends let him know that he is simply a normal human being who pushed just a little on his potential. He decided that if people he knew were no better than he was and could run marathons, so could he. The sports world is now littered with what we used to call miracle stories. Now they are just what athletes do.

The same thing holds true in the realm of medicine. We used to believe that it was up to the doctors to heal us, and now more and more people are taking responsibility for their own health.

JF: Well, it seems odd that one would think a doctor could heal you. You don't think a doctor can make you sick. Nobody can eat your food for you, and there are certain other things that you can only do for yourself. It would look as if healing is one of them. What we are finding out is that if you combine your own attitude with whatever medical science is offering, the results are far better than if you assume that medical science is the only thing working.

One of the techniques that must be very important here is being able to set goals for yourself and to focus on your goals and stick to them.

JF: Well, it turns out when you look at successful people, which is where this research starts, they are capable of maintaining their intention. If you are going to walk up a mountain, every once in a while you have to remember which direction is up. You don't have to keep the top of the mountain in mind, because the mountain itself has a lot of hints, but now and then you have to remember, "What am I doing here, and what's my intention?" So daily, perhaps more often, people remind themselves what they are really doing.

One of the nice things about schools, since I have said nasty things about schools, is that school continually reminds you that for an hour we are going to think about geography. If you say, "I'm having a problem in division," the teacher says, "Now, wait a moment. We're all thinking about geography for a while. Can you pay attention?"

What we are seeing is that in order to overcome limitations, to transcend whatever you used to be, takes a little bit of information, and it takes reminding yourself. Those are the secret, occult doctrines of twentieth-century psychology.

OVERCOMING COMPULSIVE BEHAVIOR

WITH SHINZEN YOUNG, PH.D.

A Buddhist monk and scholar of Buddhism, Shinzen Young is director of the Community Meditation Center of Los Angeles.

According to Buddhist philosophy, compulsive and addictive behavior are common to all "normal" individuals. Through meditation, says Young, one learns to recognize the root cause of addiction as a lack of mindfulness. Gradually, through increased awareness, the compulsive impulse loosens its grip on the individual. Addictive behavior, when addressed through meditation, thus affords an opportunity for spiritual growth.

W *hen we talk about addictive and compulsive behavior, it would seem that from a Buddhist perspective most human behavior would be viewed in that light.*

SY: That's correct, and when I work with people who have addictive or compulsive problems – overeating or substance abuse or compulsive gambling or whatever – one of the things that I emphasize is that their behavior is not fundamentally different from the average person's. It is just that the compulsiveness or drivenness, which is my word for it, is all concentrated in one object, and that object is very self-destructive. The average person is driven constantly; and that quality of drivenness, which is largely unacknowledged in the so-called happy or adjusted person, is what blocks that person from experiencing the really deep spiritual self or the transcendent spiritual experience. When a person has a compulsive disorder, such as overeating, undereating, or something like that, on one hand we can say that person has an immense personal tragedy. But on the other hand, there is a bright side to the picture from the perspective of the spiritual path, in that

that person is forced to come to grips with the whole issue of drivenness per se, whereas the person whose drivenness is distributed among many different objects may be able to postpone that confrontation. And so, the person who has a problem with food, or what have you, in order to survive, may be forced to attain a spiritual state. The motivation will be there; and my job as a meditation teacher is to teach them the spiritual dimension of the path to sobriety or abstinence.

One of the basic teachings of Buddha is that all of life is suffering.

SY: Let's put it this way. As long as there is drivenness, then we cannot experience our true nature. Our true nature is effortless. It is the nature of nature itself – an effortless, spontaneous flow. Whether we realize it or not, all of us, from infancy on, start to acquire drivenness, compulsiveness, grabbiness; and that covers over our true nature. As long as that is covered over, then yes, life is going to be suffering. On the other hand, we could just as well say that Buddhism teaches that life is heaven on earth if we see what is really there.

The basic model that I usually use for dealing with compulsiveness is that when a person is abusing a substance – whether it is food or a drug or whatever – what they are doing is using that substance as an anesthetic or a coping mechanism for unconscious subliminal pain or discomfort. What has been discovered in the meditative path is that there is an alternative coping mechanism. Instead of dealing with one's discomfort by trying to stuff it down, as they say, there is a special state of consciousness that is sometimes called the witness state, wherein you are able to simply observe and experience that discomfort without being caught in it. And when you are not caught in it, it doesn't get exaggerated into a suffering that must be relieved by doing a self-destructive activity. We teach people how to enter this witness state of consciousness and then simply observe the discomfort in a way whereby it doesn't drive them. We have step-by-step, very specific techniques that allow a person to develop the witness state, just the way they could develop their game of golf as a skill.

The American Medical Association has recently come up with a new term, addictive disorder, to include all of the different addictions. The body might choose one or another object, but it's still something that is called an addictive personality.

SY: I personally like to use the word drivenness, and that is the way that we look at it – that any drivenness works on the same mechanism. And when people overcome their eating problems using a meditative technique, they will not just be overcoming that problem, but it will cause an immense revolution in their total lives, because if they use the meditative path they will deal with the real issue; they will get down to drivenness per se.

Now, what happens when you enter the witness state is that the discomfort that you ordinarily would cover over by, let us say, overeating, you just observe; and you are able to see that it is changing and insubstantial. It loses its gripping power, and you don't need therefore to engage in a self-destructive behavior. The other amazing thing is that this is not just a temporary substitution. If you can consistently observe in this witness state, as the months and years pass, the pain that is driving the behavior actually starts to dissolve of its own. We can't make it go away, because if we were to try to push on it, that would be manipulating and would cause more pain. But by our just observing, it breaks up of its own. And so the actual compulsion itself goes; and not just the compulsion around the food, but the overall sense of drivenness that that person may have with respect to anything – having a conversation, making love or what have you.

The conventional thinking in programs such as Alcoholics Anonymous is that an alcoholic may learn not to drink, but will always remain an alcoholic.

SY: There is a very good reason why the 12-Step programs say that, and what I am saying in no way contradicts that; because unless you practice a very deep meditative technique for a long period of time, you probably are not going to contact and uproot that pain. Although you may deal with some of it, the seeds of the compulsion will always be there; and it is typical of the addictive personality to have what they call the phenomenon of denial. If you start thinking, "I'm cured, so I can take a little drink," you are going to blow it. So that is why the 12-Step programs teach that.

And they seem to be effective.

SY: Yes, they seem to work quite well. But if you conquer an addiction with a meditative technique – and not everyone does – the advantage is you will uproot it; you will be cured.

You used the term, "the seeds of the compulsion."

SY: Right. The seeds of the compulsion are the underlying pain.

Where does that arise?

SY: Basically it arises from past experience. Whenever we have any experience, we have sensations that arise, pleasant or unpleasant feelings. If this interview is going well, I get pleasant feelings; if we run into a hitch, I get tension and unpleasant feelings. Feelings are with us at all times. If a person has feelings in a skillful way, in that moment those feelings will simply be full and complete and they will pass through. Whether they are painful or pleasant makes no difference; they won't leave any ghosts.

That's an interesting phrase – to have feelings in a skillful way.

SY: We study all sorts of skills – skill at tennis, skill at computer languages. But very few people realize that the most fundamental skill for any human being is how to experience pleasure and pain in a wholesome way. Now, skill implies two things – that there is a complete awareness of the feeling, and that there is a non-interference with the flow of that feeling. To the extent that a person can have pleasure and pain in that way, to that extent the pain will not cause suffering and will not leave ghosts of fear. And the pleasure will not cause frustration; it will be completely fulfilling and will not leave ghosts of dissatisfaction. From infancy on we begin to feel. In fact, that is all we did when we were infants; we did not think very much, but we sure felt. We are totally feeling beings. And we start to develop the habit of doing two things around feeling – diverting and tensing. As soon as you are doing that, you are not having the feeling skillfully. And as soon as you have any feeling that's unskillful, it is going to leave ghosts – unresolved remnants of itself, residues.

Most of us are taught as children not to cry, not to have painful feelings.

SY: Well, there is a difference between expressing externally and expressing internally. Skillful feeling means that you totally experience it internally. Whether you express it externally or not is an independent dimension from that. Whenever you fully internally manifest a feeling, it will leave no ghost. Most people do not do that. Therefore, they start to accumulate ghosts, or residues, of pain, and that builds up and builds up and builds up. Everybody carries with them enormous subliminal, hidden pain, whether they know it or not. Some of that pain can start to come to the surface, and when it does, in order to cope with it we sometimes begin to engage in negative behavior, to anesthetize ourselves to it.

You asked where the pain comes from. It is essentially the remnants of thousands, hundreds of thousands, of past experiences – not just one or two that may come up in psychotherapy, but hundreds of thousands of moments of unskillful feeling, each one leaving tiny little ghosts. What happens in the meditative state is that we begin to watch those feelings in an uninvolved way; we have specific techniques that teach people to do this. As we watch these feelings, we realize that they are impermanent, they just come and go; they are like waves of energy.

Let's take a devastating disorder like bulimia. When you actually get down to experiencing the real pain that underlies that, it is not all that horrible. But if you cannot experience it with full awareness, it impacts at a very primitive level of consciousness which is very sensitive, and it seems like the end of the world – like "I've just got to overeat," or "I've just got to vomit," or "I just can't handle anything." But when that pain is actually brought to the surface and observed specifically, it is not all that intense, really.

The way we bring it to the surface, in the particular form of meditation that I teach, is very interesting. If I were to ask you to get in contact with the stored unresolved pain of your lifetime, where would you look? If somebody says, "Where's Jeffrey?" I can point with my finger and say, "Follow the finger, and there's Jeffrey." But where is the stored pain of your lifetime? What is the finger that points us in the direction to look, so that we can start to resolve this stuff? One of the great discoveries that was made in the Buddhist tradition is that the ordinary sensations that we have in our body, if we start to pay attention to them, will direct us down into the core of pure feeling within us, wherein are stored these ghosts of the past. And so we teach people step-by-step techniques to sensitize the body so that they can feel this pain coming to the surface in the body, and just observe it as a three-dimensional, impermanent wave passing through. Once they can do that, they find that, number one, they don't have to act on that pain; and number two, they work through. It is as if a layer of discomfort percolates up to the surface, and then it dissolves in the light of dispassionate observation.

In other words, you ask these people to do the very thing that when they are involved in their compulsive behavior they fear the most, which is to feel their pain.

SY: That's correct; and that is why the meditative path is very tricky to give to somebody with a compulsive disorder. It has to be done in a very skillful way, because you are giving them a new coping mechanism which happens to be one hundred and eighty degrees in the opposite direction from their old coping mechanism, and therefore you have to be very careful about the transfer of the coping mechanisms. You mentioned the 12-Step programs earlier. When we teach this technique, we usually encourage people to enter a 12-Step program while they are learning Buddhist meditation for their compulsion. The reason is unless there is a strong networking from their peers to keep their behavior in line, their behavior may well get worse before it gets better, because we are digging down into the source, and we want to keep that under control with a behaviorally oriented program such as a 12-Step, Overeaters, or Alcoholics Anonymous.

I guess what you find in meditation is that the pain is never so great it can't be tolerated.

SY: Absolutely. Ultimately, I sometimes find myself saying, "I don't know whether to laugh or cry," because when you actually see what is there, you see somebody who has been destroying their life over something that is not all that painful, if they could just get in contact with it. But getting in contact with it is very difficult. One passes through, I would say, three basic stages. The first stage is where you do not experience it as specific bodily discomfort. You just have urges; it is all "I just gotta" – I just gotta have a drink, I just gotta do this or that. That's the stage where the sensations are completely covered over by ignorance. Then there is a second stage where the sensation rises to the surface, and you actually feel what you are trying to relieve by indulging in the compulsion. I call this stage detection. At this stage it will usually be all over the whole body; we teach people how to scan the body, how to get in contact with every bit of it. At the third stage they see that it is really insubstantial, it is impermanent, it is not nearly as painful as they might have thought. At that stage the urge vanishes; you have abstinence without effort. And at the same time, the spiritual self, which has been covered over all those years by that subliminal pain, that transcendent self, starts to manifest; and that opens up a world of fulfillment that is simply unimaginable to the average person.

Does this process also work with hard-core physiological addictions such as alcohol or heroin, where withdrawal can become a major problem?

SY: Absolutely; it would work. My experience has been that if the person has a very high motivation, and if they can get very competent, clear instruction in meditation, then they can conquer the disorder, and not only that, but go far beyond that. In other words, the people we so much pity in the state of having the disorder, if they use the meditative technique to conquer it, now become the people to envy. They become enlightened and liberated.

Stronger than they would have been if they had never had the problem.

SY: Incomparably stronger; I sometimes call that the bright side of addiction. My life companion, Shelly, runs a special program for eating disorders, and she came to this because she almost died from her own problem; she had an eating disorder. Not many years ago she was living on the streets, penniless and on the verge of suicide. She used this technique; she now has her own center, she is an established teacher and a source of enormous strength and encouragement to all the people around her.

In the meditative traditions, a lot is said about the higher realms of meditative practice. Are people who have been through addictive disorders as capable of reaching into those higher realms as anyone else?

SY: In a sense they are more capable; that is the point I was trying to make. They have an enormous motivation, and so yes, they will be drawn to that. Actually, a rock-solid addictive-compulsive disorder is not going to be cured by anything short of enlightenment, because you have to go to the core of the ego to deal with it. But it can be cured. Enlightenment will cure it.

There seem to be so many obstacles in the path of enlightenment. Is it a path for everybody?

SY: I can only say that in my experience it is a path for anybody that really wants it. But people should realize that this word enlightenment is thrown around rather loosely. As I use the word it has a very specific definition in Buddhism; it is not something that you are going to get in two weekend seminars. It represents a fundamental understanding of the nature of the oneness of all things – not as a belief, not as wishful thinking, but as rock-bottom reality. You would not expect to go to the moon without having an enormous endeavor. Look what it took to get us to the moon. You don't just wish your way there; you make step-by-step endeavors. But if you really work at it, you can do it, and go to the moon. Enlightenment is like that; it is not just something that you are going to wish your way to.

QUALITIES OF HIGH PERFORMANCE

WITH LEE PULOS, PH.D.

A clinical psychologist, Lee Pulos is the author of Miracles and Other Realities *(with Gary Richman) and* Beyond Hypnosis. *He served as Sports Psychologist for Team Canada at the Commonwealth Games and has worked with a number of Olympic and professional athletes. As a successful businessman and entrepreneur, he experienced another dimension of high achievement.*

In this interview, Dr. Pulos describes his work with outstanding achievers in athletics and business, as well as with individuals who have overcome cancer. He identifies many characteristics they hold in common — including goal setting, high self-esteem, and a passion for life — and suggests how we can begin to develop these qualities in ourselves.

You have worked with peak performers in many different fields – in business, in athletics. You have also spent a lot of your professional career working with cancer patients.

LP: My ideas on high-performance people are based on my work as an entrepreneur, on my cancer counseling, and of course on working with business people. I have noticed that all of them have certain qualities in common that seem to motivate them and help them get where they wish to go.

One of the most important qualities they have is a burning vision, a goal, something they can see in their minds. The goal is something that they see in the future, but they bring it into the present, as if it has happened. Every single person has this vision, and goal setting is critically important. There have been a number of studies on this; more and more psychologists are beginning to look at the issue of goal setting. For example, in a study at Yale working with convalescent patients, a psychologist named Judith Rodin separated them into two groups. One group was given a potted plant; this sounds so mundane. They were told to take care of the plant. The other group was told, "Don't worry about it. The nursing staff will take care of it." After eighteen months they looked at three variables – social factors, medical factors, and longevity; the life expectancy in a convalescent home like that is about eighteen months. The group that had no purpose, no goal, died within the expected period. Members of the other group had actually increased their life expectancy almost twice as long, about fourteen months longer than had been expected.

In other words, all other factors being equal, simply having a potted plant to take care of made a big difference in the life of these convalescing patients.

LP: Absolutely. Then they began adding to that, and compared the control group versus an experimental group who had more say as to what kind of clothing they wore, planning their meals, their television program – in other words, who had a sense of control and power and purpose in their lives.

You've got to have a goal; that seems to be the real message.

LP: That's right. But related to this whole issue is a feeling of empowerment. Once you have a goal, a vision, you feel much more empowered. There was another classical study at UCLA called the learned helplessness experiments, where an animal learned how to get through a maze, and then they put him into a leather harness and shocked him and shocked him and shocked him. Then they released him from the leather harness, and even though the animal knew how to get out, it just stood there and received the shocks. It had learned helplessness. If you were to extrapolate this into the work situation, factories for instance, the people on the assembly line seem to have more psychosomatic disorders, and so on, because there is this learned helplessness. Things are happening to them rather than from them.

I suppose as a psychologist you would say that a lot of that is their attitude rather than what is really true about them.

LP: That's right. It is strictly in the attitude of perceiving that you have given your power away to someone else. This is one thing that high-performance people do not do; they are totally in charge of what happens to them.

Often in therapy clients give enormously elaborate rationales about why they can't control this, why they can't control that.

LP: Blaming others, lacking control, is related to self-esteem, which is the second quality of high-performance people. They create situations in which they are always building on their self-esteem, their reputation with themselves. One of the things that detracts from self-esteem is blaming someone else, giving your power to someone else – blaming the weather, blaming this, blaming that. High-performance people do not do that. When you blame someone, or even take on a martyr role, which is part of our Judaeo-Christian ethic – you know, having to work hard and suffer and struggle – that really detracts from your sense of potency or empowerment and self-esteem. So there is no blaming in high-performance people; there is no martyrhood or struggle. These people view life as something to be lived joyously, impeccably, and they go through it having fun. If you keep programming your unconscious that everything is going to have to be hard work, then it becomes just that, and success becomes difficult.

Can people learn to change those attitudes?

LP: Absolutely; and this gets to another factor of high-performance people – that they are constantly monitoring their self-talk. Every single person self-talks between one hundred fifty and three hundred words a minute – forty-five or fifty thousand thoughts a day. Now, most of it is innocuous like, "I wonder what I'm going to wear tonight?" or, "How is it going to go? Where are we going to go for dinner?" But a lot of it, especially with people with low self-esteem, is, "I'm so stupid. Nothing works for me. I can't lose weight," and so on.

It's negative.

LP: And it's over and over and over.

You seem to be saying that this level of great competence and high performance would be a natural state for virtually everybody if we didn't program ourselves somehow into having low self-esteem.

LP: Yes, because our self-talk is one of the things that keeps reinforcing information in our subconscious, our reputation with ourselves. High-performance people are very conscious of that, and they will stop it right away and change it to something else. You never hear them saying things about themselves that are deprecatory like that.

There was a rather interesting study at Iowa. They went into the homes in a typical Iowa community where there were children and took a count of the number of positive or negative utterances that a parent would make to a child in the course of the day. They averaged it out over a three-week period. In the course of one day an average of four hundred and thirty-two negative utterances were made to a child.

What would be an example of a negative utterance?

LP: "Oh, you stupid child. There you go again, you've done it again. You're such a mess."

Something that would lower the self-esteem of a child.

LP: Precisely. That happened an average of four hundred and thirty-two times a day, versus thirty-one positive statements a day.

And that's in your typical Iowa household.

LP: In middle America. So that's another aspect of it – that high-performance people very, very carefully watch their self-talk. As a matter of fact, they are constantly programming positive self-talk.

Do you find, in looking at these individuals, that they have gone through periods of low self-esteem and then come out of that? Do people actually transform themselves in the process of becoming high performers?

LP: Well, I think a lot of people will take models. A lot of high-performance people read biographies of people in their field; they find out what these people think like, what they feel, what they do, and they begin emulating. They have a role model and begin incorporating some of those qualities and characteristics.

This must involve a good deal of visualization ability.

LP: Well, visualization is another one of the qualities – mental rehearsal. In their mind's eye they are constantly running a mental movie of what it is that they wish to achieve. For instance, I worked with a couple of Canadian swimmers who would visualize every single stroke of the race, the feeling of the water, the sound of the crowd as they were going up and doing their flips, everything. As a matter of fact, they would take turns timing each other, and they would be within one second of the splits in the various laps; that is how close their visualization matched the actual performance.

I think everyone is aware of the sorts of things that have been done in cancer counseling using mental imagery. This is based on the work of Carl Simonton, a radiological oncologist, who used relaxation techniques and mental imagery to augment the chemotherapy and radiation, the regular medical treatment that people were receiving. For example, one woman with lung cancer would imagine herself going into her lung with a vacuum cleaner and vacuuming away the diseased tissue, and then coming in with a medicated spray. A fourteen-year-old boy with terminal leukemia went into his bloodstream dressed like the Lone Ranger, all in white, and every time he saw a leukocyte he would pull out his six shooters and kill the leukocyte and haul away the dead leukocytes.

And these people were then successful in overcoming a disease like cancer.

LP: Well, with terminal patients, after five years, twenty-six percent of Simonton's population were still alive, many of whom would otherwise probably not be alive. There was an increase in the quality and quantity and longevity of life. There have been a number of other studies on mental rehearsal, particularly in the sports field and in business. For example, for the 1980 Olympics in Moscow, the Russians wanted to set up a showpiece for the world. They split their athletes into four groups: Group A, one hundred percent traditional physical practice; Group B, seventy-five percent physical, twenty-five percent mental; Group C, fifty-fifty; and Group D was seventy-five percent mental practice and twenty-five percent physical. Now these were all world-class athletes; they had all the skills. At the end of the Moscow Olympics and the Lake Placid Olympics, they counted the number of medals that each group had won. Group D, seventy-five percent mental, practice and twenty-five percent physical, had won the most medals, and there was an inverse relationship.

Seventy-five percent mental, twenty-five percent physical – that was the most optimal way to prepare.

LP: Absolutely. When I first started working with athletes in 1967, with the Canadian national volleyball team, to my knowledge I was the only sports psychologist in Canada; there may have been three or four in the United States. Today every single team in Canada has a sports psychologist whose primary function is teaching them how to mentally rehearse, make mental movies, mentally prepare themselves, build up self-esteem, and so on. It's critical.

There is one other example I wanted to give with respect to goal setting. A friend of mine, when he took over as chairman of the board of a large corporation, sat down with the vice presidents and asked what their goals or vision was for the company. The response was somewhat disjointed. He went out and purchased a thousand-piece jigsaw puzzle; he took away the top, put all the pieces on the floor, and said to them, "This is an exercise in communication and team building. I'd like to see you work together as a team and put the pieces together." They said, "Oh, great." After about fifteen minutes, with a little bit of jostling, he could see that things were getting a little testy.

They didn't have the picture.

LP: No picture. Then he said, "I've got the picture in the next room, but I'm going to take you in there one at a time and show you the picture, since this is an experiment in team building, in communication. The trick of the experiment was he showed them nine different box tops, so they had nine different pictures. When they came out, of course it was absolute chaos. He finally said, "Stop. I cannot stand this," and he showed them the picture, and they put it together in a matter of ten or fifteen minutes. Question: how many of us are in a relationship, in a company, in a corporation, in a team, that has no idea what the big picture is?

So the key to a really successful, high-performance team is that everybody is working towards the same goal, and they all understand that goal.

LP: That's right; and of course high-performance people are also always looking for ways to build up self-esteem in their people.

How do you overcome years and years of programming since childhood, if you grew up in Iowa and have been inundated with negative remarks?

LP: You change it the same way you learned it. You begin replacing the negative self-talk, the negative images, the negative expectations, with positive ones. It is exactly the same way you learned in the first place.

And how do you do that?

LP: Well, you begin being aware of the kinds of things you say to yourself. You are affirming things to yourself, negative or positive, all the time. If I were trying to lose weight, it might be: "I can't lose weight. It runs in the family. Diets never work for me." I would change that to: "Every day in every way I'm finding it easier and easier to meet my goal of weighing one hundred and sixty-five pounds. I'm finding it easy to lose weight. I feel good about myself as I'm looking healthier and feeling better," and so on.

Really we are all hypnotizing ourselves all the time.

LP: Constantly.

And hypnosis is a powerful force that we all need to learn how to use in a positive manner.

LP: Precisely. First of all is de-hypnotizing yourself from your old suggestions, because if you have forty-five to fifty thousand thoughts a day, that's an awful lot of subliminal input that you are putting into yourself and that you are not aware of. We know from the research that subliminal programming is very powerful and very effective. So we are doing it to ourselves. You're not aware of forty-five or fifty thousand thoughts a day, are you? It just goes on. As you begin becoming aware of them and stopping them, that is critically important.

The second thing, related to companies, is that there are high-self-esteem companies that really foster and build the sense of self in people, and low-self-esteem companies. My image for a low-self-esteem company is a pyramid where there is power at the top, control, and the employee is there to be of service to the employer. For the high-self-esteem company the image I think of is a circle, and there instead of power at the top they are looking for ways to empower their employees – sending them to seminars, increasing their training, and so on; and instead of control, influence. Have you ever tried to control and influence a child at the same time? You can't. Influence is a much more powerful motivating factor than control. Thirdly, instead of having the employee be of service to the employer, high-self-esteem companies have it just the other way around – how can we, the company, be of service to you, the employee, to make you a better person?

In today's work environment, more and more of the labor force are demanding high-self-esteem companies, as they come to realize that they want self-actualization out of their work. It's not enough just to take home a paycheck.

LP: That's right. And there are other factors too. High-self-esteem people are aware that we learn and process information in different ways – the old right-brain/left-brain hypothesis. Even though it's a metaphor, it is a useful metaphor– intuitive with simultaneous processing of all kinds of information. There was a recent article in the *Harvard Business Review* on left-brain planners and right-brain managers. They found that the left-brain planner prefers long written memos, whereas the right-brain manager prefers direct contact – looking at body language, facial expression, voice tonality, and so on. Right-brain managers are networkers; they are connected to all kinds of things going on in the community. Their doors are always open. You can come in and go; the phones are ringing. There is simultaneity of activity, versus the pipe-smoking, sitting-up-in-a-lofty-office left-brain planner. High-performance people realize that it is important to oscillate back and forth between two modes of consciousness depending on the task, and not look at the world through gun-barrel vision.

So they try to live really balanced lives. And yet, we often have a sense of high-performance individuals almost being compulsively neurotic, putting in sixteen hours a day in training or at the office. Is that not true?

LP: Well, that's more like a workaholic who is always looking for a score of ten, who is demanding perfection when a nine is good enough, when just excellence is OK.

You mean you don't need to be compulsive to be a high performer?

LP: No, not at all. As a matter of fact, a lot of compulsive workaholics always have the "better than" attitude – "How can I be better than someone else?" whereas the high-performance person is asking, "How can I be more than what I am now?" It is a subtle distinction, but an important one.

But still they must have a lot of drive.

LP: They do. There are a number of factors involved. One is the desire. You've got to have that fire in your belly, the desire to do what you are going to do; and secondly, the absolute expectation that what you are going to do is going to work, no question about it. Third, the imagination, using some of the things we talked about – mental rehearsal, self-talk, and so on.

If you don't have that drive, if you are basically lazy, and yet you want to make something more of your life, what would you do – set a goal to have more drive?

LP: Yes, absolutely. At times I have found that my desire, my fire in the belly, has waned, and so my self-talk and my visualization have been to ignite that desire. And even though it doesn't happen right away, gradually I notice things start happening, and all of a sudden, boom! I get into it. We have been talking mainly about the intrapsychic factors in individuals – that you can change what goes on inside. But for high-performance people the context in which they work is also very important. Some years ago I went to the Philippines. I have been gathering data on traditional healing methods all over the world, and I was able to observe two groups of Americans seeing the same healer. They were evenly matched groups; let's call them Group A and Group B. No one in Group A at the end of the two weeks got healed. Everyone in Group B had various degrees of healing. I wondered how this could be. They were seeing the same healer. And so I went back and reviewed my notes and listened to my tape recordings. I discovered there were two people in Group A who would say every time someone would get off the table, "Oh, I don't know; you don't look any better to me. I don't think this stuff works. Do you think they're faking it? I don't believe in it." I called that group the psychic bleeders. Every time someone got up on the table in Group B, someone would be touching them. The moment they got off the table, they would embrace them and say, "I love you. You look great. You're doing terrific. You're looking better than you ever looked." I called them the psychic fountains. Question: how many of us are in a context with psychic bleeders who bleed off the energy, bleed off the enthusiasm, and depotentiate a lot of things from happening? High-performance people avoid bleeders, and they look for nourishing rather than toxic kinds of people.

I suppose it's because they have enough self-esteem to say, "I deserve better than this."

LP: Precisely, and they attract high-self-esteem people.

The exciting thing about what you are saying is that, by studying the character-istics of high-performing individuals, people can actually learn to change their lives.

LP: Absolutely. It is critical to have a model, a hero, an ego idea, whatever you want to call it. One further element that we observe in high-performance people, in addition to goal setting, mental rehearsal, watching your self-talk, and being able to use both sides of the brain, is that they are very health conscious and very careful about the sources of stress in their lives. There are physical sources of stress, nutritional sources of stress, and psychological. They are very careful about the way that they allow those to impinge on their everyday lives.

INTUITIVE RISK TAKING

WITH PATRICIA SUN

An eloquent and charismatic speaker, Patricia Sun is a spiritual teacher, healer, and expert in communications and conflict resolution. She has shared her "philosophy of wholeness" with academic and business audiences worldwide.

According to Ms. Sun, intuition is a natural part of our intelligence which functions in a holistic, non-linear fashion. In this interview, she points out that developing intuition involves opening up to our vulnerability, being more loving and accepting of ourselves and others.

L*et's start out by defining intuition as you use the term.*

PS: I feel that intuition is actually part of our intelligence; it is an aspect of our capacity to grasp reality. One of the reasons I think we have so much difficulty with it is that when we talk about our intelligence we usually mean the logical, cause-and-effect side.

The left brain, so to speak.

PS: The left brain, exactly right; and intuition, being the right brain, thinks in an entirely different style. It thinks in metaphor, feelings, pictures, a spatial whole. It governs all those intangible things that are incredibly essential, like love and beauty and art and music; that is why the arts and powerful emotions like love and joy seem to be gifts of the gods – because they just pop into your mind. In fact, that right brain is where genius comes from – where the ideas that never existed before just pop into being. They don't have to have a logical origin.

It sneaks up on you sometimes.

PS: It definitely does; it just comes in. It is interesting that you say it sneaks up on you. That is the linear mind's interpretation of the lack of control that characterizes the intuitive mind. The intuitive mind is proclaimed by no control. You can't create it; you can't make it. It is already there. What you can do is receive it, and most of us don't like to do that because we like to be in control all the time.

The Greeks called it the muse – the muse has to hit you. All those ideas about intuition show our logical belief that it is somehow magical; that is why we are uncomfortable with psychic phenomena – telepathy, precognition, clairvoyance, healing, just knowing something. All of those phenomena have been made occult. The word psychic, as opposed to intuition, implies occult, and occult means hidden. So yes, it is hidden, because we don't know how we get it; but there is an implication of something sinister or some other kind of magic, which is what the linear mind tends to do with things it doesn't understand. It gets a little afraid of them.

Some scientists say that what intuition really is, is that your brain can work so fast, that it can perform logical computations faster than you can realize that they are going on, so you can instantly have an answer.

PS: I don't think it is computation; again, there is our attachment to linear thinking. Intuition comes to conclusions, it gives you information, more than any linear computation could give you. You know the old parable about the six blind men touching the different parts of the elephant. They are asked to tell what an elephant is. The guy who's got his tail says, "Oh, he's like a rope." His leg: "He's like a tree trunk." The guy who's got his belly thinks he's a wall; the one that's got his nose, that he's a serpent; his tusk, he's a spear; his ear, he's a fan. Now, they are all correct in their observations, except they're all wrong about what an elephant is.

For us, as evolving people getting to be on good terms with our intuitive mind, all our experiences are true; but not quite, because we don't really allow that intuitive mind to give us all of its information. That is why a picture is worth more than a thousand words – because there are no words in all the universe to tell you what a picture tells you; because if I gave you all kinds of ropes, tree trunks, walls, fans, spears, and serpents, you would still never get an elephant.

So in a sense we are like these blind men if we don't use our intuition.

PS: Exactly right.

We operate through partial information, and intuition is holistic; it gives us an overview, a whole sense of things.

PS: Exactly. It gives that richer information that you know in one second. And so you can get information from that logically; you can extrapolate. The word genius comes from genesis, and genesis means creation and creativity. Creation and creativity are, "Out of nothing, something." The linear mind rejects that; it doesn't like it. It doesn't even like the word infinity: What do you mean? What's the end? What's the beginning? It wants to contain. As soon as we get on good terms with using the linear mind happily, and using it as a tool – knowing it is a tool for sorting reality but not equivalent to it – then the intuitive, acausal mind will have more room to speak in metaphors that we won't have to take literally, but we will get the meaning of the parable or the insight into the greater whole of reality.

One way in which people discuss intuition is to use terms like, "Listen with your heart," or "Open up your heart."

PS: When you are genuinely loving, you trust the world; you trust the universe; you trust who you are with. And that state of love is the most optimum state for intuition to move in, because one of the reasons we naturally block our creativity and our intuition is that are afraid. We are afraid mostly of being wrong, especially if we can't deduce why this could be a right answer. And so there is this sort of controlling aspect in trying to understand it.

I guess part of it is trusting ourselves ultimately.

PS: We judge ourselves very harshly; I think that is one of the difficulties. We are hard on ourselves. We want to be good; we want to be right so much and we know all the ways we fall short of that. Also, in our linear-thinking dominance, we think there is only one answer to things; of course, one of the first things intuition tells you by seeing an overview is there are many, many parts to something. There are many, many perspectives, and that is where our real creativity comes in.

There is an aspect of intuition which opens us up to spiritual experience. That seems to me to be a crucial aspect of it; and yet on the other side, in the material world, many great inventions come out of intuition, many very practical things.

PS: Absolutely; but living well – practical things – are part of the spiritual phenomena. I think it was the linear mind that made spirit separate from matter; the intuitive mind knows that it is the descent of spirit into matter. In other words, it isn't God versus man, it is God in man, it is God in the earth. It is heaven on earth, not heaven separate from earth. Even Jesus said, "Pray for this. Pray for Thy kingdom come, Thy will be done on earth as in heaven." Make it here. We are spiritual beings, and that is inspirational, and it is practical, and it is creative, and it is delightful, and it is part of being very alive – being able to dance and sing and have art. If we are only linear we get very computer-like, and a computer is only as good as whatever information you put in it. So we have to keep being open to the source.

That is what intuition ultimately is – being in touch with that source.

PS: Exactly – not disqualifying it with your linear mind but letting the linear mind step aside for a moment. I use the example of the earth being round. Intuitively we knew the earth was round; after all, the sun was round, the moon was round. And then we got logical and said it can't be round, or we'd fall off; obviously it was flat, because just look. And then we realized, after going around it, that it was round. Later we went to the moon, we looked back, and yes, it is round. The point is that on a sphere north, south, east, and west are wonderful linear coordinates that help us perceive and understand and coordinate, and they are tools for discerning. But on a sphere, if I am facing east and I want to go as far west as I can go, all I have to do is turn around. In other words, on a sphere there is no such thing as up or down, north or south, it is something we have made up.

To play devil's advocate for a moment, it sounds as if you are making the linear, left-brain mind into the bad guy here.

PS: Yes, it does sound like that, and I apologize if it does. I am really trying to boost the intuitive, acausal mind more than make the linear mind the bad guy. It is our attachment to it that is causing us the pain. I am obviously very logical and verbal, and I love it; I think the linear mind is a wonderful part of us. It's essential. The thing is, because of its style of thinking it tends to preclude our feeling comfortable with intuition – trusting that a mother knows how to take care of her baby, or that you do know what is wrong with your body. Maybe you don't know it totally linearly or logically, but you do have a sense, particularly if you ask yourself. It is an asset that a doctor or a healer could have in working with a patient; instead of having to go super-technological and statistical, they actually can look at the person and feel them and know more about what is going on.

If they can open up to that.

PS: You see, the key thing about the intuitive mind is that you are not in control. I think that is one of the reasons we dislike it so much.

And the linear, logical, rational mind is so well geared to being in control.

PS: That's right. It just gives us the wonderful illusion that we are.

Patricia, you have quite a reputation as a healer. Let's talk a little bit about how intuition relates to healing work.

PS: Well, for me, it is almost entirely intuition – although now that I say that, that's not true either. I do pay attention to medical information and how things work, and I always respect listening to medical models; I just don't hold them as literal truths. That allows me to get the best out of that and to use the best out of my intuition. But in terms of the actual experience of healing someone, the phenomena that happen, it is very intuitive, very non-controlling; it is almost always purely love and wishing the person well and wanting to feel them whole. You see, I really believe, from lots of experience, that everybody's body is naturally healthy and wants to be healthy. There is a nature, an order, a harmony that holds the planets in place, and the molecules and the atoms inside your body and mine, that make us as we are. There is a reason why snowflakes take their shape, and why when you cut yourself it grows back together. And for all that science has to say, we really don't know why if you have a cut it grows back together. It is part of that other energy. What I find in that other energy that makes things heal, whether it is with animals or plants or people, is that the feeling of love is a very real thing.

If you want to heal yourself, feel love in the area where you have a symptom, or where you feel numb or unconscious. People say, "How do you do that?" Well, just imagine how it feels when you love something – a flower, a baby, someone you love – when you are in awe, and you go, "Aaahhh, isn't it wonderful?" Instead of being angry at a need because that doesn't work, send a lot of love. Feel it glowing. Use imagery of any sort, with feeling.

I don't think healing is a big mystery. I think it is something that we are all going to do, and in a fairly short period of time. I think it is going to speed up more and more; it is going to get more and more normal.

One of the things everyone can do to speed up the process of their own intuition and healing and empowerment and authenticity on the planet is to begin to consider from this moment forward that everyone can read your mind. That puts you at the level of really being authentic; now you know what I am talking about. It also gives your linear mind, your little computer, a new program. Instead of having to keep track only of what you said, it now has to be a little bit more aware of what you think. This causes you to become more conscious of what you do think, which is very empowering. I believe this is going to happen anyway, so we might as well start practicing while the fog is down; it is a little easier to do.

That's a beautiful thought, and yet in some ways it goes against the grain of our whole tradition of privacy. You are saying that to really be ourselves, we need to be transparent – that's a term that is often used in psychology.

PS: I think that is what real liberty is. I think you have true liberty when anything can come in and anything can come out. The reason we have needed privacy is because we have been such dogmatic thinkers, and if anyone didn't think like we thought they should, we persecuted them. But as you become more open and more empathetic, you just see yourself, you understand, and you don't invade anyone's privacy. That is the essence of communication. It is a mutual desire to understand one another which creates that link.

I suppose ultimately when we hide from other people, when we get defensive, we are really hiding from ourselves.

PS: That's right, absolutely.

And denying ourselves access to that source.

PS: Precisely. That is of course why, whether it is on a personal level or on the level of nations, it is really always projection when you dislike someone. It is a form of projection; it is some area in your life you are not understanding well enough yet, some place you haven't given yourself compassion, to be real.

That's a key insight. It reminds me of the famous statement of Will Rogers: "I never met a man I didn't like."

PS: Yes, that's true. I agree. I think intuition is part of feeling God, and it is part of being free, of being artistic and beautiful and joyful and spontaneous and innocent, and I don't think it is an accident. As Jesus said, the only way to the kingdom of heaven is to be as little children. There is a point there; that is a real energy statement. And when we stop worrying about how we are performing, and just be who we are, we really are free.

STRESS MANAGEMENT

WITH JANELLE M. BARLOW, PH.D.

Janelle Barlow is a human development consultant and author of THE STRESS MANAGER, a self-improvement workbook. Dr. Barlow's work focuses on practical, easy-to-use methods for monitoring and managing stress at home and in the workplace.

In this interview, Dr. Barlow offers suggestions for becoming aware of how stress influences the body and for discharging the effects of stress before they become toxic.

L*et's talk about the mechanisms of stress. Many people have heard of the fight-or-flight syndrome, when you get really tensed, and you don't know quite what to do. That has been specifically delineated, hasn't it?*

JB: Yes, it was described by Walter Cannon a number of years ago, and that has pretty well stood the test of time. Basically what happens is that when the body is exposed to something from the outside that it feels it needs to get activated towards, then the brain does that for the body automatically. The whole purpose of the stress response is to enable the human to survive. For example, say a dog attacks you; that's a more reasonable example than the tiger that's usually talked about. If a pit bull comes after you, your body needs to do certain things for you to survive. If you are injured in a car crash, your body needs to organize itself in such a way that you can survive. Basically it is a survival response.

So the stress response is a normal human response.

JB: Absolutely. Sometimes when I talk with people about the stress response, they say, "Well, maybe we can get rid of it." But if you got rid of it you wouldn't be human. Part of defining who we are is to have this response.

In your work as a trainer, you focus on the practical things that people can do to deal with stress in their lives. One of the most important things that comes up is their awareness of whether or not they are having a stress response, and just how it manifests for each individual.

JB: That's right. That awareness is the biggest part of the battle – getting people to be aware of how they are responding. In today's world – and there is quite a bit of research now to support this – it seems as if the things that are really getting to us are not the big things; it's the little tiny things that go on all the time. It is missing a parking place; it's the people in the grocery line with eleven items in their baskets when they're only supposed to have ten. Or, it's calling up somebody and then getting disconnected. There are so many small things that are going on all the time.

These things that activate or trigger the stress response are called stressors.

JB: That's right; you can think about them as stressors. And then the body does something in relationship to these stressors. That is a really useful model to have, because then you can always do one of two things. You can either change the stressor – if you can, but sometimes you can't; or you can change the way you respond to it, and you probably can always do something about that.

When people are experiencing a lot of stress, does that mean they are not managing their stress response very well? For example, two people might be under identical conditions, and one person might be fuming, with hunched shoulders and barking at people, and another person might appear very relaxed.

JB: It is a question of how they are processing this particular event inside their minds. You can put people in exactly the same situations, and they will have totally different responses to it. I remember a news story I saw on television once about mudslides that were taking place in Southern California. A TV interviewer came up to one man whose house had been destroyed. His reaction was what you would typically expect. He was very upset; his house had been destroyed; what was he going to do? He was crying. It was a very strong presentation for the evening news. Then the reporter went down the street to another man who had suffered the same fate, and his response was a little different. He said, "Well, my family got out all right. We can save a lot of this stuff. It's been buried in the mud, but we can dig out the pictures." His last comment was the telling one; he said, "You know, I've always wanted a third bedroom." The same situation, and a very different response.

In other words, the attitude with which we approach life actually seems to affect the way our physiology reacts towards outside stress.

JB: As long as it is a social stressor. When it is a physical stressor, I'm not so sure that's true. For example, if you put people in a sauna for three hours and the temperature is close to two hundred degrees, I don't know how many people could control their response to that; that is a physical stressor. But today we are dealing primarily with social stressors, so the physical question is sort of moot.

I have heard a lot about the Holmes-Rahe Scale. This is a list of social circumstances that people go through in their lives, ranked according to how much stress they typically induce.

JB: That's right. For example, the death of a spouse was given one hundred points; that was the top of the scale. What the Holmes-Rahe Scale was trying to look at was change. But when you look at the research closely, the correlations on that research are not very strong. But some interesting things have been done with it. A researcher named Suzanne Kobasa at the University of Chicago identified people with high scores on this scale and then she said, "I'm going to look at the ones who remain healthy. Who are the people who have a lot of change in their lives who remain healthy?" Basically she concluded that they have high self-esteem. She said they were actors rather than vegetators; when they had a problem they tended to move towards action rather than sitting with it. And they had their life goals in order; they knew what their priorities were, so when something happened they could measure it against that. They also had what the psychologists call an internal locus of control; that is, when something happened to them, they saw that they were responsible for it, rather than that they were victims of their surroundings.

Some people, if they have a stress response, may get upset, they may get angry; they get the various physiological concomitants of that response. But they are able to discharge it right away; they get it out of their system. They may go out and have a run, or they exercise, or they hit a punching bag. They get rid of that, and then they're back to normal.

JB: They're back to normal, and then the body can endure some more. It is very important for people to understand that their bodies can endure enormous amounts of stress. What the body can't endure is enormous amounts of stress for prolonged periods of time; that is to say, with no break from it.

So if you get stressed and you don't know how to discharge the stress, that could be a problem.

JB: That is the problem; or you may not even know that you've got it, and that can be one of the big problems. In my workshops people are often carrying a lot of stresss that they are not aware of. They have no idea that their shoulders are up, or that their jaws are clenched. Frequently people in my seminars tell me that they didn't learn that they had a problem with bruxism, which is the unconscious grinding of the teeth, until they went to see a dentist. Only when their dentist told them that they were grinding their molars flat were they aware that they were doing this. It takes quite a bit to grind your molars flat, and to be unaware of this is quite a state of denial. This is extraordinarily common. One of the jokes that I make in my seminars, after people list all of the indicators they have that they are under stress, is to say to them, "You know, you may think that you are the sickest group in the world, but you're not. If you went out in the street and asked people randomly as they went by, you would see that they've got the same problems."

Many people must go through their lives thinking that a state of living with a clenched jaw or a tight stomach or tight shoulders is normal/natural.

JB: Right. And that's how you get people dropping dead of heart attacks, and their friends will say about them, "You know, he was never sick a day in his life. How did that happen?" Well, it doesn't happen like that. You really have to work hard to destroy your heart. You have to work hard to destroy your body. It's built for the long haul.

At one time you yourself were experiencing a high degree of stress. You became a stress management trainer by learning how to manage and control your own stress first.

JB: It came out of my own personal experience. I had heart disease as a child, and I was hyperkinetic. As a child I got out of things by getting sick and breaking bones, and it's something I have to watch even to this day. If I am doing something that I don't want to do, I'm very likely to hurt myself; that's my flight mechanism. I don't like that in myself, but I have to admit that it is a part of my personality. I grew up with the notion that people who couldn't do whatever they wanted were weak, and that if you needed to sleep more than two hours a night, that there was something wrong with you. And so I drank enormous amounts of coffee, and I ate No-Doz pills straight. I was so hyper that there were times I literally couldn't feed myself; the food would fall off the fork.

So one of the ways that we stress ourselves is through using coffee, sugar, tobacco, alcohol, and things of that sort?

JB: Oh yes, the coffee especially. You sit down and the waitress or waiter comes up to you, and it is assumed that you are going to have a cup of coffee. Most people have a hard time getting started in the day without that cup of coffee.

How does that cause stress?

JB: It is a central nervous system stimulator, so it affects the adrenal glands, and the adrenalin makes the heart beat faster, makes the muscles get tighter, and makes you think more clearly, at least initially. It's if you use too much of it that it is a problem. It's a total body system response. You don't just stimulate one part of it; everything gets stimulated. And that can happen as a result of the pressures that people put on themselves towards achievement, and that is where a big part of the stress comes from. In my own case, it came from an overachiever's attitude when I was eighteen, nineteen, or twenty. I graduated from high school when I was eighteen. I had my first Master's degree before I was twenty-one, and I also had my first set of ulcers. I was in pretty bad shape. I finally made some decisions to change my life when doctors told me that I wouldn't live to forty otherwise. What I found – and this has been the most interesting thing in the field of stress to me – is that you can learn how to manage your stress without having to reduce the amount of your activity in the world. You don't have to become a low achiever to manage your stress well. I'm forty-four now, and I feel in better shape than I have ever been before. But because I do a lot of traveling in my work, I can also feel when it gets out of control for me. If there is one advantage I have that other people may not have, it is that because I teach this subject I am constantly monitoring, constantly aware of what my body is doing, so I don't let it get to a point where I am out of control.

So your first rule, if you were to tell people how to handle their stress, would be just to be aware of it.

JB: Exactly. There was quite a telling study done at Stanford Medical Center a number of years ago. They were interested in why so many people had lower back pains. The number-one cause of disability in the United States is lower back injuries or pain to such a point that people have to quit their jobs. How they conducted the study was they put a belt around the participant's hips, and on one side of the belt was a sensitive biofeedback device which would measure muscular contractions. It had electrodes which came around and attached to the lower back. When the lower back got tight to a certain degree, the machine registered this, and then it emitted a high-pitched sound. At this point the participants were instructed: "Go to this side of your belt, take off the pad of paper and pencil and write down what you were doing." It was very clever. Now they could say that if the participant walked by somebody's office, that person was the stressor; or if it was the telephone. The problem was that after three weeks the researchers had to discontinue the study. It is interesting why the study had to be discontinued.

I suppose it was because it was going off all the time.

JB: That's what most people would say; or that they ran out of paper and pencils because there were so many stressors. But the answer is that the beeper stopped going off; in other words, the participants stopped tightening their lower backs.

In other words, because they were becoming aware; through awareness we can learn to relax. And relaxation itself is the antidote to the stress response.

JB: Letting go of it, yes. Relaxation doesn't have to mean sitting down with your eyes closed for twenty minutes, or taking a nap. Once people learn how to do simple relaxation techniques, and if they are aware of the stress so they don't let it get too bad, then if you have it just a little bit and then notice it and let go of it, and have a little bit more, notice it and let go of it, that's what the body is really built for.

There is a lot of research lately that suggests that the immune response is related to the stress response.

JB: Not just lately; that has been known for some time. Hans Selye was the father of the concept of stress, and that was part of his original research. The immune system definitely gets involved with it. There is a lot of recent research in connection with this – for example, if somebody is in a bad marriage, seeing if their immune system is affected by this, and yes, it is. The thymus gland, which is partly responsible for the production of white blood cells, actually atrophies when a person is in a highly stressed state for a long period of time. You can't say that stress causes illness; that would be an overstatement of what stress does. But in every case where you have illness, what you will probably see is that some piece of stress is involved with it.

You frequently use the concept of self-talk – monitoring your self-talk. How does this relate to stress?

JB: Our self-talk affects what we think about a situation. When you are dealing with a social stressor, you are not really looking at reality; what you are looking at is your interpretation of that reality, and your self-talk is that interpretation of that reality. Here is an example. I read in the newspaper about a woman who was fifty-six and widowed for the first time. Her children were grown, and she decided she wanted to fulfill a long-term fantasy to become a Roman Catholic nun. She agreed to do this on one condition – that the convent that she joined would allow her to work in a Mexican jail. Now, most people would say, "Do everything you can to avoid being in a Mexican jail." Well, this woman's self-talk about that Mexican jail is obviously different from the self-talk of someone who is trying to avoid being in that Mexican jail.

In other words, your mind is always saying about situations, "This is horrible. This is terrible. This is bad."

JB: Or, "This is a problem." A very simple piece of research was done on that. They looked at people who used the word "problem" and they looked at people who used something like "This is an opportunity." For example, they compared people who said, "We've got a problem down in marketing," or, "We've got a problem with that person over in the typing pool," versus the people who said, "You know, there's a situation down in marketing that deserves our attention," or, "There's somebody over in the typing pool who needs a little more careful supervision now." Those people who used the latter phrases had a reduced stress response compared to the people who identified their situations as problems. A simple shifting of a word seemed to make a difference in a person's reaction to the same situation; that is why self-talk is important.

People like you are now going into corporations and teaching executives to do things that would have once been considered unthinkable, like meditation.

JB: Let me just say how unusual that is. Ten or eleven years ago, I think I may have been one of the first people to go in and do practical workshops in businesses. Now everybody is offering stress management courses. It's not considered a weakness to go to a stress management course today. Everybody wants to hear about it, even if they have heard it before, because they need to be reminded.

People are very receptive to a wide variety of strategies. In my programs I try to hit as many different people's needs as possible. Some want to hear about exercise; some people want to do relaxation/meditation kinds of exercises. I put a heavy emphasis on what I call quick-and-dirty techniques, things that people can do without taking time – things that you can do in a meeting, for example. I teach people how to breathe with their eyes open, to relax their diaphragm, to relax their muscles, simple kinds of things, because people aren't going to do difficult things.

One of your techniques is just to put up little reminders near the telephone or the refrigerator, reminding people to watch their level of stress, to watch their breathing.

JB: Right, it is easy to make yourself relaxed.

One or two deep breaths can really make a big difference.

JB: Absolutely. It starts the cycle of moving towards the parasympathetic nervous system response, the relaxation response. Just as something can move you into the stress response, something can start to move you out of it.

It seems as if these kinds of skills, which in the last ten years have just been moving into the business community, will have to become more widespread in our culture because the stressors are increasing.

JB: That's right. Most of our social stressors are here to stay – for example, economic instability, differences between races, social and religious differences. Those things aren't going to go away. The crowdedness isn't going to go away. We have to learn how to adjust to some of these things – deadlines that people face in their businesses; leaner and leaner staffing; people's jobs getting larger and larger, with fewer and fewer resources to do them. We have to be more efficient, and that sort of thing you really can't do anything about. So what you have to do is to learn to accept it and learn how to gauge your own response in relationship to it.

SELF-OBSERVATION

WITH CHARLES TART, PH.D.

Charles Tart, a Professor of Psychology at the University of California at Davis, is internationally known for his research with altered states, transpersonal psychology, and parapsychology. He is the author of ten books, including OPEN MIND, DISCRIMINATING MIND; WAKING UP: OVERCOMING THE OBSTACLES TO HUMAN POTENTIAL; ALTERED STATES OF CONSCIOUSNESS; and TRANSPERSONAL PSYCHOLOGIES.

Our culture discourages self-observation because we tend to equate it with the judgmental superego. In this interview, Dr. Tart explores the methods and benefits of allowing our awareness to become conscious of itself. With practice, this can become a simple yet powerful discipline.

When we talk about self-observation, I think a lot of people feel a little embarrassed. If they begin to observe themselves they get self-conscious; they blush a little bit. It's almost as if there were a subconscious agreement not to look too closely at ourselves.

CT: Yes, that is one of the sad parts of this whole field. So many of us have been taught or conditioned in childhood that we are lacking, we are not good enough; and that makes us very reluctant to look at ourselves. And yet, if we don't learn how to find out what we are really like, then we don't use our mind efficiently; we make all sorts of mistakes. So we have to learn to self-observe, but it has to be done very carefully. You know, anthropologists have distinguished several ways of controlling people. One way is to follow them around with guards. The trouble is that is an expensive way; those guards aren't doing anything productive, and they are watching you all the time. A much more efficient way is to put a guard in someone's head – to take someone as a child and split their mind, so that a part of their mind absorbs all the standards that the parents and the society want them to have and watches for transgressions. And it's not even that simple, because that part of the mind is also given the power to make you feel rotten. Freud talked about it as the superego, the part of us that is over our ordinary conscious self and can make us feel bad.

Now, I want to talk about the value of self-observation, but I am not talking about superego observation. Most of us already know how to do that, and it makes us feel bad. We selectively watch ourselves; we catch ourselves in a fault, or sinning, or lacking, and then we feel rotten about it.

Often when other people want us to look at ourselves, it is for the purpose of making us feel guilty about something we have done.

CT: Exactly. We lay a lot of guilt trips on each other to try to control each other. So it is not surprising that most people don't want to look inside. They will distract themselves with anything, but not look inside themselves.

Probably most people can think of times from their childhood when they were in a difficult situation and were trying to get out of it, and one or the other parent said, "Be honest. Look at yourself. Tell me the truth." And so that whole idea of knowing the truth about yourself, or revealing that truth to others, became associated with fear, punishment, and feeling rotten.

In a religious sense, it even gets associated with sin. It's not just your parents; it's like God is up there.

CT: Exactly. That's what makes the superego so powerful. See, there's another distinction you can make. Anthropologists say that in some cultures people are controlled by shame – if people knew what you did, you would be so ashamed. That's pretty good, but it still has a little out. If you can get away with it and nobody knows it was you, you are tempted. The superego is one step better, because even if nobody else knows, you know and God knows, and so you get punished for even thinking about doing things.

Are you suggesting that in some primitive cultures people don't have superegos – that it is something unique to our culture?

CT: It is certainly not unique to our culture, but yes, there are some cultures in which the superego is a very minor part of a person's mind. Our culture today is mixed on that question. We have drifted more toward a shame sort of culture, where what the public knows, what other people know, is more important; but we were primarily a superego culture. Of course that comes from our whole Judeo-Christian heritage – you know, God is watching.

So guilt, and the fear of punishment of the superego, is one of the forces that mitigate against self-observation. What are some other major obstacles?

CT: We are not taught to do it. The whole culture gives us a picture that we are not good, so we don't want to look. Take the Freudian notion, for instance, that basically we are wild animals with a thin veneer of civilization on top, keeping us from running amok. I mean, who would want to look inside that picture? Or if you are born in original sin, and basically you are rotten and going to hell, who wants to look at that? Our culture has invented a multitude of ways for us to distract ourselves from ever having to look inside. But the result is that although we apparently avoid the pain of seeing what we fear we will see, we then go on to really mess up our lives because we don't know ourselves. We don't know what we are really like, we don't know what we want, we don't know our resources well, and we make mistakes.

And yet we have this ancient philosophical tradition, going back at least to Socrates, "Man, know thyself." But when I studied philosophy in college, there was none of that.

CT: You didn't have Introspection 101 and 102?

Not at all. Introspection is pretty much outlawed even in psychology these days.

CT: Not only is it effectively banned, but we don't have the skill to introspect very well. It is one thing to tell somebody, "Start observing yourself. See how you really feel, what is really going on." But if people take that seriously, what they often find is that it is very hard to concentrate. Their attention drifts. They get confused as to what they're looking at, and pretty soon they end up watching TV, distracting themselves again.

I would think that ultimately knowing oneself should be the goal of psychology.

CT: I wouldn't want to make it the only goal, because we have also learned a lot by concentrating on observing people from the outside. One of the things that you learn when you practice self-observation is that you fool yourself, that you are a very biased observer, and so getting feedback from somebody else can be very helpful. For instance, take a classic case in therapy. Somebody goes into therapy, and the therapist tries to find out the problem, and asks something like, "Do you get along with your father?" The client says, "Yeah, I get along just fine." The therapist says, "Really? No problems at all?" "No!" The client isn't observing himself very well; in fact, we now know there are systematic psychological blocks to his knowing that. But the therapist can see there is a big discrepancy between the behavior and the report, and that suggests a line of work that you might learn a lot from. So we need both; we need feedback from other people as to how they perceive us, as well as learning to perceive ourselves from the inside.

Is this art of self-observation the goal of any particular discipline?

CT: No. Many spiritual disciplines put very little emphasis on self-observation, because they already know what's right, and they simply give you a prescription: "You behave according to this set of rules, and that is what salvation is about." Other spiritual disciplines practice a very biased self-observation. It is a superego type of thing: "Here are the sins you have to watch out for." So you become very sensitized to signs of those.

The kind of self-observation I am talking about involves making a commitment to learn the truth about yourself and your world, no matter what it is – not to observe yourself to catch yourself in your sins; not to observe yourself only when you happen to be doing something you like. Not to observe yourself in order to support what you already believe; but to try to observe yourself in your world to see what really is. And that is a commitment. I like to quote a famous American spiritual leader of a sort, Patrick Henry: "Eternal vigilance is the price of freedom." If you aren't vigilant about yourself, with a commitment to knowing reality as it is, you will build up fantasies. You will live in this state that I call consensus trance. You are lost in fantasies, and they are widely shared in the culture; everybody else has similar fantasies. So we all think we are normal, but we are seriously cut off from the world around us and do a lot of stupid things as a result.

There is a paradox there, because not only is the world as it is, but it is as we create it. We are not just passive in this process.

CT: That's right. One of the things you learn from observing yourself is that you aren't just taking it in. You are looking at this and not that. You are selectively listening to this part of the conversation and not the other. But that's fine; that's what you are seeking to learn – how do I run my psychological machinery, as it were? You see that, and you say, "OK, can I see it more clearly? Can I see what's behind that? What else can I learn about this?" But again, it has to be done with this commitment too: "I'll accept whatever I learn." It can't be: "I'd like to have an insight that shows me how wonderful I am or what an awful sinner I am." It has to be "I want to see what's in myself. I'm looking for the truth." And the truth is very rewarding in a subtle kind of way, even if you don't like what you see in yourself. I don't know how many times, in practicing self-observation, I have seen things in myself that I don't like at all, that I am ashamed of; and yet there is a sort of authenticity that comes from the fact that you know you are trying to be as honest as you can, and that's satisfying.

I'll give you an example of self-observation, which I began doing systematically many years ago. I began to notice my mental attitude when I was driving, and I realized that I was very angry at drivers who did not follow the rules. If they followed too closely behind me, or cut in too closely in front of me, I didn't like that. In fact, as I observed it more I realized I was so angry that I wanted them to die; I mean, anybody who followed me too closely and threatened my life deserved to die. Well, it was hard to make that observation; I think of myself as a kind, understanding person. But there it was, and I was going to stick with it and watch it for a few more times until it went away. Well, it wouldn't go away for three years. Every time I got in the car, part of me wanted to kill whenever anybody followed too close. It didn't matter that I didn't like it; I had to stay with it. Eventually, keeping the focus of consciousness there it made some changes occur.

So you are saying that you can't change yourself simply by observing yourself that way.

CT: Well, sometimes observation alone will change you. There are a lot of things that in a psychological sense aren't very potent; they are not hooked in with really deep, powerful emotions. They are habits of thought and feeling and perception, and they have to run in the dark, as it were, without too much consciousness. Once the light of consciousness is put on them two or three times, they just sort of fade away. But some of the things you find won't go away, and you have to commit yourself to observing them even more closely, observing the feeling states associated with them. Eventually you may get some insights to make them go away, or you may eventually have to get yourself involved in some kind of training or discipline to do something specifically about those kinds of things.

So now when you drive the car you don't get that way anymore?

CT: It's not anywhere near as bad now. I don't pay as much attention to it. When I first started self-observation I thought, "Right; I should be able to do this for a month and become a perfect being." It's a long haul, but it's satisfying.

Are there particular techniques that you would recommend for people?

CT: Yes. It is no good just to tell somebody that you should observe yourself. That's like saying, "Be good." Lots of people have already told us that. You have to practice. You have to do things, for example, just to learn to focus your attention clearly. Most people, if they try a concentration exercise like, "Look at the sweep-second hand on your watch, or the little digital display, and don't think of anything else. Just be aware of it," will find that they are lucky if ten seconds can go by before they are wondering, "When will this be over? I wonder what I'll have for lunch tomorrow?" You know, the mind goes off – in all directions. As you begin to observe yourself, you find that is one of the main qualities of ordinary consciousness. We are constantly distracted and drift to something else. We can't concentrate, in a very real sense.

Once you see that this is difficult, you can begin practicing in simple ways. For instance, as we sit here right now, this is an interesting conversation, but are you aware of your position in the chair? What do your arms feel like as you sit there in that chair? Are you breathing fully? Can you notice whether you are breathing, and still be aware of what I am talking about at this moment? When you shook your head just then, how much was that a conscious decision, and how much was it a habitual sort of thing? You can't expect to say, "I'll start self-observation, and I'll see these fantastic things about myself right away," because that is a biased observation. You have to say, "For the next five minutes, I am going to see every little thing that comes along, even if it's trivial, even if I don't think it's important," because that trains you to pay attention, and that is really the foundation stone.

In other words, you would recommend that people isolate a small block of time, like five minutes, to really pay attention, to really notice everything.

CT: Sure. If I tell somebody, "Observe yourself for the next hour," they will observe themselves for two or three minutes if they are lucky. They will forget about it, and then they will remember it again and feel guilty because they forgot. To try to do it for an hour right off is too hard; you are setting yourself up for failure. Set yourself up for thirty seconds of really noticing what's happening in your body; or when you get good, five minutes of noticing when you walk down the street, how do you move your arms? When you sit in a room with nothing to do, what do you look at? Is there a pattern to the way you look around the room? Start with simple things, and things that aren't that threatening. If you have to start right away with, "I'm going to observe the way I'm nasty to people while I'm being kind to them," that's heavy. That is going to produce a lot of resistance. But if you learn to focus on the simple things then you can get more into the complex things, and the things that are emotionally relevant; and of course that is the most important source of things.

Do you recommend that people keep a journal of these observations?

CT: I have ambivalent feelings about that. If you self-observe in order to get interesting material to write in your journal, you are going to be selectively self-observing. Who is going to write in their journal, "I noticed an itch in my left elbow, and as I noticed the itch in the left elbow, it spread down to my left wrist?" Nobody is going to write that in a journal; people want a dramatic, important journal. But that is selective attention. There is nothing wrong with selective attention at certain times, especially if you do it voluntarily.

But you're suggesting it is really important to notice the seemingly trivial things.

CT: Yes, to be able to stay in the here and now. That is what self-observation ultimately leads up to – an ability to be present, and present in what is really going on. And let's face it, sometimes in the present, nothing spectacular is happening. You are sitting and your elbow is itching. Our bodies are full of sensations. They form an excellent reference point to start self-observation. But I am not limiting it to that, of course. If something emotional happens, it is very useful to try to observe your emotions as if you were a fair witness, a neutral observer. Suppose you were a reporter having to write up an objective account of what this person feels like. At the same time they are happening in you, so you are not completely distinct. But try to see how much you can see: what do you really feel like, instead of what you would like to feel like, or what you ought to feel like? Then you have insights in yourself.

Now, if you already have a harsh superego, as a lot of people do, if you systematically try to pay more attention to yourself, you are going to see a lot of things you don't like. Your superego is going to say, "Ha! Gotcha! Look at that nasty thought that you have about that person." Then you have to move up a little bit and try to observe the superego in action, instead of just identifying with it, instead of just being carried away with it.

Don't underestimate the power of the superego. Whenever you see someone who has suicided, you see the power of the superego in action: "You are so bad that only death will begin to do it." Another of my favorite examples: there have been a number of cases in England where a house caught on fire, and the firemen knew the person was right inside the front door and could have gotten out. They saw movement through the curtains, but the person died from smoke inhalation or being burned to death. Well, it turned out they were naked. They couldn't go out the door with people out there when they were naked. The superego made them feel ashamed enough of being naked that it amounted to a choice to die instead. The superego is very powerful, far too powerful in many cases.

So in self-observation we want to observe our superego in order to begin to understand its power over us.

CT: Yes, but don't start with the superego. Start with simple things: how do you feel right now? We mentioned focusing on the body. That is actually more subtle than you think, because a lot of our emotions express themselves as certain kinds of bodily feelings. So while you think you are mainly looking toward your physical sensations, you are actually learning to tune in more to the subtleties of your emotions.

An itch might not be just an itch; it might be reflecting some deeper level of experience.

CT: And what does the itch turn into? What is the feeling tone that goes with the itch?

And as we observe ourselves, and then observe ourselves observing ourselves, gradually, layer by layer, we become enlarged as human beings.

CT: Yes, we get a much wider idea of who we are. When we get conditioned into consensus trance, our human potentials are narrowed. We could be so many things, but society says, "This is good, this is good, that's bad, don't do that," and our self-concept gets narrow and squeezed and tight, and it gets very sad after awhile. G.I. Gurdjieff expressed it very powerfully when he said a lot of people you see walking around in the street are dead. They have been so squeezed in terms of their inner psychological self that it is all habit and conditioning, and the essence, the vitality, is all gone from it. It is very sad.

Now, there is another obstacle to self-observation that is also important. Sometimes people will do limited self-observation. They know something is wrong. Their life isn't going right, or there are obvious problems, or it is empty. They observe themselves for awhile, and they see a part of what is wrong; but they want to change so badly that as soon as they get one or two ideas of how they are not living right, they become converted to some religion or growth movement that claims to save you from that particular thing. They concentrate exclusively on changing that, without having gotten a good idea of what the rest of their mind is like. They stop the process.

We talked earlier about how people try to make each other feel guilty in order to manipulate each other. Sometimes we try to make each other have insights, but I want you to have the insights I approve of. There was a time when consciousness-raising groups were very popular; but as near as I could tell, consciousness raising meant that when you agreed with my views, your consciousness was raised. You should not start self-observation with the idea that there are certain truths that somebody else has already figured out that you've got to observe for yourself and then you will have arrived. Rather, start with a much more open-ended idea that you want to know for yourself, want to see things the way they are. I don't want to leave the impression that all you ever see are these negative, horrible sides of yourself. A lot of the sides of ourselves that have been repressed are very positive. Our vitality, our childlike joy at being alive, a lot of our creativity and talents – that has been squeezed down too. And you can find that.

Do you have a sense of where this all ends?

CT: No, I have no sense of where it ends, and I don't want to have a sense of where it ends. It is easy to fall into this trap of, "You've only got ten sets more to go, and then you reach some final point – like being dead, or something.

I think it is much more exciting and adventurous to just realize there is more. It is an infinite universe. Why set limits on yourself? As a psychologist, I know that if you set limits on yourself, those limits will become true most of the time. So why set limits on yourself? And observing myself as I talk about this, I see that I really feel like a kid all excited inside when I talk about how limitless we can be.

PERSONALITY DEVELOPMENT AND THE PSYCHE

WITH HELEN PALMER, PH.D.

Helen Palmer is a noted psychic intuitive, psychologist, and founder of the Center for the Investigation and Training of Intuition. She is the author of THE ENNEAGRAM.

Certain paranoid and neurotic states can open your mind to a range of intuitive and psychic states, according to Dr. Palmer. In this interview, she suggests that through inner practices you can observe your mind and recognize these experiences as they occur.

Many mystics, many parapsychologists and psychic teachers say that everybody really has psychic potentials. Yet most people experience consciously being psychic only on rare occasions, not all the time.

HP: Many people experience an opening into psychism, a realm of information that just is not available to the thinking self, in an extraordinary moment, when they either come under pressure, or come into some state of grace, and so they are moved into a point of view that is not a usual one. Many of the rest of us were not so graced by a higher experience at the beginning, but found a great deal of unusual perception, an unusual form of knowing, in the middle of extraordinary moments that might be called neurotic. I think that is a very common experience. People don't realize that a great deal of the source of their own information is actually not from their linear, thinking self, but from other parts of themselves that are equally intelligent, but not the thinking self.

So if we could reflect on the shifts of attention that we have during the day in our stream of consciousness, we might discover quite a bit of psychic activity going on that we are unconscious of.

HP: And yet in a way our whole style of life depends on these kinds of shifts of attention that are particular to individuals. We might call them neurotic, or unfinished, from early childhood; these are the points of view that we get attached to. We don't realize that there are extraordinary kinds of perception that support those points of view. For example, children who have been traumatized, frightened children, may for protective reasons become extraordinarily sensitive to the potential of anger in other people, without realizing that they are focusing and recognizing through their body and through their inner mind the aggressive possibilities in adults. As an opposite example, children who are dearly loved may learn how to tap into the available affection in people, how to keep the love flowing in their direction, usually by merging with the wishes of others, knowing how to please, and being very sensitive to minute changes in temperament in adults. These are actual psychic potentials that can go way over the line of linear thinking, without the individuals realizing that they are doing something unusual.

You're reminding me of the story of the late great Dutch psychic, Gerard Croiset, who was hit on the head by a rock as a child and fell into some water and nearly drowned. Thereafter much of his career was devoted to locating the bodies of missing children who had drowned. It's as if some kind of wrinkle got created through this early experience that opened up his own psychic perception in that particular area.

HP: If we could do some expert plumbing and focus our attention deeply into our own neurotic functioning, we would find a wellspring of particular ways we use our attention to derive the information that supports our point of view. Often if the undercurrent is ready to have an opening, a psychic experience of some kind, then there is a kind of collusion, where in the unconscious that wants to express itself, the psychic potential that is lying dormant will instigate a situation for the individual to experience, like the example of your Dutch psychic. In my own experience, I placed myself, without realizing it, in a very frightening set of circumstances that went on for a number of years. In the midst of those experiences a great deal of truly psychic information came forward, but it was so embedded in the context of my survival that I didn't realize I was trying to access a really important part of myself. I think that we engineer circumstances, so to speak, so that we can recognize our own potential in a conscious way; and then it becomes a conscious ability, and used very specifically, rather than in an unconscious, repetitive way.

What you are suggesting is that what we normally call neuroses or psychological problems are really an effort by the deeper layers of the psyche to achieve freedom or psychic liberation. We put ourselves under stress in order to create psychic openings.

HP: Yes. I have interviewed several people who were under objectively dire circumstances for prolonged periods, and had unusual experiences during the time that they were under pressure. These were survivors of the concentration camps during the Second World War. They experienced both healing powers – self-healing and sometimes affecting other people who were ill, transferred healing – as well as precognitions of the events that would befall their group that were helpful to their survival in the camp.

Such experiences are not that unusual, when ordinary people like ourselves are put under extraordinary circumstances. We always have the example of the mother who in an extreme case lifts the car off the child, finding some resource in herself to affect the situation. And in a smaller way, I think we do that all the time. We need to put ourselves under some sort of circumstance where we have to revert to a part of ourselves that we are not usually used to dealing with; that is a real indicator. In fact, I think that neuroses, instead of being seen as something dark or negative, are a wellspring of buried, latent, almost-on-the-surface, almost-ready-to-come-up psychic abilities. For example, the child who loved, who is able to merge with the wishes of another, can be a real neurotic burden to an adult – always putting the other first, selling out his or her own priorities in order to receive affection, always being a doormat kind of personality. It can be seen as a burden rather than as a talent. But the neurotic preoccupation, the need to be loved, is an indicator of what that person might do if he adopted an internal practice and recognized the moments when his attention shifted into this merger, this replacement of oneself with the wishes of another.

The term internal practice seems crucial here. I suppose that is what distinguishes a neurosis from a real growth or breakthrough kind of experience.

HP: Yes, that's a very good point. I think that when we are still identified with the neurosis – say, if we are still attached to our paranoia – then our psychical talent for recognizing other people's unexpressed aggression may get referred to ourselves. We might feel this within our own body, and we might feel somehow under attack, if we are predisposed to paranoia. Rather than seeing that as negative, you can see it as a talent. But a practice would have to be adopted where the individuals who are so-called afflicted with paranoia, though perhaps blessed in another way, would have to be able to distinguish between the times when they were just identified with the idea that the world is a terrifying place and looking for it in every corner – you know, falsely projecting their own terror, attributing it to the other – and those times when they are actually recognizing something unexpressed. And so it is an internal practice of recognizing the difference between projection and a truthful impression coming from outside the self, which registers as a psychic impression.

Another example might be in a romantic situation, where one person may be experiencing telepathic merger with another person, and not be aware of it.

HP: I think that happens in intimate situations of all kinds – with parents and children, or lovers, or mates; we have these experiences of becoming the other. I had a very striking example of that; in fact, it was one of my very first clearly psychic experiences. It involved myself and my son, who was then quite young, seven or eight years old. We were in some conflict; I forget what the situation was. At the time I had an internal practice of self-hypnosis. A very interesting shift occurred through a self-hypnosis technique I had been using to modify my own reactions. It led me into what you might describe as a merger with another person, actually taking on the characteristics and the viewpoint of another person. This is quite different from something like psychological empathy, where you kind of imagine what it would be like to stand in someone else's shoes; that would be a close approximation. In real psychic merger you become the other person, sometimes even with their own thoughts and inner feelings, which might be quite unknown to you, and which you never could have imagined because they are alien to you.

This experience of merger happened in a very ordinary setting. I had gone into an inner state of attention to focus on modifying my reaction to my son's behavior. I wanted to be more calm and not to try to convince him that he was wrong, because he was having a bad reaction to my convincing him. He was opposing me in a sturdy way, and that upset our family scene. What I did was try to affect myself by visualizing both of us in an inner room in my mind. I went down many, many stairs in my hypnotic induction, and then I wound up at the bottom of these flights of stairs, and there I was with my little son. I was viewing myself as I was looking out from behind my own eyes toward my son, who was seated at the other side of the table in my imagination. Within the confines of the practice, my attention shifted in a way that it never had before, so that I was no longer myself, seeing his face through my own eyes, but I was inside him, seeing my face from his position. When that happened, it was extraordinary, because his perception of me was quite radically different than I had supposed.

That would seem almost one of the key experiences of anybody who is developing psychic abilities – seeing yourself through the eyes of another. That must be frightening. I imagine it is one of the reasons why so many people are afraid of ESP, or would rather deny that it exists.

HP: I agree with that. That is a specific practice, actually, that I did for many years – seeing myself through other people's vision, and sometimes with great shock and surprise at the discrepancy between what I thought I would observe and what I actually observed when I was in the altered state. You see, I don't get freaked out by things like that. My interest draws me into it; I would rather know than not know.

I suppose for many people it is not that the experience is so bad, but it is the fear of it.

HP: Well, you can't be too attached to this simple reality. There are many, many versions of reality. The psychic world, actually, is kind of a lightweight version; many spiritual realms are far superior to the psychic realm. But the psychic realm has an interesting relationship, really, to the stable personality, and often the stable personality gets a little upset if you start having perceptions that are alien and even contrary to what you would like to see. There is a very popular psychological theory called the social masking theory, and I absolutely agree with it. In childhood, it says, we build certain defenses that keep us unique and keep us operating, and we would rather not know the information that our defenses keep out. We really want to believe that what we see is the truth; but it is extremely distorted and modified in order to keep the personality feeling secure. We need those defenses. When you start altering your perception to see, in the altered state, the discrepancy between that broader reality and your own finite view of things, it raises the specter of all that we suspected in our early childhood was so – that at times we weren't loved, and that a great deal of our perception was distorted in order to keep us feeling more secure. And we can't stand that, so we close the door and we become afraid of altering our own awareness, and become very afraid of those people who do. So the psychic person, the intuitively inclined person, comes in for a great deal of speculation and projection from those individuals who are afraid of what they might see about themselves, their own unconscious material. If you are really going to pursue an inner practice, as soon as you modify your awareness you have taken away the guard of defenses, and the first thing that floods out is buried, unconscious material. In a way the practices are very safe, because they are gradated in difficulty, so you don't get flooded.

But if it is subconscious material, undoubtedly it must have a lot of libido, sexual and aggressive drives, which Freud says are the very things we want to hide the most.

HP: When you are in a state of inner vision, you have taken down the guard of the thinking self – projection, denial, and the various defenses that we have – and you are in a state where any old thing can shoot out from your unconscious and be revealed to you. I have seen things about my own unconscious aggressions and my own sexuality that would turn most people blue, frankly, because they can't stand that this might be part of their own nature.

I suppose the only ultimate saving grace is that everybody has it.

HP: Oh yes, and it is only a question of time until the neurosis and its defenses become thin enough, or limiting enough, that we rebel against it because we know it is limiting and we are inspired to get rid of it; the unconscious colludes to engineer a situation that becomes more than what we can tolerate with our defenses, and so they become explosive. And then, sure enough, intuition and its abilities come forward. But first we really have to see what our limitations are, because as soon as you see a bigger picture in an altered state, and then you recognize the limitations of your own point of view, it can be very depressing.

The inner practices are really no big deal. They are simply to learn how to modify your own inner attention and how to stay constantly aware of the very subtle impressions that are there all the time, but that we never really have quite sharp enough interest to pay attention to. These images, and these senses of things, are there all the time; they are happening to you and to me right this moment. But we happen to be focused in a conversation; we are not paying attention to that realm. If we shifted our attention and went into an inner vision, or an inner sense of things, we would immediately find that we do have impressions – about each other, about God, about nature, about whatever object you are focusing on.

Our culture certainly supports us in denying our intuitive faculties.

HP: And I think our culture in some ways shows that. We are very individualistic, and we need to support the idea of individualism because we are competitive. We have the idea that somehow if I win, nobody else loses, that my direct action doesn't affect other people in some way. As soon as you move into an intuitive realm, or you realize the degree of actual merger between individuals who think of themselves as separated, it's shocking. If I injure myself, the other guy gets it too; if I boost myself at someone else's expense, I also suffer from that, though I may not know it. In the merged state, you are immediately aware of those things.

The role of these inner practices, I guess, is to tease these things out, to become aware of these little subtle currents that are in the backdrop of our lives.

HP: Well, they seem subtle when we think about them and far away. Actually, it is not that difficult to tune your attention, to close your eyes, and to be able to tell the difference between a spontaneous image with respect to an unknown situation, and a thought; or the difference between an emotion – my own, belonging to my own particular personality – and a reaction with respect to my attention to an unknown situation. Once you turn the attention inward, those discriminations are really not that difficult. I want to encourage people, because this realm seems so far away and so glamorized. I think our fears want to keep them glamorized and far away, because we don't want to realize the extent of our merger with other people, the extent of what we could know. We don't want the responsibility. We don't really want to have to guide our lives from that kind of perspective.

The practices are actually very modest. They depend on an ability to stabilize your attention in a non-thinking state. You have to get past the thought barrier and into a relatively empty space where you can recognize the observer, also called the witness or the aware state of mind, depending on your nomenclature. Actually, if you go inside, close your eyes, and make an image, like a color spot, you realize that there are two aspects to your perception. There is a color spot, and we think, "Oh, that's where the information is; it's in the image." In a way it is; but the more important aspect of the perception is that which is aware – the observing part of the mind that is able to tell the difference between the color spot and a thought, an emotion, or something like that. So the training is to strengthen this capacity to observe. In the West we rarely have any time during the week where we shift inward and even recognize that there is an observer. We are so preoccupied with the objects of attention – the thoughts, the car on the highway, the emotions. But the actual training is to strengthen the ability to stay present, observing these very subtle impressions as they go by. They are not so subtle, actually; when you get into being able to tell the difference between a thought and an image, the images become super strong. They are not intangible or weak; they can become as strong as billboards inside. So you are really dealing with very, very subtle objects of attention; but they are as describable as furniture in a room.

What you are saying is that the essential difference between an average, supposedly nonpsychic individual, and an individual who is using intuitive capacities daily, is this capacity for self-observation.

HP: That's really all it is. I mentioned that I had this so-called opening, where I recognized that I could merge my observing state of mind with inner images of unknown situations – a distant part of the world, for example, or a person I haven't met. I could make an image, a symbol, of that individual, and observe it, and merge the observer with the image, so that a small dream, a small set of spontaneous impressions would come with respect to this unknown situation. Well, I had been doing that for years, but I never realized there was any truth in it. I had never set up a test situation where I actually performed an internal practice of moving my attention around, trying to merge with an object or a vision, trying to separate, trying to engage and disengage. It is actually quite pedestrian, you know, like moving your hand forward and backward.

THE MIND-BODY PROBLEM

WITH JULIAN ISAACS, PH.D.

Julian Isaacs, a professor of parapsychology at John F. Kennedy University, is a council member of the British Society for Psychical Research and an applied psychologist specializing in training psychokinetic abilities.

Most brain researchers believe we will eventually explain the mind in terms of neurological functioning. In this interview, Dr. Isaacs challenges this materialist view. He says that new developments in areas such as theoretical physics, as well as the evidence of parapsychology, may eventually lead to an understanding of the common ground connecting mind and matter.

I n mainstream science it is generally assumed that the mind is an epiphenomenon, an emergent property of the brain, a by-product of the physical, material universe.

JI: That's right. The consciousness of each individual is taken to be simply the inside view of what is going on in that brain. This is very important for modern science, because modern science says that nothing exists in the universe except physical bits and pieces, including the molecules and atoms of which the brain is made, and that consciousness itself is not a physical or even a non-physical existent. In other words, there is no such thing as consciousness. It is simply a process which we are somehow, rather mysteriously, aware of; but perhaps a computer could also be conscious, and therefore the computer would be aware as an insider of the currents in its transistors and their parts.

There is a paradox here, because modern science is based on the notion of empirical testing, verifying things through experiment; and to say that nothing can exist outside of the physical universe is to postulate something metaphysical and not really testable.

JI: That's true; consciousness has always had this paradoxical, difficult-to-pin-down property. It is the central problem, in some ways, of a great convergence of the different sciences, and of course there is no test for consciousness per se. We normally say people are conscious because we contrast that with their being asleep or unconscious; but there is no real way of telling whether people are conscious or not, in some final sense.

In fact psychology means the science of the psyche, or the mind. But most psychologists will tell you that is not what they really are anymore; they are behavioral scientists.

JI: That's true, but that is changing too. The cognitive move within psychology has made looking at conscious processes much more respectable, because we expect to be able to model those processes in computer and mathematical terms.

There is also a small but prestigious minority who maintain that the materialistic viewpoint that the mind somehow emerges from the brain doesn't really hold up.

JI: Yes, there have always been outstanding neurologists such as Sir John Eccles and Wilder Penfield, both of whom believe that the brain in some sense is an instrument which is played upon by a nonphysical mind. Of course this view is very ancient; I am sure it goes back to paleolithic times, when people believed in the survival of the spirits of their forebears. One of the reasons why I'm so interested in this dualistic viewpoint, as it is called these days, is that it is one of the possible theoretical explanations for the phenomena of parapsychology.

Mainstream scientists and positivistic behavioristic philosophers get a little upset if you use the terms mind or soul. They claim you are making a categorical error – that you are describing a process as if it were a thing.

JI: That's true. For example, the British philosopher Gilbert Ryle in *The Concept of Mind* sought to prove that mind talk was a way of talking about behavioral dispositions. Later philosophers have seen that this clearly cannot be the case; there are very powerful technical problems in reducing statements about people's behavior to statements about intentions or beliefs or consciousness.

In other words, to view the mind as an entity, as a thing in and of itself, is now considered acceptable in mainstream philosophy.

JI: I'm not saying it is acceptable. I am saying that the attempt to reduce mind to just being the brain seems to have failed in some way, and that the philosophers are aware of that. But the people who have bright hopes for artificial intelligence in the computer world still expect that the reduction of consciousness to some form of brain process will occur. And of course we mustn't forget that if we are talking about the existence of a nonphysical mind, that is importing into the universe something very strange and very different from the regular matter which the physicists have so far told us does exist. What interests me is that view of man as consisting of at least two separable elements – that is, a body including the brain, and a mind which can separate from it at death – seems to have been consistently held by very widely divergent groups in different parts of the world, in different forms of culture, and at different times and places. If we look at parapsychological phenomena – the phenomena of the out-of-body experience, the apparent survival of people through death, the deathbed experience itself, where people allegedly see their departed relatives coming in to welcome them into the nether lands, and many other forms of psychic happening – these are all explicable on the basis that there does exist a mind separate from the body. The real problem is to produce a theory which is modern, which describes this in terms that make sense to us as twentieth-century psychologists, rather than in the seventeenth-century terms of René Descartes, who was the paradigmatic dualist theoretician, or the old forms of the anthropologically interesting but obviously scientifically invalid view of the spiritualists, the occultists, and the different sorts of primitive groups who believe this.

One of the reasons that many mainstream scientists today reject the evidence of parapsychology is because it does challenge their materialistic view of the brain-mind system.

JI: Unfortunately, as parapsychologists we have a set of phenomena which seem to be very, very naughty, in the sense that they won't lie down, they won't go away, and they won't behave themselves and become normal physical residents of the universe. For example, in precognition people seem to be able to pick up information about the future. This simply shouldn't be possible. Equally, ESP – telepathy between people, for instance – doesn't fall off with distance as radio waves would. In addition, we have people at my laboratory affecting instrumentation in ways that we simply don't understand, which really don't look as if they are normal physical processes. All of this suggests that perhaps we are dealing with a realm of phenomena where somehow we're transcending the normal limits of space and time. This was a very clear position held by many parapsychologists throughout the history of the subject.

The crux of the argument boils down to what we mean by the normal limits of space and time. The fundamental philosophical foundations of physics are in great uproar right now. There are big disputes as to whether the equations of quantum physics can be taken to literally mean that there are multiple dimensions of space, or that time could run in both directions.

JI: We are in a very interesting period, because it looks as if the whole issue of what interpretation should be given to the mathematics of quantum physics is virtually up for grabs. Perhaps a form of dualism may come in through that particular approach. I know that the physicist Evan Harris Walker has said that essentially what makes a quantum reaction finally get to some determinate end point is a human consciousness observing it. I'm not sure that is really all that need be said about that area, but this is certainly one position which is being advocated.

That same point was made thirty years earlier by John Von Neuman, the great mathematician who invented the Von Neuman machine, which is the basic architecture of all computers. He suggested that the collapse of the quantum wave function, or the basic observation in quantum physics, occurs when some conscious entity becomes aware of that.

JI: That's true. According to this viewpoint, the mathematical descriptions of the quantal process cannot give you an explanation for why the collapse should occur.

Julian, neither you nor I are physicists, but can you try and explain what we mean by collapse of the quantum wave function?

JI: When a quantum reaction occurs – say two particles collide – there are various different possibilities which could actually occur as an outcome of that particular encounter. What the quantum terminology of the mathematics says is that the system actually is in every one of those possible states, of which there could be thousands. When you then observe the system you find the electron or the particle in only one particular place. What is said to happen is that the realm of possibilities which was inherent in the situation becomes collapsed from being diffused out, almost like some kind of spatial cloud, into one particular event; and hence we talk of the collapse of the state vector.

There is a sense, then, in which the very physical world, as we observe it, is actually created by our act of observing it.

JI: That is a very interesting viewpoint, because working in psychokinesis one is very aware of the way that events are apparently being created by people's conscious or unconscious intention. The idea is around in parapsychology that perhaps large aspects of the world are created by people, and that maybe what we are living in is a mind-dominated universe where the human race has come to a consensus as to what things should be like, and the world therefore operates along those lines; and if as a group we totally changed our minds, then the planet might operate in a different way. This kind of viewpoint was first clearly summed up by the German philosopher Kant, who said that it is only human beings who impose the notion of space and time on what is really a sort of smeared-out existence without things being separate from each other. This is very much like the English philosopher and physicist David Bohm's notion of the implicate order, in which the universe exists most of the time, and what we see are just eruptions out of this sort of void.

In other words, we have a physical world, or we observe the world around us to be physical; we have the laws of physics. But in effect, all of our laws of physics, all of our observations are generated by our brains, or by our nervous systems, or perhaps by our minds.

JI: That's true. Now, some parapsychological theories of the existence of minds separate from bodies is that parapsychologists have wanted to produce a more detailed picture of the relationship between the mind and the brain than anybody ever has done before. Two British theoreticians, Thouless and Weisner of Cambridge University, produced a theory of dualism which said that the mind in its relationship to its brain uses psychokinesis, the ability to affect matter, to initiate the voluntary action of the body; and it uses ESP to scan the brain. In this case the brain becomes a very sophisticated sensory system for scanning its environment, preprocessing information, and then displaying it to the mind entity which reads the information off the surface of the cortex by ESP. This is an important theory, because in some final sense it gives a place for ESP and psychokinesis. It gives a reason why they should be in the world, because otherwise they just appear to be rather strange and bizarre, rather meaningless peripheral features of the world.

It also suggests that anyone who is able to use their brain to function in the world is automatically psychic, at least internally.

JI: And the problem of using psychic ability then becomes the problem of taking the attention of the mind entity away from the brain and going directly into the physical world, as in clairvoyance; or into somebody else's brain or perhaps somebody else's mind, as in telepathy; and then, if you are able to use your mind power directly on the physical world, you have psychokinesis.

This brings up an interesting question. When out of an act of pure will I decide, say, to lift my hand, how do I do that?

JI: The neurophysiologists such as Eccles and Penfield would say that what happened was that your mind manipulated your brain in such a way as to initiate that series of voluntary actions. This view is not taken seriously at all in sciences, because it is not yet proven. The difficult thing about dualist theories is that it is very difficult to prove that they are true. One of the things I have been interested in doing is to see if we could deduce provable, empirical, experimentally testable consequences from dualist theories of mind.

Insofar as science is a search for order and elegance in the universe, it would seem that a dualistic theory would always somehow be unsatisfying – that people would always want to get to the ground of existence in which mind and matter are somehow really unified.

JI: J.B. Rhine, the founding father of parapsychology, certainly thought that. He thought that we had to acknowledge that there was a mind entity, but that on a more fundamental level of existence, in order for mind and matter to interact at all, there must be some more fundamental substratum which was the ground in which that interaction occurred. That view is called neutral monism, because the ground of the interaction is neutral as between mind and matter.

Parapsychologists use the word psi to describe psychic phenomena, extrasensory perception, and psychokinesis; and yet in physics psi refers to the probability functions that underlie physical phenomena. Maybe that is the ground.

JI: Yes; in fact Eccles, Thouless, and Weisner thought that how psychokinesis affected the brain was to very subtly and very slightly change the probabilities of transmission between different nerve cells across the synapses of the brain, and that what you saw was a very gentle but mass effect on thousands and millions of different neurons, so that the steering could be very subtle and very well coordinated. This in many ways is very consistent with our picture of psychokinesis, because it seems to have the property that it is independent of the complexity of the task that is involved. Psi as a whole seems to have this independence of complexity, in the sense that if you give somebody an ESP task, and you give them a psychokinesis task, and then you give them a task which involves both, they seem to have about the same level of success at doing the two tasks separately as they do if they have to do both tasks to get the outcome. This suggests that somehow the extra complexity doesn't matter.

When we talk of the underlying ground of the physical universe as being not particles, not even energy forms, but rather probability waves, it is interesting to think that we would emerge at all out of these billions of probability waves.

JI: It is a very boggling thought. The philosopher Austin in England was always very amusing because he understood this point. He said that philosophers and scientists generally, other than physicists, dealt with the world of medium-sized dry goods; what we are dealing with is a world of tables and chairs. And as a result, the properties of the microworld boggle us, because we cannot use analogies derived from our normal experience of medium-sized dry goods to actually understand how that strange world of probabilities works. Yet it seems that we really have dematerialized matter with quantum physics, and that the world does dissolve into a sea of energy and probabilities, and this view is what we are finally left with; we cannot go back to a classical view. And yet the diffusion of this change in viewpoint is occurring only very slowly, because it is so counter-intuitive and so against our normal experience of the world. My fellow applied psychologists certainly are not aware that the universe has changed in that way. I do want to sound a note of warning against a tendency I find around me in California. People assume, because we have some very interesting speculative ideas to link quantum physics with large-scale questions about reality and with parapsychological phenomena, that therefore automatically we have solved the problems. I want to say this is a starting point, and we need to do a very large amount of precise research to really check this out, rather than simply assuming that our views are true.

It's likely to be many generations before we are able to integrate quantum physics with something as fundamental as neuropsychology or neurophysiology, let alone parapsychology.

JI: I am seriously hoping that reincarnation is a fact, because I would like to be around when that synthesis occurs.

What do you see as a viable mind-brain relationship that may emerge from all of this?

JI: I really don't know; I think it is too soon to say. I am seriously interested in trying to elaborate a dualist theory with enough detail to allow us to produce predictions. The sort of view which seems to emerge from that picture – and I am not saying it is true, but it is interesting enough to try and test – is of a mind which may be located in some sense out of space and time, which therefore can perform psychic things, and which is in contact with its brain which is located in normal physical space and time. Now, supposing that you have a nonphysical mind, the next question is, where do nonphysical minds come from? There are some very difficult questions here. For example, at what point does the nonphysical mind become attached to the body? The Catholic Church has a wonderfully bureaucratic answer to this which is that at three months it kicks in, and that's that. There are other questions too, such as, where does mind arise first in nature?

Arthur Young, the cosmologist who invented the Bell helicopter, suggests that there are aspects of mind apparent even in photons.

JI: That is a very interesting viewpoint, because there are two really difficult positions. One is on the horns of a dilemma when one asks that question. One of the horns is to say, as Arthur Young does, that inert matter has properties of mind. The problem is that those properties seem to be quite different from what we associate as being properties of mind. Do we really mean it is the same thing? Photons simply don't understand what is going on, or write letters to each other, or talk to each other in the way that we would understand as being mindful. And yet, if you talk of mind as being some nonphysical entity which is associated with the body, the whole issue arises of how that association takes place, and where minds come from.

Another view, which comes out of systems theory, is that mind emerges as a property of the whole, as a property of a complex system like a human brain. You can't find it in any of the atoms, in any of the cells or organs or structures within the brain, but when you see it as a whole, there it is.

JI: One can have both materialist forms of that emergence, and also dualist forms, where there is some basic, pure awareness which belongs to some nonphysical entity, and consciousness per se – structured, socialized, individuated consciousness such as you and I presumably have – arises through the interaction of mind and brain. This is Professor Charles Tart's view; he talks of an emergent interactionist view of the mind-body relationship, where consciousness is actually an emergent property of the interaction of mind and body.

Tart hypothesizes that perhaps there is some form of overall, total mind stuff, of which we become individuated small subsections, when somehow – and he hasn't explained this – there is an association between this basic awareness and the brain. And what happens is that the consciousness we know has been shaped by the society that we live in, by our individual personal psychology, our goals, our social environment; that then constitutes our normal state of consciousness, and only certain states of consciousness are permitted within any given society. You can be drunk, you can be asleep, you can be dreaming, or you can be various other things; but for example, in terms of our society certain states of consciousness are not valued which might be much more common amongst primitive peoples.

It seems as if on the one hand you've got the absolute, materialistic view – that mind emerges from matter and is conditioned by it. It seems that Tart is getting close to that, except he is adding the social dimension as a materialistic form of conditioning the mind. On the other hand is the dualistic view that you have mentioned. I suppose we ought to add that on the other end are the idealists, who suggest, in the vein of Bishop Berkeley, that the entire physical universe is simply a subset of the mind.

JI: This brings us back to Evan Harris Walker, who has produced an experiment which is very Berkeleyan in the sense that he seriously believes that quantum systems are indeterminate except when they are being observed by human beings. You can test that in an experiment, and that will be very interesting to see. If the Berkeleyan view is true, it will allow parapsychology to be much more readily explicable, but the problem is, how on earth do you prove the Berkeleyan view?

Well, it is dismissed in philosophy as solipsism.

JI: Yes, but solipsism isn't just that everything is mind; it is rather that there is one single mind, which happens to be me. That is the solipsistic point of view, whereas idealism allows there to be lots of other minds. As a parapsychologist I think that one would like to take the view that if the universe is created by mind, we all have a democratic vote as to which way the universe should be.

THE HOLOGRAPHIC BRAIN

WITH KARL PRIBRAM, PH.D.

One of the foremost contemporary scholars exploring the mind-brain relationship, Karl Pribram is a professor of neuropsychology at Stanford University. He is author of LANGUAGES OF THE BRAIN, and the originator of the "holonomic" theory of brain functioning.

In this interview, Dr. Pribram explores the similarities between current findings in neuropsychology and in quantum physics. With a better understanding of neurological function-ing, he says, we may find the groundwork for a new approach to understanding spiritual and mystical experiences.

Many academic psychologists over the years have taken a perspective which laymen tend to laugh at. They claim that the mind doesn't exist. I wonder if you can explain that perspective and talk about what you mean by the mind.

KP: I don't like the term the mind because it reifies – that means it makes a thing of – something that is a process. We pay attention; we see; we hear. Those are all mental processes, mental activities. But there isn't a thing called the mind.

You are very well known in neuropsychology as the developer of the holographic, or holonomic, model of the brain. Can you talk about that a little bit?

KP: The holonomic brain theory is based on some insights that Dennis Gabor had. He was the inventor of the hologram, and he obtained the Nobel Prize for his many contributions. He was a mathematician, and he was trying to develop a better way of making electron micrographs, to improve their resolution. With electron microscopes we make photographs using electrons instead of photons. He thought that instead of making ordinary photo-graphs, what he would do is get the interference patterns. Now, what is an interference pattern? When light or electrons strike any object, they scatter. But the scatter is a funny kind of scatter; it is a very well-regulated scatter. For instance, if you defocus the lens on a camera so that you don't get the image falling on the image plane and you have a blur, that blur essentially is a hologram, because all you have to do is refocus it.

Contained in the blur is the actual image.

KP: That's right; but you don't see it as such. So one of the main principles of holonomic brain theory, which gets us into quantum mechanics also, is that there is a relationship between what we ordinarily experience and some other process or some other order, which David Bohm calls the implicate, or enfolded, order, in which things are all distributed or spread; in fact the mathematical formulations are often called spread functions, that spread this out.

What you are talking about here is the deep structure of the universe. Beneath the subatomic level of matter itself are these quantum wave functions and they form interference patterns. Would I be wrong in saying it would be like dropping two stones in a pond, the way the ripples overlap?

KP: That is certainly the way interference patterns work, yes.

And are you suggesting that at that very deep level of reality, something similar is operating in the brain itself?

KP: Well, no. In a way, that's possible, but that is not where the situation is at the moment. All we know is that when we map the mathematical descriptions of single-cell processes, and the branches from the single cells, and how they interact with each other – not only anatomically, but function-ally – we get a description that is very similar to the description of quantum events.

There are billions of these single cells operating in the brain.

KP: That's right; and there are trillions of connections between them. And these operate on the basic principles that have also been found to operate at the quantum level. Actually, it was the other way around. The mathematics that Gabor used were borrowed from Heisenberg and Hilbert. Hilbert developed them first in mathematics, and then Heisenberg used them in quantum mechanics. Gabor used them in psychophysics, and we have used them in modeling how brain networks work.

In other words, in the brain, when we look at the electrical impulses traveling through the billions of neurons, and the patterns of their interaction, you would say that is analogous to the processes that are going on at the deeper quantum level.

KP: Yes. But we don't know that it is a deeper quantum level in the brain. And analogous isn't quite the right word; they obey the same rules. It is not just an analogy, because the work that described these processes came independently. An analogy would be that you take the quantum ideas and see how they fit to the data we have on the brain. That is not the way it happened. We got the brain data first, and then we saw that it fit the same mathematics. The people who were gathering these data, including myself, weren't out to look for an analogous process. I think this is a very important point, because otherwise you could be biased, and there are lots of different models that fit how the brain works. This is based on how the brain was found to work, independent of these conceptions.

So you've got a mathematical structure that parallels the mathematical structures of quantum physics. What does that tell us about the mind?

KP: What it tells me is that the problems that have been faced in quantum mechanics for the whole century, or at least since the twenties, those paradoxes also apply at the psychophysical level and at the neuronal level, and therefore we have to face the same sets of problems. At the same time, I think what David Bohm is showing is that some of the classical conceptions which were thought not to apply at the quantum level really do apply at the quantum level. Now, I am interpreting Bohm; I am not sure he would want to agree to my interpretation of what he is doing, but to me that seems to be what is going on. So the schism between levels – between the quantum level, the subatomic level and what goes on there, and the classical, so-called uncertainty principle and all of that – that applies all the way along; but you've got to be very careful to apply it to the actual data, and not just sort of run it over.

Why would the average layman be interested in this? Is there some significance for our everyday lives?

KP: Sure, and this is the critical thing. If indeed we are right that these quantum-like phenomena, or the rules of quantum mechanics, apply all the way through to our psychological processes, to what is going on in the nervous system, then we have an explanation perhaps, or certainly a parallel, to the kind of experiences that people have called spiritual experiences; because the descriptions you get with spiritual experiences seem to parallel the descriptions of quantum physics. That is why Fritjof Capra wrote *The Tao of Physics*, and why we have *The Dancing Wu Li Masters,* and all that sort of thing. In fact Bohr and Heisenberg already knew; Schroedinger talked about the Upanishads, and Bohr used the yin and yang as his symbol. The conceptions that grew out of watching the quantum level – and therefore now the neurological and psychophysical level, now that it is a psychological level as well – seem to have a great deal in common with our spiritual experience.

Now, what do I mean by spiritual experience? In human endeavor many of us seem to need to get in contact with larger issues, whether they are cosmology, or some kind of larger biological or social issue, or it is formalized in some kind of religious activity. We want to belong; and that is what I define as the spiritual aspects of man's nature. And that part has this implicate order. It has the explicate order, too – the ordinary space-time order.

Let's stop for a second, because you are using Bohm's term implicate order. We haven't really quite defined that.

KP: It is the holographic. You described it very well with the pebbles. You can talk about it in terms of waves, or you can talk about it in terms of mathematical matrices which have vectors in them, and so on. When you look at a photographic plate that has a hologram on it, you can either look at some of the swirls in there, or you can look at the individual grains of silver. So there are lots of kinds of mathematics, but they all fit together. This is not relevant to the ordinary person, but I just want to say it here, because otherwise we get stuck in the wave, as if it were all waves, and that's too simple.

But what you're saying, if I can try and simplify it, is that there's a level of reality at which things are what they appear to be. I look at you and I see a body and a face. That would be the explicate level, where things are what they appear to be.

Then there's an implicate level, which is just as real, but if you were to look at it, it doesn't look at all like the other.

KP: We experience it entirely differently, as a spiritual aspect of our being. This implicate order is also a potential order; we are not in it most of the time. For years we have had this whole idea of human potential, and I think that is what we are talking about.

Human potential may be embodied somehow in the implicate structure.

KP: That's very nice, yes; that's a good way to say it.

Prior to the development of quantum physics and the holonomic model of the brain, people based their notion of how their minds worked more on the classical Newtonian models of physics; and perhaps if they bought into those models, they would tend to deny their spiritual experiences.

KP: Very definitely, and that recalls a remark by De Tocqueville, who wrote *Democracy in America*. After writing his histories, he said, "Maybe I have been interpreting it the wrong way, because I have been doing it in terms of classical mechanics, with cause-and-effect relationships. But when the human being acts, this is not a cause; this is a challenge." When we act it is a challenge, and that is very much a quantum-type, holographic, implicate-order kind of idea. The whole system can reorganize on the basis of this challenge, and you never find out where the cause is. The whole system does it. There isn't a start and a midst and so on, because time and space are enfolded, and therefore there is no causality. You can challenge the system, and it will respond in an unpredictable way.

I must say I'm a bit surprised, because earlier you described yourself to me as a positivist of sorts, and a behaviorist. In a way the language that you are using seems very much like the language of the Buddhists, who talk about no self, and just process.

KP: You know, the hard-nosed kind of scientists, in my experience, who were the stimulus-response scientists, became very soft after awhile. That was the hardest, hard-nosed kind of science; and the cognitive, which was soft, became the hard-nosed one. I am quite sure that the kinds of definitions I am giving are just as hard as anything that ever was in stimulus-response psychology.

You see, the beauty of science is that it is based on sharing. The reason we want to quantify is not because we are interested in quantities, but because then you can communicate and share much more clearly than if you can't have quantities. So all of science is based on the notion of sharing, and we need to define things clearly. If some Buddhist tells me, "I've just had a high experience," or "I've just seen the light," and I don't know what the hell he's talking about, then I can't share that. But if he gets me to have the same experience, that begins to be science. And if I can make definitions so I can describe to you what is going on – let's say the pineal is secreting some substance that makes you suddenly flash, or something of that kind – then we have some way of sharing this experience. That goes deeper than just being stunned when somebody says, "Yes, I've seen the light." That may be just metaphorical, or it may actually be that they did produce a reaction akin to stimulation of the visual system.

The point is simply that this business of what's soft and what's hard keeps changing, and my prediction is that the kind of thing we are dealing with here will be seen as solid and scientific. In the twenty-first century we'll look back and see some of the fuzzy stuff that was done in the name of behaviorism. I think that in the twenty-first century we are going to be able to do an awful lot that we weren't able to do up to now, simply because science will be admitted to the spiritual aspects of mankind, and vice versa. These have been segregated for at least three hundred years, since Galileo; the spiritual aspects, in Western culture at least, have been sort of relegated over to one side. We build buildings, and we do surgery, we do all of those sorts of things. And then we have a spiritual aspect to ourselves; and we go do that somewhere else. Now I think these things will come together, and it will be perfectly all right for what we today call "faith healers" to come and help with reduction of pain and to ease all kinds of things. I wouldn't even be surprised if preventative therapies could be instituted that deal with controls of ourselves, so we aren't as prone to get cancers, and so on. It will be a different world.

MIND AS A MYTH

WITH U. G. KRISHNAMURTI

U.G. Krishnamurti is a philosopher and author of Mind is a Myth *and* The Mystique of Enlightenment.

Does the mind exist as a distinct entity apart from our thoughts? Sometimes thought of as an anti-guru or a reluctant sage, U. G. Krishnamurti in this interview challenges our belief that the mind is real.

I n *your thinking, if I may call it that, you seem to suggest that the mind isn't real – that there is no mind separate from the body. Is that fair?*

UK: Yes. What is there is only the body. So where is mind? If there is a mind, is it distinct from the activity of the brain? It is very difficult to deal with the question of mind. Our topic is "Mind As a Myth," but your series is called "Thinking Allowed." This raises a very fundamental question – what is thinking and why do we think? These questions arise from the assumption that thoughts are self-generated and spontaneous; actually, the brain is only a reactor, not a creator. For centuries we have been brainwashed to believe otherwise. It is very difficult to accept my statement that there are no thoughts at all.

You seem to be taking a very materialistic and mechanistic position – that the brain is nothing more than a machine or a computer.

UK: It actually is a computer, but we are not ready to accept it. For centuries we have been made to believe that there is an entity – an I, a self, psyche, a mind, and so on. And even though most people will not hesitate to reject the fact, there really is no such thing as a soul; soul is created by the thinking of man. We have been fed on this kind of bunk for centuries, and if this diet were to be changed, we would all die of starvation.

If you do not want to think, is there thinking? Wanting and thinking go together, and thought is matter, you see; so you use thought to achieve either material or spiritual goals. Unfortunately, we place the spiritual goals on a higher level and consider ourselves very superior to those who use thought to achieve material goals. So actually, whether you call it spiritual or material, even the so-called spiritual values are materialistic. Thought is matter; thought is not a creator of thought, it is a response to stimuli. What is there is only stimulus and response. Even the fact that there is a response to the stimulus is something which we cannot experience except through the help of thought, which creates a division between stimulus and response. Actually, stimulus and response are one unitary moment. You can't even say that there is a sensation; even the so-called sensations we think we are experiencing all the time cannot be experienced by us except through the knowledge we have from the sensations.

And so we infer from all of this that there is a self, that there is a mind that is mediating between the stimulus and the response.

UK: What is there is only the knowledge we have of the self, the knowledge that we have gathered, or have had passed down to us, from generation to generation. Through the help of this knowledge we create what we call self, and then we experience the self as separate from the functioning of this body. So, is there such a thing as the self? Is there such a thing as I? For me the only I is the first person singular pronoun. I use "I" and "you" to make the conversation simpler; but really what we call I is simply a first person singular pronoun.

Other than that, is there any such thing as I? Is there any such thing as the self? Is there any such entity, different from the functioning of this living organism? You see, somewhere along the line of evolution – if we assume that there is such a thing as evolution – the human species experienced this self-consciousness which doesn't exist in the other species on this planet.

The whole of nature is a single unit. Man cannot separate himself from the totality of what we call nature. Unfortunately, through the help of this self-consciousness which occurred somewhere along the line, he accorded himself a superior position. He placed himself on a higher level; he treated himself, and we still continue to treat ourselves, as superior to the other species on this planet. That is the reason why we have created this disharmony; that is why we have created these tremendous ecological problems and other problems. Actually, man, or whatever you want to call him, cannot be separated from the totality of nature. That is where we have created one of the greatest blunders, and that unfortunately is the tragedy of man.

But you yourself say at times that there really is no problem – that since we are part of the totality of nature, nothing really is wrong, even if we are doomed.

UK: But we are not ready to accept the fact that there is no problem. Actually, yes, there is no problem; but we have only solutions offered to us, and we accept the solutions offered by those we consider to be in possession of truth and wisdom. Those solutions do not help us to solve the problems at all, you see. So we replace one solution with another solution. The problem is the solution, and the solution has not helped us to solve the non-existent problem. So actually, it is the solution that has created the problem, and we are not ready to throw the solution out the window, because we have tremendous confidence in those who have offered these solutions as the things that will free us from the problems that the solution has created for us.

What I am trying to suggest is that there is no such thing as your mind and my mind. For purposes of convenience, and for want of a better and more adequate word, I can use the term world mind. The world mind is the totality of man's thoughts, feelings, and experiences passed down to us.

The world mind?

UK: The world mind is that which has created you and me, for the main purpose of maintaining its status quo, its continuity. That world mind is self-perpetuating, and its only interest is to maintain its continuity, which it can do only through the creation of what we call individual minds – your mind and my mind. So without the help of that knowledge, you have no way of experiencing yourself as an entity. This so-called entity – the I, the self, the soul, the psyche – is created by that, and through the help of that you will be able to experience these things. And so we are caught up in this vicious circle, that the knowledge gives you the experience, and the experience strengthens and fortifies that knowledge. Is it possible for you – let alone the mind, or the entity, or the I, or the self, or the soul – to experience your body as a body, without the help of that knowledge? For example, when you look at your hand, is this hand yours? We have only the senses. The sensory perceptions do not say that this is a hand. The knowledge that we have tells us that this is a hand, and that this is your hand and not my hand.

This knowledge is put into us during the course of our life. When you play with a child, you tell him, "Show me your hand, show me your nose, show me your teeth, show me your face. What is your name?" This is how we build up the identity of the individual's relationship with his hand, with his nose, with his eyes, and with the world around.

We have to accept the reality of the world as it is imposed on us. Otherwise we have no way of functioning sanely and intelligently; we will end up in the loony bin, singing merry melodies and loony tunes. So it is essential for us to accept the reality of the world as it is imposed on us by culture, by society, and leave it at that, and treat it as functional in value. But it cannot help us to experience the reality of anything. We assume that there is a totality of thoughts, feelings, and experiences. But are there thoughts? Even that I question. There are no thoughts; what is there is only the activity about thoughts. What we call thinking is only a dialectical thinking about thinking itself. We use these nonexistent thoughts to accomplish, to attain a goal; whether it is material or spiritual doesn't really matter. We need this to achieve our goals; so if you don't want a thing, there is no thinking at all. Whether you want this material goal or spiritual goal – whether you want to be an enlightened man, or a god-man, or whether you want to run away with the beautiful girl living next door to you – society may condemn such a thing, but basically the instrument which you use to achieve your goal is only through the help of thought. Otherwise any thought that is born out of that creates misery for you, because any thought that is born out of thought is destructive in its nature; it is interested in protecting itself.

Thought is a protective mechanism. It isolates you from the totality of nature, which cannot be separated from you. The difficulty is that you cannot accept that you are not separate from the totality of things, from what you call nature – that every form of life is also part of this nature. When I use the word nature, I use it in the general sense; nature means the world around you. All the species on this planet are integral parts of what we call nature; they cannot be separated from that. But unfortunately, we have succeeded in separating ourselves through our thinking, and through the help of this knowledge we continue to maintain the continuity of knowledge. That is the reason why we have invented all this integrity – becoming one with nature, and all that kind of thing. And we are not going to succeed, because we don't understand that what separates you from the totality of things is thought; and thought cannot be used to bring about an integral unity. Basically, we are all integrally united; and unfortunately, through our thinking we have separated ourselves and are acting from this point of separateness, and it is this that is responsible for the chaos in your personal life and in the world around you.

Let's step back for a moment. You seem to have said that all that we know is by virtue of thought; and yet we can't even know thought itself, because every time we look at thought we don't see thought, we just see thoughts about thought.

UK: Even the thought we are talking about is created by the knowledge that is given to us. So thought is a self-perpetuating mechanism. And when I use the word self, I don't use it in the sense used by the philosophers and metaphysicians – like a self-starter.

Or self-perpetuating.

UK: Yes, perpetuation – the body is not interested in that at all. The actions of the body are responses to stimuli; thought has no separate, independent existence of its own. Unfortunately, thought is what has created beginning and end; it is interested in permanence, whereas the functioning of the body is immortal in its own way, because it has no beginning, it is not born, so it has no death, you see. So there is a death for thought, but not for the body.

Let me try and paraphrase you; you seem to be suggesting quite a fabric of intertwined notions here. One of them is that thought tends to perpetuate itself.

UK: It does not want to come to an end.

The mind doesn't exist, but even so it wishes to believe it is immortal.

UK: It is interested in creating an artificial immortality – of an entity, a soul, a self, whatever you want to call it. It knows in a way that it is coming to an end somewhere along the line, and its survival, its continuity, its status quo depends upon the continuity of the body. But the body is not in any way involved with the thought, because it has no beginning and no end. It is thought that has created the two points, birth and death.

So our illusion that we have a mind is born out of fear.

UK: And so we do not want fear to come to an end, because the end of fear is the end of thought. If thought comes to an end, the body drops dead there.

What is left after that is something the body does not know. For you, I am alive and not dead because you hear me responding to your questions. But there is nobody who is talking; there is only talking. It is like a tape recorder, you see; you are playing with the tape recorder for your own reasons, and whatever comes out of that is what you want to hear from this tape recorder.

You seem to be taking a position almost equivalent to that of the physicists who look at matter; they look at molecules and atoms and then particles, and beneath particles at quarks, and finally they say there is really nothing there.

UK: One of these days the scientists, in their quest to find what they call the fundamental particle, will have to realize that the fundamental particle does not exist. They are not ready to accept that. One day they will come to terms with that, and accept that there is no such thing as a fundamental particle, and that there is no such thing as the big bang, or whatever they call it; it is an exercise in futility. They will continue to dabble with that, to find answers to the question only for the Nobel Prize.

You seem to be saying that the body exists, that the brain exists, and that nature exists.

UK: But they have no beginning and no end; that is all that I am emphasizing. And since the body is not born, it has no end. It is thought that has created the body, and has established a point and says it was born here, and is going to end there. So it is thought that has created the time factor. We are caught up in the field of logical thinking; and that there is no beginning and no end is something which shatters the whole fabric, the foundation of our logical thinking. We are not ready to accept that at all.

I can see how this notion of no beginning and no end might apply to time and space, but not to the body.

UK: You talk as if this body is separate from the totality of nature, or whatever you want to call it. It is thought that has created the body, a separate entity, and says that it has a beginning and an end. Thought creates space; thought creates time. It is thought that has created space and experiences space; but actually there is no such thing as space at all. What is there is a space-time-energy continuum, which has no end. You see, thought cannot conceive of the possibility of a movement without a beginning and without a point where it is going to arrive sometime. So that is the problem of thought; its actions are limited to its perpetuation, its continuity, its permanence. But if it tries to talk about anything, or to experience the body, it cannot do that, because living thought is something dead.

You seem to be saying that we are trapped in the prison of our own thoughts, and this prison creates the illusion that we are separate, that we are not part of nature. And yet the prison itself is also an illusion.

UK: The prison also is created by thought, and that is why it is trying to get out of the trap it has itself created. There is a simile given in one of the scriptures in India. A dog picks up a dry bone; there is nothing there. And then it bites, and the bone hurts the gums, and blood comes out of them. And the dog believes – imagines, experiences, feels, whatever word you want to use – that the blood which is coming out of its own gums is from the bone. That is the kind of trap in which the whole structure of thinking is caught up; and it tries all the time to get out of the trap it has created. That is the human predicament.

BIOLOGICAL AND SPIRITUAL GROWTH

WITH JOSEPH CHILTON PEARCE

Joseph Chilton Pearce is an expert in the development of intelligence and author of the influential books Magical Child, The Crack in the Cosmic Egg, and Magical Child Matures.

Optimal development in children today is thwarted by a variety of factors peculiar to modern technological society, ranging from hospital delivery methods to the educational system. In this interview, Pearce suggests that current problems are so immense that it is virtually impossible for children to develop their full human potential. Parents who are truly concerned, he suggests, must begin by cultivating within themselves the spiritual power of love.

In Magical Child you suggest that there is human potential in the child, in the human organism, that gets stifled by our child-rearing and educational practices. Perhaps you can elaborate on that.

CP: We hear constantly that we only use a small percentage of our full potential; we tend to ignore it. Some recent information, I think from Cornell Medical School, points out that the capacity of the brain to think, to learn, and to adapt is determined not so much by just the neurons, the major cells that make up the new brain, but by the neural connections between the neurons – the dendrites and axons and all those things. The more lines of communication you have between the cells of the brain, the more efficiency the brain has, and the more intelligence it will display.

In other words, we've got about twelve billion neurons or so.

CP: A lot more than that, I think.

But each neuron might connect to a thousand others, or ten thousand others.

CP: Yes, you run into the neighborhood of quadrillions and trillions of these neural connectors. At eighteen months of age, when a little toddler's head is about one-third adult size, he has the full number of neuronal connectors that we have as adults. By age six, that child has at least four to five times more neuronal connections than we have as adults, or than he had at eighteen months – a fantastic neural mass of networks prepared to match or adapt to or imprint to any conceivable kind of model.

One would think, then, that a six-year-old would be able to learn much better than an adult.

CP: A six-year-old is able to adapt to, modify to, modulate to, imprint to anything. That is, the capacities of the brain at that point are infinite beyond all infant calculations. Now, you see, he is ready to imprint to the whole social body of knowledge, the whole social idea system of his world, all the ideas of his limitations, his capacities, and everything else. Then at age twelve, a chemical is released by the brain and starts dissolving that neural mass that has not been activated by being given the proper stimulus of models out there, who represent these capacities for the child.

In other words, if the neural pathways aren't being used, then they atrophy.

CP: No, they get dissolved, all of a sudden, with a chemical released into the brain. They'll get literally absorbed into the cerebrospinal fluid, and become just kind of food for the rest of the brain. Now, what protects the neural connectors is a fatty sheathing called myelination, and myelination takes place any time these neural networks are involved in patterning, according to the nature of the stimuli given them by a model out there in the world. Mama comes along, and she uses French language; that immediately will start myelinating the patterns of the brain according to that unique pattern above all patterns. By age six, the child has this infinite capacity of adapting to any kind of pattern given. And eighty percent of that neural brain mass is dissolved by age fourteen from disuse. That is what has just come out, after many years of some of the most painstaking work that has ever been done in medical research. You then have an adult brain which has at its disposal only twenty percent of the potential which it had at age six. And at least a dozen research papers have come out over the past ten or so years which have shown that of that twenty percent remaining in an adult brain, we utilize approximately five percent. So we are dealing with approximately one percent of our potential that we ever utilize. This is on the new brain, the neocortex – not so with the two ancient, primitive animal brains.

Your theory involves what you call the triune brain system.

CP: Any theory of the brain has to include that now; it is based on Paul McLean's work at the National Institute of Mental Health's Brain Research Center – pure, hard-core research.

Could you just explain what those three portions of the brain are?

CP: We have three brains in our skulls, not one; and they are three uniquely separate brain structures, developed throughout all evolutionary history on earth. We have a reptilian brain, which includes our spinal cord and the brain stem, which is identical to the brain found in all reptiles. Ours is a little bit bigger, slightly more elaborate, but essentially it is the same structure. That is our sensorimotor brain. Superimposed on that is the great limbic structure, which we share with all mammals; that is our emotional-cognitive brain which handles emotional energies. Now, emotional energy proves to be the most awesome thing in the universe. Emotional energy is the energy that hold all patterns in their pattern form, that relates everything together. Emotional energy pulls everything into its formal relationship and maintains all relationships; it is the great glue, the great bonding power, of the universe, this emotional energy. And then superimposed over that is the neocortex, which occupies eighty percent of the skull, five times bigger than the two animal brain structures. That is our thinking brain, our intellectual brain. That is the one we use five percent of, the one that loses eighty percent of its neural mass at adolescence. But the two animal brains we utilize one hundred percent of, and they never lose anything. As McLean has clearly shown, the vast bulk of our ego awareness – our personality, our awareness of selves in the world – translates into our awareness through the two animal brains, and only the tiniest fragment of it through the intellectual brain.

I gather from what you said earlier about the brain tissue dissolving that it must be very crucial in certain stages of children's development that they get a lot of stimulation.

CP: Surely, and it depends on what kind of stimulation. Hilgard at Stanford said about age seven the child becomes acutely susceptible to suggestions about the ideas implicit in his society – that is, the ideas his society gives him of his place in the universe, what the whole show is about, his capacities, his limitations, and so on – and imprints to those through his intellectual brain. And so our brain imprints, makes all its neural patterns, according to the suggestions given. They don't even have to be spelled out to the child; they can be psychologically implied within the child's whole ambient. A whole raft of recent studies have shown that fully ninety-five percent of all learning and memory that the brain lays down in that neural patterning takes place beneath conscious awareness. Only five percent of those neural patterns will result from all of our training and discipline of our children; all of our teaching can only account for about five percent.

That is, we are unconscious of most of what we impart to our children.

CP: Totally. Ninety-five percent of what the child is picking up from us, we are not aware of and the child is not aware of. There are a lot of good, solid reasons for that, and they are all physiological. None of it is occult or just hypothesis; we know how this thing works. If you look at what most of us think about our child, we want a better world for our child than we have had. We don't want our child to have the bad behaviors that we have had. We want him to avoid the pitfalls we have fallen into, and we want him to have a lot more of the few joys we have had, and not know all of the miseries we have had. So immediately, the minute they can use language, we start prescribing to them the behaviors that we intellectually think might help them to avoid all the pitfalls. Now, we are trying to hand down verbally, through our teaching, prescriptions for their behavior that will help them keep from being who we actually are.

But our nonverbal signals are just the opposite. They are who we actually are.

CP: And the child is simply imprinting with ninety-five percent of the whole psychic machinery of the brain to our states of being – to who we are physically, who we actually are emotionally, and to who we actually are intellectually. And every intellectual ideal I have of myself – "I am no good, I'm isolated, I'm estranged, I don't work in the world, I'm this, that, and the other" – the child is automatically imprinting through this non-aware process. The slightest suggestion becomes sort of a command to the child in

Jospeh Chilton Pearce | **271**

this respect, and particularly we know that the child is continually imprinting to our emotional states through that emotional-cognitive brain structure. Of course they do a lot of imprinting to our physical postures, stances, and gestures, but those are almost incidental compared to the overwhelming power of the intellectual-emotional.

Now, that would all be simple, but that five percent, our prescriptions for the child's behavior, he has to try to follow, because the child is driven by one of his greatest instinctual intents, to follow the model of the parent or the teacher at all costs. We may not believe it, but he is trying desperately to follow our models with that five percent. But since we are telling him to be something that we are not, since we want a better world for the child, the other ninety-five percent is simply imprinting automatically to who we are; and since who we are radically outweighs who we tell the child to be, the child is simply split right down the middle. And then, when he fails to be who we tell him to be, this whole system simply imprints to who we are in the states that we're in, we then accuse him of moral failure to measure up to the lofty standards of our prescriptions.

That lowers the self-esteem even further.

CP: And splits him even more. As my teacher, Gurumayi, says, until that which you think, that which you act, and that which you speak and feel and so on, are all a single integrated unit, not only are you robbed of your own power and efficiency in the world, but you fragment every child that you even pass on the street, since the child is simply influenced by the whole emotional-cognitive-intellectual ambient of everyone as he passes.

I gather from your writing that there are stages of development at which the child is more susceptible to one or another kind of influence. For example, you mentioned that at the age of seven suggestion becomes a very strong influence on the child.

CP: Well, we are talking about social suggestions at age seven. That is when throughout human history we recognize the emergence of the social ego, and also the emergence of logical thinking – somewhere between six and seven. The church started administering the sacraments at age seven two thousand years ago for a very good reason – because at age seven the child can begin to catch on to some real rules and regulations. Well, we could go on throughout history to show how they recognized six to seven as that big turning point when the child shifts from the family as his major model to the society as his major model.

The peer group.

CP: Not so much peer group as the society of adults around him. He'll shift to peer group if this adult model is failing, and therein lies our current failure. We get this very strange peer group orientation of children to other children. They are trying to model for each other because their other models have failed them so tremendously that they have lost faith in them. That kind of generation gap is absolutely unique in history. We have never had that before, where because we are not giving the child any models that follow the needs of the child, they try to pick up cues from each other about what they can do in this abandoned kind of state. Howard Gardner of Harvard, in his theory of multiple intelligences, has outlined eight or ten distinct, unique intelligences inherent within us at birth. Each of these intelligences unfolds when the optimal period for its development is ready. You can't have one intelligence unfold until the prestructures of other intelligences on which it draws are there, and it is ready. For instance, sexuality unfolds – or always did universally until recently – somewhere around age fourteen. You had to wait until all the physiological and psychological and emotional systems were mature for it.

Recently it seems to be happening at an earlier age.

CP: Do you realize that menarche is now at epidemic outbreak in the United States? Menstruation begins in eight-year-old girls, and we have a very serious outbreak of pregnancies in nine-year-old girls, and an even more tragic and serious outbreak of violent, hostile rape against females and males under age ten. Forty years ago it was inconceivable to anybody that this would happen.

And this, I understand from your writing, is a result of hormones getting into our food.

CP: That is only one of about five major causes. Another is premature pressure for early academic education, which forces the brain to fire in patterns of thinking related to adolescence, which produces entrainment of the entire brain. Television is another major cause of damage to the young child. Hospital technological childbirth is another major contributor, for a lot of reasons. All of these interweave; they are all self-supporting, interweaving factors, and never have we had any of them before; they have no historical precedent. The child's sytem could compensate, perhaps, for one of these damaging influences, but not all of them put together – including day care, and a whole raft of things that are breaking up the genetic unfolding, the actual genetic timing. It would be as though all of a sudden half the children in the United States started developing twelve-year molars at age six, or else didn't develop them at all – just as we find seventy percent of our child population not really moving into formal operational thinking at age eleven, which we always considered genetic and built into the system. That is a breakdown of the whole genetic unfolding.

What is formal operational thinking?

CP: It is pure intellectual, abstract thinking – the ability to think in pure abstract logic, pure semantic language structures, to move into pure mentation without any objects. Eleven to fifteen is the development stage for that. This is Piaget's term, but all the rest of the developmentalists also recognize this at that point.

And that's not happening now?

CP: It is not happening in about seventy percent of our teenage population. We have about a seventy percent functional illiteracy rate in the twelve-, thirteen-, and fourteen-year-old groups. Functional illiteracy means they can go through the sensorimotor motions of literacy, but there is no carry-over into contextual meaning, so they can't grant it meaning. This is a breakdown in the relationship between the three brains. It is a breakdown in the limbic structure's ability to transfer information from one part of the brain to another.

It sounds like a massive overhaul of our educational and child-raising system is going to be essential to correct this.

CP: We have known that for a long time; but we knew it back in the sixties, and it has only worsened since, and I see no possibility of that happening. I don't think you change institutions at all. There is no possible way to change the American educational system as I see it now. It is just like hospital technological childbirth, which is without doubt the most damaging, destructive thing on earth, including the bomb and pollution. And yet that comes as a great shock to people. Research has gone into this now for forty years, and the evidence has been conclusive over a long period of time, but you are dealing with a fifty-billion-dollar-a-year industry, and there is not one chance of changing that.

You mean the child comes out, and you whack him on the back.

CP: That's only the beginning. It is a series of serious disasters, all of which do primary damage to the limbic structure of the brain.

Perhaps we can't change the whole educational system, but you might have some recommendations about what individuals can do.

CP: What individuals can and must do is examine their own hearts, examine their own lives, and remember that there is no way on earth to heal the children except to heal the adults and models that they are following – the teachers, the parents, the people who are working with children. If they are fragmented, if they are at war with themselves, then they are going to pass that on to the child. You find, for instance, the total lack of love in a child's life. The child is absolutely starved for emotional nurturing and love. But how can you love until you have first been loved? Love is the greatest of all intelligence, the intelligence of all intelligences. We know from developmental psychology that no intelligence can unfold in the child from its potential state until it is given the stimulus of an intelligence developed already out there in the world.

You need a model.

CP: Language learning begins in the seventh month in the womb – provided the mother is a speaking mother.

The infant in the womb shows distinct motor responses to particular phonemes that it hears.

CP: It has one muscle for each of the fifty-two phonemes that it responds to; there are fifty-two muscles in the child's body. It varies with every child; each one will respond to each of the phonemes as he builds up his sensorimotor aspect of language. The point is, this happens if he is given the model; no intelligence can unfold without a model being given out there, a person who has developed that intelligence. Furthermore, the intelligence that then unfolds in the child, from his potential intelligent state into its actualized state, is determined virtually one hundred percent by the character, nature, and quality of the models that the child follows.

And so for parents who are really concerned about their children's development, the number one thing they can do is work on their own development.

CP: They have to bring themselves into wholeness. Now, wholeness is determined, strangely enough, by the heart. All of the new research which is now piling in, in mass amounts, is that the heart is one of the major governors of the entire human experience. The heart governs the limbic structure, which governs all of our immune and healing systems, so the heart is intimately connected with the whole healing process.

You mention in your book that the heart is directly related to the middle of the three brains.

CP: That is the emotional-cognitive structure. The heart directs all the emotional energies of the brain, all of our response to the world out there in relationships.

So there is something to the notion of the heart being associated with love.

CP: The heart is a universal consciousness. As McLean says, the individual ego translates through the brain; universal consciousness translates through the heart. That is why the heart can relate all information together. What has happened to us in this day and time is a breakdown in mind-heart dialogue – a breakdown literally in the mind-heart connection. The way to reachieve that mind-heart connection is to come across someone who has opened up that mind-heart connection, and who operates out of the heart. In my yoga, we believe that God dwells within the heart, and that until you open up and get in touch with that God in the heart, you are isolated and estranged from everything. The minute you are opened up to the heart, you are intimately related and a part of and one with everything. The heart immediately integrates the brain structure, so that which we are thinking, that which we are feeling, and that which we are acting are a single integrated whole. That gives us a great deal more power and effectiveness in our life than we ever had before. And so meditation is the answer to the whole thing. That may sound phony, but you see, meditation is one of the natural circadian rhythms that we are born with, and it is lost in ninety-seven percent of the population. I have been following siddha meditation, an ancient system, for ten years. All I can say is it has radically transformed my life.

You also seem to be saying that more important than providing children with intelligent role models, or athletic role models, are loving role models.

CP: The work in Guatemala by Kagan of Harvard proves conclusively that strong emotional nurturing of a child is the whole determining part of the development of intelligence. They can be brought up in a pigpen with an abysmally low standard of living, but with a high quality of life, because the only quality of life for a child is the emotional relationships. Give them a high quality of emotional relationships and you will have a brilliant, happy child. But who can do that for a child until they themselves are integrated and well-knit? You cannot love until you have first been loved.

SPIRITUAL DEVELOPMENT

CREATION SPIRITUALITY

WITH MATTHEW FOX, PH.D.

A member of the Dominican Order, Matthew Fox is founder and director of the Institute in Culture and Creation Spirituality at Holy Names College. He is the author of numerous books, including CREATION SPIRITUALITY, THE COMING OF THE COSMIC CHRIST, ORIGINAL BLESSING, and ON BECOMING A MUSICAL, MYSTICAL BEAR.

According to Fox, spirituality is a joyful response to life itself, and our ecological crisis is a result of the lack of a true cosmology. In this interview, he advocates a deep ecumenism that draws on the wisdom of all religions to recover our inherent divinity and preserve the diversity of life on our planet.

You are a pioneer in developing a new kind of ecumenical spirituality within the Catholic Church, one that recognizes the spiritual thrust in all religions and cultures.

MF: I call it deep ecumenism, and I think it is something that is long overdue. When the Western churches went out in the sixteenth century and encountered the African, the Native American, and the native Asian religions, they had lost their cosmology and mystical traditions; and so the encounter was extremely severe, and that contributed to the genocide against these peoples. When you are looking for wisdom in the world today, you have to look at the native peoples the world over and the wisdom of their religions; and this forces one to look at the wisdom of one's own. This whole tradition of mysticism has been ignored in ecumenism. Ecumenism is not meant to be the reading of theological position papers. It would be best to meet in sweat lodges or in processes of ancient ways of prayer. We do this in our Institute; it is an essential part of recovering a living cosmology. I think the only hope that mother earth has of survival is that the human race change its ways from violence to cosmology and mysticism.

In your writings you suggest that religion itself works against genuine spirituality.

MF: It often has. Perhaps it doesn't have to, but religion often becomes a sociological phenomenon. You certainly see it in the right-wing television preachers, where religion is being manipulated for political reasons and economic gain. Of course that is what Jesus took on in his own day and what any prophet does – criticizing religion. Gandhi was in fact criticizing the Hindu religion of his time when he proposed the intimate connection between social justice and moral development. Hinduism in his day had split the two things, as religion does whenever it goes corrupt. So the renewal of religion is always out of some kind of spiritual awakening, of the community as well as of the individual.

How do you define spirituality?

MF: Meister Eckhart talks about the innermost part of our being. It is the innermost commitment and experience which is also the cosmic experience. I think it is impossible to separate authentic spirituality from community celebration, community healing, and social justice; but it comes from living out of our depths, instead of out of superficiality – what Paul calls the inner person instead of the outer person.

Spirituality is a way of life. It dictates our response to everything in life, whether it be the beauty of the trees, the winds, the suffering, the pain, the creativity. It is our response to all of this. The creation tradition maintains that our basic response to being here is, "Wow!" It is awe and wonder. Rabbi Heschel says that wisdom begins with awe, and spirituality is that experience of wisdom, as opposed to just knowledge. But awe is really our basic experience. The more science tells us about the amazing story of the universe and our being here – how there were decisions made in the first millisecond of the fireball nineteen billion years ago, on our behalf, without which earth wouldn't have evolved to be a hospitable place for us – the more you have to begin with awe and wonder, and that is where the mystic always begins.

In your writings you suggest that compassion is absolutely essential, and that it has been lost in the Christian church.

MF: Not altogether; but I think that yes, in Western culture too, compassion has been trivialized and sentimentalized. People often think of it as dropping crumbs from the table, as feelings of pity, whereas really the Biblical tradition is that compassion means justice, as Eckhart says; it means the healing that comes out of our yearning for unity and the sharing of our common experience. It also means celebration, though. Compassion is fifty percent healing, and it is fifty percent about enjoying and celebrating. And it is not just anthropocentric. We have compassion with the other animals of the world, and the trees and the soil; and all the suffering that mother earth is under today is really an invitation to wake up to our capacity for compassion.

You have referred to Meister Eckhart, who was also a Dominican priest.

MF: Right; a fellow heretic.

He seems to be a very important figure in the original development of creation spirituality.

MF: Definitely. Eckhart was a fourteenth-century mystic, a social activist, who got himself in trouble because he was involved with the peasants of his day, and with the women's movement, the Beguines of the fourteenth century. But he is recognized as the foremost Western mystic we have produced.

Dr. Suzuki, the Zen Buddhist, was in a dialogue with Thomas Merton in 1959, and he finally gave up. He said, "Tom, you're just like every other dualistic Westerner I've ever met. You'll never get Zen, except there is one outside chance. If you read your one Zen thinker of the West, Meister Eckhart, you might get us." Merton said, "Well, Eckhart's been condemned." And Suzuki said, "Well, I can't help that." So Merton spent 1960 reading Eckhart and Zen poetry, and it converted him from being basically a romantic monk of the fifties to being a really prophetic figure in culture and the church in the sixties.

He had a strong influence on you personally, didn't he?

MF: Yes, Merton did; in fact, he sent me to Paris to do my doctorate. He told me that would be the place to go. He was a good man. But Eckhart is so amazing because he speaks out of a deep feminist tradition and out of the deep Jewish tradition of the wisdom literature. He brings together the justice struggle and the deep mystical experience in a way that is very hard to find in any other writer in the West. His influence has been very great outside the church. Carl Jung says that Eckhart gave him the key to opening up the unconscious. He was a big influence on Karl Marx, which has been proven by some Marxist historians. George Fox, the founder of the Quakers, was very influenced by Eckhart. So he has had all this influence on cultural figures; but what I am trying to do is show the Church that Eckhart lies in the real center of the entire Christian message. His writing is immensely Biblical.

To this day, some six hundred years later, Eckhart's works still stand condemned by the Church.

MF: The Catholic Church is not always swift in changing its mind. They just let Galileo off the hook a few years ago. You have to be kind of patient. They burned Joan of Arc at the stake and then canonized her five hundred years later, so it takes a good sense of humor, in the sense of history, to remain Catholic in these circumstances. Actually the Dominican order has petitioned Rome to lift the opprobrium over Eckhart, and the rumors are that that is going to happen. But I don't think that's the heart of the matter. The heart is, is this man a spokesperson for wisdom, or isn't he? And everyone I know who has encountered him finds that kind of truth in his writing.

The Catholic Church, as the epitome of a religious body, seems to be a great paradox. On the one hand it proclaims saints and pronounces miracles, and it holds up examples of exalted and pious and holy people for us; and on the other hand it represses that very same thing. It must be quite a struggle for you to work within that context.

MF: It's a challenge; but I suspect that this is a phenomenon that happens in a lot of institutions. The distance between the ideal and the practice is often vast whenever humans get together and start guarding their privileges. I think the whole issue of institutional corruption is part of the human dilemma, and this is why you need prophets and mystics. Carl Jung says, "Only the mystic brings what is creative to religion itself." And so the prophecy offered religion, the renewal of the Church and the synagogue, has to happen through the mystical tradition. So you are right. The Catholic Church can produce a John Tetzel, or someone like that. It can also produce a John XXIII. It is full of paradox that beauty can come through.

Who was John Tetzel?

MF: He was a notorious Dominican at the time of the Reformation who went around selling indulgences. He was one reason that Luther got hot under the collar about the Catholic Church.

You talk about needing prophets and mystics. The prophet is often the one who condemns the unholy practices; so in your view, creation spirituality involves pointing to things that need to be changed, as well as standing in awe of the beauty.

MF: That's right, exactly. It's a wonderful dialectic between yes and no. Yes is the mystical affirmation of the beauty of our being and the beauty of the universe, and the no is that prophetic critique which is also part of compassion. Gandhi said he learned to say no from the West; that goes right back to the Jewish prophets. The Jewish prophets said, "No, this is not what fasting means; fasting means doing justice and cleaning your heart out, not just being seen not to eat food." So that marvelous prophetic tradition of Judaism, which Jesus belonged to – in Luke's Gospel, the first time Jesus opens his mouth he says he is from that tradition – that is saying no to institutional injustice and the evils that corrupt us at that level. So you have that marvelous dialectic, and I think we all have it. As Heschel says, we are all called to be prophets, and I think Jesus was saying the same thing. We are also all called to be mystics, to be childlike, in awe and wonder at our being here, and in gratitude.

You also borrow somewhat, perhaps, from Marshall McLuhan, in talking about the global village.

MF: I don't know how much I owe Marshall directly. But yes, our generation has seen the astronauts' picture of mother earth, and it is extremely holy and special; and again, it is a paradox. On the one hand we are living in a time where for the first time we have seen the beauty and begun to understand the immense fragility and uniqueness of this planet, and on the other hand we are despoiling the planet as never before in history. We are destroying in our country alone six billion tons of topsoil a year; the forests are disappearing at the rate of half the size of California every year. What we are doing to the soil, the forests, the other species, the waters – these are the capital sins of our time.

Yet most of the churches and synagogues are just quiet about it. Why? It is because they have no cosmology. They are so anthropocentric, as the rest of our culture is – meaning that they zero in only on the two-legged agenda – that we don't have the scope to realize what we are doing to ourselves as well as to the other creatures when we destroy the forests, the soil, the air, the waters. The issues of creation spirituality are the fundamental moral issues of our time. There are also the fundamental aesthetic experiences of the whole human race, and that is why we are in a time of deep ecumenism. There is no such thing as a Jewish ocean and a Lutheran sun and a Buddhist river and a Taoist forest and a Roman Catholic cornfield. Once you move to the level of creation, you are into an era of deep ecumenism. And I think for mother earth to survive we need this awakening of wisdom from all world religions – and not just the five-thousand-year-old patriarchal ones, but the goddess religions, the religions of the native peoples of America, Africa, and Asia. This and this alone, this combination of mystical wisdom is going to awaken the human race to its own salvation, if you will, its own getting its act together.

That is what we are working at in our program. I have working with me scientists and artists, and then Native Americans, native Africans, native European tradition people, goddess tradition people, along with Protestant, Catholic, Jewish, and Sufi people. This is where our education has to take us.

I gather then that you see yourself as catholic with a small c in the universal sense of the word.

MF: Yes. But what I am doing is also Catholicism at its best – medieval Renaissance of the twelfth and thirteenth century, of which Hildegard of Bingen is a great example; so is Chartres cathedral; so are Francis of Assisi and Thomas Aquinas. Meister Eckhart is the culmination of all this in the fourteenth century. This is a tradition we are trying to reawaken, and I think it is very important, because that was the last time in the West when we had a living cosmology – when we had a combination of a scientific world view and a religious tradition, a mystical tradition, agreeing that here was the basis of a world view. Since that time the West has splintered between science and religion; they have been fighting each other for four centuries. All this, of course, is changing under the Einsteinian paradigm today. Einstein, being a good Jew, has moved us from the mechanism of Newton to a realization that the whole universe is mysterious, including our bodies and our minds and our imagination; and therefore it is all mystery, it is all a source of mysticism.

And I suppose it is in that same sense that you seem to regard all religions as a response to life itself, to existence.

MF: Of course. Even the Second Vatican Council of the Catholic Church said the Holy Spirit has always worked through all religions and all cultures. That statement is one of the most important sentences in the entire experience that was the Vatican Council. I don't think much attention has been paid to it since, but it is very important that God works through all religions. That is why we have to draw forth the wisdom of all religions today to recover our own divinity, and to encourage one another in going the better route, which is our capacity for compassion. The human race is obviously capable of so much folly, of so much militarism, of so much destruction of humans and other creatures, that we need all the help we can get in choosing a better path.

One of your critiques of established religions is that they are basically geared to children, to the Sunday school process. We grow up thinking about such important things as prayer in a way that it is taught to children, and not really quite as adults.

MF: The sentimentalizing of religion really occurred in spades in the nineteenth century with industrialism and capitalism, when the real moral choices moved from the farm to the factory. Religion became more interested in children, so we invented kindergartens and Sunday schools for kids. But the fact is, if you look at the Gospels, Jesus never taught religion to children. He used children as examples of spirituality for adults, time and again. It seems to me that spirituality is natural for children. Every child is a mystic; we were all mystics once. It gets driven out when we move into the adult world, and we make so many compromises with the child inside. This is why you need spiritual leaders like Jesus or Isaiah or Gandhi or whoever – to awaken healthy spirituality in adults again. This is a very important need today, because many adults are frozen in a fifth-grade religious world view, and it is just pitiful.

A good example is these people who are still fighting scientists over whether evolution happened or not, because they think God couldn't work through evolution. The fact is, in the twelfth century Hildegard and others dealt with this issue. They concluded that it shows more of God's power that God

I am expecting to happen today – a renaissance, a global renaissance; a rebirth of civilization based on a spiritual vision, a new cosmology born of the new science and the ancient mystical traditions, creation mysticism. And you know, we in America have a special role to play, because the Native Americans have so much wisdom in their creation-centered sixty-thousand-year-old way of praying on this soil.

You asked, how do we awaken the child? How do we awaken the ecstasy in us? A sweat lodge, where you go in the dark together, is a return to the womb, only it is a communal womb. You are in there with others praying, and it gets very hot in there, and it's very scary. My first twenty minutes in a sweat lodge, I was looking for the fire exit, or a fire extinguisher, and finally I decided, well, I was going to die there. And once I did that, I went through a process of yielding, and then it was a very mystical experience. All mysticism really is a process of letting go and yielding, or surrendering. So there are these ancient ways of prayer, and we have sweat lodges on our campus, and it is amazing to experience these kinds of prayer with Christians and Jewish people and native people together. This is what I mean by deep ecumenism – praying together instead of just theologizing together. I have never prayed with native people without it being very genuine and cosmological. They have a cosmology. They wouldn't think of experiencing the divine except within the universe itself. They have not succumbed to the split of religion versus science.

You've used the word deep ecumenism on several occasions. What you seem to be saying is that as we go into the mystical experience we go deep within ourselves, and the cultural conditioning falls apart – what the churches say or even what some scientists say – and at that deep level we get in touch with what really is true.

MF: Exactly. In fact, deep is a synonym for me for true spirituality – what Eckhart calls the innermost part of the soul, the innermost part of the person. That's deep, as opposed to superficial, external, or dictated by external forces. Eckhart says God is a great underground river; so we come to this common ocean of being. This is why we have different wells of wisdom. There is the Jewish well and the Sufi well and the Buddhist well and the Catholic and Protestant; but they sink into one deep underground river. There is only one divine source of all this wisdom, you see.

SPIRITUAL TRAINING

WITH IRINA TWEEDIE

Irina Tweedie is the author of Daughter of Fire, *a diary of her intensive spiritual training in India with a Hindu Sufi master.*

In this moving and personal interview, Mrs. Tweedie, who is now a Sufi teacher in London, describes the bliss, peace, and love – and the despair and loneliness – of her years of training in the Sufi tradition.

T*hirty years ago, at the age of fifty, you would have had a hard time imagining what a very profound transformation you have gone through in your spiritual training.*

IT: The problem with the spiritual path is that you know how you begin, but you never know how you will end. It is like putting your foot in a wasp's nest. All sorts of things can happen to you, usually quite unexpected; one really doesn't know where one will be finishing.

In your book you refer to what the Sufis call "the glance" – the look of your guru that affected you so profoundly. At that moment you realized you were on the path, you were with that teacher.

IT: According to the Sufi tradition, the moment the teacher looks at you for the first time, you are born again. That is a very important moment; it is your second birth, as the Sufis say. So really I am not very old as yet – not eighty, but very much less. I was born in 1961, on the second of October, when my teacher looked at me.

One of the first things that he told you, as part of your training, was to keep a diary, day by day, of the experience; and it's a marvelous document. You mention in the Introduction that the lessons keep getting repeated, with different nuances, in different ways, until you finally arrive at an understanding of the process of letting go of your little self to awaken to a larger sense of things.

IT: That is quite right. You see, it is exactly like in school. The lessons are repeated and repeated again, so that the student will learn. And also, each lesson triggers off a slightly different psychological reaction. Spiritual life, any spiritual path, is exactly like programming a computer. Our mind can be compared to a computer; it can be programmed to a certain path. It is really a programming of the whole human being – body, emotions, and mind – to a certain way of thinking, a certain way of realizing the potential within oneself. And also it leads to a complete change of values.

One aspect of your training involved dream interpretation. Your guru asked you to tell him your dreams on a regular basis.

IT: According to modern psychology, dream interpretation is of the utmost importance. I personally feel that dream interpretation is the modern equivalent of the ancient Sufi teaching stories, which were very much used in the past.

These stories are designed to open something inside us.

IT: That's right; and dream interpretation is the modern way. There is a kind of communication, or rapport, on a different plane of thinking in a different space. We believe that a dream has much more meaning than just a dream. It is a message to us from our unconscious. It is a guiding line how to behave, what to do, in life or the spiritual path. So dreams are usually very important, and to interpret a dream is to contact a human being at a different level of consciousness. It helps him to be accepted, to be the center of attention, which everybody likes. And of course the whole group learns from the interpretation of the dream, because it is done in a group, like the Sufi stories.

I was really struck by your description of the doubts you experienced. Your process seemed to alternate between moments of great peace and great ecstasy, and moments of profound inner torment and pain.

IT: I think that is natural. Don't we all experience a lot of doubts if we are faced with something absolutely unknown to us? Here I was, alone, in a country I didn't know, in the hands of a man who I knew would do absolutely anything for the sake of training. It was a very frightening experience.

In the Christian tradition they refer to the dark night of the soul as being an essential part of the mystical path. You must have gone through something corresponding to that.

IT: Yes, but not quite at the beginning. The dark night of the soul is really the inner moments of utter dejection. This is what happens on the mystical path. Sometimes the meditation is easy; everything is wonderful. We call God or That, the Beloved, and the Beloved is near. It is all wonderful. The next day I am alone. I can't find the Beloved. God doesn't exist. It is awful. We call it the yo-yo syndrome – up and down, up and down, up and down, endlessly. And that provokes a kind of loneliness, and a kind of frustration, which St. John of the Cross calls the dark night of the soul.

You can compare spiritual life to a spiral; the experiences repeat themselves in a higher and higher spiral, at higher and higher frequencies. And the dark night of the soul gets deeper and deeper and deeper. At the end I was practically suicidal. I wanted to commit suicide twice, but I didn't, of course. My teacher saved me from it, with some very simple words. First he told me, "You are absolutely hopeless. You are nowhere. You will never reach spiritual life." He treated me so badly that I really thought I was wasting my time. I knew I couldn't go back to London without having achieved at least a little bit; I wouldn't respect myself. So I said, "Well, I'll just go out of this world." I was in terrible desperation; the heat was 120 degrees in the shade, and he was treating me in a terrible way. I had very little to eat, because I couldn't eat in that heat. I got thinner and thinner. You know, at a certain point the physical body just can go no further. I decided to throw myself from the bridge at Kampur, the city where my teacher lived; he has died in the meantime. This was a big, long bridge on the Ganges, and the Ganges is deep, so I thought, "Well, it won't hurt very much." He seemed to know my thoughts, because suddenly he turned to me. We were sitting in the garden, and I was so disgusted I didn't want to look at him. He said, "Mrs. Tweedie, look at me." So I just looked at him, and Ahhh! He was full of blinding light. I just looked, speechless. He said, "Mrs. Tweedie, look at me. Do you think I would waste my powers if you really were hopeless?" And only half a day before that he had told me that I was utterly hopeless.

You say he seemed to be doing these things to stop your mind – to get you outside of your intellect by throwing curve balls at you, always behaving in inconsistent ways.

IT: That's probably correct. You see, it is said in all the scriptures, in the Hindu Upanishads, in Christianity – that it is the mind that is the greatest obstacle on the spiritual path – the constant automatic thinking of the mind, constantly churning memories and desires and thoughts of the future, and so on. This mind has to be stilled somehow, in order for spiritual experiences to come through. Deep down, the mind may be thrown into confusion; but you know, the law of nature is everywhere. It is "As above, so below," on the spiritual plane, and also in this life. The pendulum goes backward and forward; this is one of the laws of nature, going one way and then going back. So it is kept artificially between the desperation and the nearness.

It's as if the further away you were the more desperate you got and then the more desire you developed to finally break through.

IT: Absolutely, you have put it just right. And not only the teacher does it, but your state of mind is also like that. It is as if the Great Beloved, or God, does the same thing to you. You can pray, and then you can't, and you are desperate. Actually the idea is that when the mind is completely desperate, at one moment it sort of stops in the middle, utterly helpless; and it is in this moment that so-called illumination can come.

Your teacher referred to two different paths, or two different methods of attaining enlightenment. One is through meditation; and the other, I suppose, has to do with the fire in the title of your book – the idea of burning away the dross of the spirit or the soul. That was the more direct, intense path, which is the one that you were on.

IT: Yes. The one is called in Sanskrit the path of tyaga, which is the shortcut. The other one is the path of dhyana, which is what we practice in London. This is rather a slower path, but it is not so painful. In the path of tyaga you have to give up everything; all worldly possessions, which I had to do; and you have to give yourself away in utter surrender. But here is an interesting point. He did emphasize again and again, you have to surrender to the guru. One doesn't surrender to the guru, not really; one surrenders to the light within oneself, the light of the soul – that part in us which belongs to eternity.

You mentioned that when you looked at your guru when you were contemplating suicide, you saw this radiance coming from him. And many times he would just have you come to his house, and you would sit, and he would be asleep. But he would be working on the inner planes, affecting your soul in ways you couldn't even know.

IT: That's correct. Most things on the path of the mystics are not known to the mind. If you are on the mystical path you can go through the most wonderful experiences; the mind knows very little about it. He said to us one day, "What you can understand with the mind is not a high state. The less you understand, the better." Now for us Europeans, especially for those who lived in academic circles, that was absolute nonsense. The more you understand, the better it is. Well, it is not so on the spiritual path.

You started on this path when you were in your fifties, and yet you were willing to give up what is so important to people at that phase of life – your security. You gave up all of your financial security. You became totally devoted to this guru, even though he seemed to do things that were insulting and contradictory to you.

IT: I wanted to know the truth, and somehow, somewhere, I knew that this man could help me. That was all I needed. I am Aries. Aries's people put everything on one card; they're gamblers. So I gambled. And that's why when I thought that I hadn't gotten anywhere, I wanted even to commit suicide. But somehow I'm still here.

You know, if I may say so, you have such a serene quality and such a beautiful face. You went through that intense period with your teacher, that yo-yo phase, as you call it, for five years.

IT: Oh no, for fifteen.

Fifteen years? Did you at some point reach a phase where things stabilized, where you began to enjoy the fruits?

IT: Well, I hope it has stabilized now; now there is no doubt. You see, when you have direct knowledge, it is not even a belief, it is conviction; you know. How can there be doubt? In the state of deep meditation, which I would like to call the superhuman state – I don't like the word samadhi; it has been so abused – there, you find yourself on a plane of consciousness where you really know. There, I am the knowledge; I know. It is a plane of absolute light, of absolute omnipotence, absolute divinity, absolute everything. But the fantastic and the most disconcerting thing is, you won't find God there. There will be you, in infinity, and nothing else.

Now, for the mind that is double Dutch. One has to experience it to understand it, because there are no words to express it. This is the problem of the mystic. Often I lecture, and my greatest frustration is that the best and the loveliest things which one experiences, one cannot even express. People have to get it themselves, but it takes years.

And the purpose of the teaching is not so much to instruct people about it, but to lead people to it.

IT: Yes, and to uncover that truth within – to undress the inner truth, to take away the covering, the veils, as it is said in Sanskrit.

And the methods of your teacher, which would seem so unorthodox in Western circles, were effective methods for you.

IT: Well, I'm not so sure it is unorthodox. The training in the ancient monasteries was exactly the same. The novice had to be the last and the least and the shabbiest dog, and had to serve all the other monks or nuns. In the time of Socrates, for three years you were not allowed to ask. You were a listener; later you were allowed to ask questions. Imagine – all these doubts in the heart of a human being, and you are not allowed to ask a question. Spiritual life is so different, so foreign to our way of thinking, that you must be full of doubts.

I suppose especially to Americans, since we prize individuality above all else.

IT: It was the same for me, you know; I was brought up in Vienna. I think we in the West live on the level of the mind. The Sufis say, "Take a hammer and hammer your head into the heart and think in the heart." Plato said, "The great truths can never be apprehended with the mind, only with the heart." Plato was not only a great mystic, he was also a great sage; he left behind great writings.

You live in London and you have students there; so you must consider this method of instruction a viable method for Westerners.

IT: Absolutely, but not for everybody. Our teacher used to say, "We are never intended to be many. We always will be the few." Why? Well, who wants to get rid of the self? The sine qua non, the most important thing on the spiritual path, is really to get rid of the ego. But here again we are saying something which is very deceptive. You don't get rid of anything; but it is the me, the I, which separates me from you – that is the only evil, say the Sufis. There is no such thing as you and me. It is only absolute oneness. That is why the Sufis and all the sages call this world an illusion. But the ego is not killed, it is not transcended, it is not destroyed.

It is still there, but you must have a different attitude towards it.

IT: Yes, you have to control it. It is not the master. The master is something else, which is the soul. And what we are trying to do is to reach the level of the soul – the light within you and me and everybody else. That is Sufism. And it is not easy.

It seems like such a special path. Most people don't have this yearning to arrive at the level that you do.

IT: Well, I don't know. If the human being has got this tremendous longing, which is the famine inside of love, they will do anything. It may be this path will be for someone.

We live in a pluralistic society. We are pulled in this direction and in that direction – a little bit of spirituality Sunday mornings, and then we go to work, and then we have the family, and then we have our recreation. Most of us don't have that same burning desire.

IT: Then the spiritual life must wait – perhaps the next life, or the next after, or not at all. We have free will. You see, spiritual life is just a specialized subject, like archaeology or medicine.

THE RAPTURE OF BEING

WITH PIR VILAYAT INAYAT KHAN

Pir Vilayat Inayat Khan is an initiate of an Indian Sufi order and author of numerous books including Toward the One, The Call of the Dervish, The Message in Our Time, Counseling and Therapy, *and* Introducing Spirituality into Counseling and Therapy.

The Sufi path, according to Pir Vilayat, is one of merging our individual existence with the divine reality. Sufi practices such as dancing are an expression of the dynamic, shifting equilibriums of life, striving from moment to moment toward higher states of being. In this interview, Pir Vilayat draws upon traditional Sufi teachings as well as modern scientific thought to describe the process of unfurling our human potential.

I n your writings you often describe the struggle that we humans engage in as we are caught in between our dual nature. We are locked into a finite body, each with our own life story and melodrama, and yet simultaneously we are like God; we partake of the entire cosmos.

PK: Yes, I call that the reconciliation of irreconcilables. It is very difficult for our minds to accept this dual nature of identity, and here we are cutting right into the main problem of psychology. I think most people have a bad self-image, or overcompensate, or don't know how to assess their value in any way. It is very difficult to accept what my father calls "the aristocracy of the soul, together with the democracy of the ego"; he also calls it "the greatest pride in one's divine inheritance, and humility about one's inadequacy in bringing it through, and yet still accepting the divinity of one's being" – or as Christ said, "Be perfect as your Father."

Listening to you talk about this peculiar dilemma that we humans are in is making me feel that somehow the whole thing is very humorous.

PK: Yes, I think there is some point in laughing about things we don't understand. The Sufis say, "Oh, man, if you only knew that you are free. It is your ignorance of your freedom that is your captivity." And I would add, if only you knew what the potentials in your being are, you would realize that it is your ignorance of those potentials that limits you to your inadequate self-esteem, to denigrating yourself.

As I look through your writings, I get a sense of vast infinitudes of human potential and levels of being. You look at the spiritual writings of every religion and tradition, and somehow you assemble them all together so that it is as if we have choirs of angels and layers and layers of spiritual vibrations interpenetrating us, and that is who we are, rather than these tiny people living out their lives.

PK: You are interpreting my teaching better than I could do. You are saying it very beautifully indeed; that is how I feel. I include not just the religions, but also the teachings of, for example, Carl Jung; because what we are doing is really to individuate the collective unconscious. That is what we are really talking about – getting in touch with what I call cosmic and transcendental dimensions of our being. We only identify ourselves with, let's say, the apex of a cone that is upside down, whereas our being extends to the whole cone. And so it is just a matter of gaining awareness of other dimensions of one's being beyond the commonplace ones.

It's almost as if anything wonderful that we can imagine about ourselves, we are that.

PK: There is a great power in creative imagination. Of course there is a difference between creative imagination and fantasy, and I try to get as clear as possible about the difference. I think creative imagination is somehow monitoring the programming of the universe, and fantasizing is getting alienated from the overall order. And when I talk about an order, I don't mean a static one; I'm talking about the dynamic order. Dr. Ilya Prigogine, one of the leading scientists of our time, calls creativity a fluctuation from sclerosed equilibrium. So the order of the universe could be looked upon as potentially static if it were not continually being fluctuated away from its equilibrium. That is what we are doing in our creativity; I call it exploring "What if?" How would it look if we looked at this problem in a different way than we have been so far? That is creative imagination.

Pir Vilayat Inayat Khan | 299

In a sense then, creativity is a matter of filling those mental images with a level of being. I am reminded of a line of yours from a song by the Sufi Choir: "Sing a song of glory, and you will be the glory."

PK: That is absolutely right on. You see, I feel mentation is an act of glorification. But one can only glorify if one is willing to accept the wonder of the divine inheritance in one's being, and we are always seeking outside ourselves that which is already in us. I think it was Plotinus, the neo-Platonic philosopher of the third century, who said, "That which we fail to discover in contemplation we try to experience in our relationship with the outer world." Many years ago, when I was on the guru hunt in the Himalayas, I came across a rishi sitting in a cave in the snow. The first thing he said to me was, "Why have you come so far to see what you should be?" Actually, of course, the answer is that to become what one is, one needs to see oneself in another who is better able than oneself to manifest what one is.

You referred earlier to the scientific work of Prigogine; if I may return to that, there is always a movement from equilibrium to a new equilibrium. I get a sense from the Sufis – the dancing, the turning, the movement – that we always have to go inside and outside and to the next level, to unfurl level after level of being.

PK: Yes; I am always seeking new horizons, and I don't like to simply convey dogmatic kinds of teaching. I am trying to explore new ways of helping the human being to unfurl. The methods that I am using now are typical amongst the visionary experiences of some of the Sufi mystics in a state of reverie. Here we are coming very close to what you were saying about the relationship between the collective unconscious and the personal conscious. In a state of reverie, the door is open; one is suspended at the threshold between day consciousness and sleep with dreams. The mind is projecting forms surreptitiously; there is no way of controlling it when it is in a state of reverie. We are not using our will. On the other hand, I find that one can monitor that experience – not with one's will but with one's emotion; with one's attunement rather than one's will. It is a very delicate state; one could easily slip into the dark unconscious and get swallowed up by it. Of course I try to monitor it myself in group meditations, to keep people attuned to their highest aspirations, so that they don't have traumatic experiences, which might be very disturbing.

This level of being awake inside of the dream must be a very important level in uniting the individual consciousness with the divine consciousness.

PK: Yes. That is several levels, of course, because, you see, it is all one; this is the basic motto of Sufism. We don't think of God as other than ourselves, but as the totality of which we are, in the holistic sense, a so-called fraction which potentially includes the whole. So it is a whole new way of thinking of God, instead of thinking of God as other than oneself and up there somewhere, and kind of projecting a personality upon God that is anthropomorphic. One of the Sufi dervishes said, "Why do you look for God up there? He is here."

In your teachings you encourage people to step out of themselves, and simultaneously see themselves as a larger and larger being, bit by bit, until they can hold it all in the mind. It must take some discipline to be able to maintain these states for longer and longer periods.

PK: Of course there are techniques that are helpful – for example, breathing techniques, associated with a change in the focus of one's consciousness. There are four different dimensions, as a matter of fact. For example, one can expand one's consciousness and have this wonderful, oceanic feeling of being part of all things; that is called participation mystique. I find that the best way of doing it, instead of identifying with one's physical body, is to identify with one's electromagnetic field, and eventually with one's aura, neither of which has a boundary. This is very much in line with what Ken Wilber says in his book *No Boundary.*

You used the term aura. Can you define that?

PK: I wish I had a lot of time to do so. Let's say the physical counterpart of the aura would be simply the radiance of photons, what in science one calls bioluminescence. Plants radiate a certain amount of photons, and so does the human body, as well as electrons that are being photographed in Kirlian photography. The curious thing is that one can increase the amount of photons that one radiates purely by an act of visual representation. If you imagine that you are surrounded with light, and you enjoy looking at light, as we are doing now, then somehow the cells of your body start dividing more rapidly, their energy is enhanced, and as a consequence one's whole body radiates more light. That is something that can be observed in the laboratory – as by Dr. Motoyama, for example, in Tokyo; or a team of Hungarian-Romanian physicists who were measuring the photons radiated by the body.

I would want to take a careful look at that kind of research. But I think what you are suggesting is something on a more metaphorical level.

PK: Well, that is only the physical counterpart of what we understand about the aura. In fact I came to grief once when I was giving a talk in Oxford, and some scientists said, "Pir Vilayat, you are using a word which for us has a very specific meaning, light, and you are using it in a metaphorical sense." So I said, "Well, I don't think physicists have a monopoly on the word light; it has been used before in a sense that you wouldn't use yourself." Since that time, of course, I came across Dr. David Bohm, who said that what we know of physical reality is only a ripple on the ocean of reality; and therefore what we know of light in physics is only one very small dimension of the phenomenon of light in general. As we talk about unfurling the potentials of being, what you are suggesting is that these realms that we hear of in folklore, and sometimes on the fringes of science, are very real to you in your experience; and they are important for us to acknowledge, I gather, in our understanding of our being.

Well, what we do is take specific qualities, and work with those qualities, rather as a composer would work with a musical theme and make variations on it and try to explore all the potentialities within that theme. So basically we do have these qualities; that is what we call the divine inheritance. But how do we actuate them in our personality? That is a creative process, which is very similar to that of composing or writing or painting.

Since you have referred to music, I am reminded of your story about a time when you cured yourself of depression by listening to Bach.

PK: I had an accident, and my fiancée was killed. I was really very broken; I couldn't understand how such a thing could happen. I didn't want to live; I went through a very bad crisis. I was an officer in the British Navy at the time. I asked if I could be posted somewhere far away, and I was posted in India. Fortunately I was on an easy assignment, so every night for about three months I played the whole *Mass in B Minor* by Bach. And that is what cured me, because this tremendous glorification of heaven seems to me to be the only thing that will help one overcome one's personal pain. I remember the words of Buddha, who said, "One misses the glory by being caught up in one's personal emotions."

Bach's MASS IN B MINOR has very, very sad moments. Perhaps to reach the glory one has to go right into the pain.

PK: Yes; but then Bach has that wonderful ability to make the quantum leap from pain to extreme joy, from one moment to the other. I think that one needs to get in touch with one's anger and one's pain, instead of being heroic about it or not acknowledging it, and then harness these impulses in a positive way. In fact that is basically the Sufi teaching about mastery. Instead of repressing desire, we consider that our positive desires – to be creative in some way, build a beautiful house or compose a symphony or whatever our objective is – are expressions of the divine nostalgia. That is a phrase we use all the time, the divine nostalgia. So it is not the way of desirelessness of Buddhism, or detachment, or living in a cave. No, it's that *joie de vivre,* the joy of life – we are really experiencing the divine joy and the creativity of the universe, the way that the divine intention manifests in a concrete way; and also the extraordinary feat of generosity whereby the divine will multiplies itself by the gift of free will. We need to experience divine joy in our humanness, which is very different from the whole idea of beatitude. It is bringing joy into our daily lives, instead of opening one drawer and then closing another, being in a beatific state and then being back in life again. It is making it all one, you see.

THE PRACTICE OF MEDITATION

WITH JACK KORNFIELD, PH.D.

Jack Kornfield was trained as a Buddhist monk in the monasteries of Thailand, India, and Burma, and teaches meditation internationally. He is a founder of the Insight Meditation Society and a founding teacher of Spirit Rock Center in Woodacre, California. He is author of A STILL FOREST POOL, SEEKING THE HEART OF WISDOM (with Joseph Goldstein), LIVING BUDDHIST MASTERS, and the forthcoming A PATH WITH HEART. He is also a clinical psychologist.

As a teacher of Vipassana (mindfulness) meditation, Dr. Kornfield describes the process by which we can quiet the mind and become aware of our unconscious tensions. The act of awareness itself then serves to heal those tensions. In this interview, Dr. Kornfield discusses the factors common to all varieties of meditation.

How did you, a Western-trained clinical psychologist, become a student of something as exotic as Vipassana meditation and Theravada Buddhism?

JK: I went to Asia almost twenty years ago. I graduated from Dartmouth College, where I had first studied science when I wanted to go to medical school. I got a little bit discouraged, because I met very good, bright scientists, but they weren't necessarily wise. They didn't necessarily live with their families or their associates or the world around them in a heartful and wise way. I began to look for something in addition to science and technology, and I signed up to go in the Peace Corps to a Buddhist country, Thailand. While there, I met a number of very impressive meditation masters. I ordained, and spent five and a half years there in training, mostly in Buddhist monasteries. Then I came back and went to graduate school in psychology, trying to figure out how the two fit together – Western psychology and the kinds of training that I received in the monastery.

I would think it would be hard, studying in academia, to find the links between them.

JK: Not so difficult, because some of the issues that one faces in clinical psychology and in Buddhist practice are the same; these are the issues of human happiness. The purpose of Buddhist meditation is to make people happy, to find ways that they can release old wounds from the past, live more fully in the present, and let go of attachments that cause a lot of suffering in their lives. In some ways you can see clinical psychology as working in the same direction. It turned out there were quite a few parallels, although I will say I got better training in the monastery than I did doing my Ph.D. It was harder, and I think it was better as well. They were both good.

Let's look at how meditation might help anybody become a happier, more compassionate person, according to the ideals of Buddhism, which seem to be very sensible ideals.

JK: In Buddhism there are three aspects to practice, and all of them are oriented for people to become freer and happier in their lives. The first, as in most great religions, is generosity. One of the tenets of Buddhism is that the heart, the body, and the mind can all be trained; that is, if you practice something it will gradually grow in your life. If you practice being irritable and annoyed and angry all the time, that gets to be your habit, and after a while when someone does something you get irritated very easily. If you practice patience or kindness or generosity, and you do it over and over, even if it is self-conscious at first, after a while it grows to be your relation to the world, and people treat you differently because of it. So the first of the three aspects of Buddhist practice is generosity. The second training is that of ethics, or virtue, where you try to speak and act in ways that don't harm other people. It makes it a lot easier to meditate if you have been kind and you haven't been involved in harmful behavior or stealing or gossiping or lying; when you sit down to do some inner meditation, your mind is already quiet. The third part is a kind of training of the heart and mind. Now, how does it make you happy, is your question.

I think you've partially answered that by saying in effect that meditation all by itself isn't really enough.

JK: That's correct. The meditation really fits in a whole framework of living a life that is conscious. The Buddha was walking down the road one day right after his enlightenment, it is told, and some people saw him and were struck by his beauty and his radiance. I guess he was very happy after he was enlightened, certainly in a good mood anyway. They said, "What are you? Are you some kind of an angel, or a deva?" And he said, "No." "Well, are you a wizard, or a magician?" He said, "No." "Well, are you some kind of a god?" "No." "Are you a man?" "No," he replied. "Well, what are you, then?" And he answered, "I am awake." And in those three words, "I am awake," he gave the essence of meditation teaching. In Buddhist practice, that capacity to awaken is directed toward our own body and breath and physical being in the world around us; to our feelings and our heart; to our minds; and then to the world of the spirit, or the deeper levels of human existence. And so meditation, first of all, is a process of learning how to be more conscious, or mindful, about all that within us.

Many people have an image of meditation as being used to create a wall – to withdraw, to avoid dealing with reality.

JK: That is a very important question, because it has been confused that way, and because certain kinds of meditation practices – whether Buddhist, Jewish mystical, Hindu, or Christian – are done in remote monasteries where you remove yourself from the world. There are two major categories of meditation. One is where you try to make yourself quiet – by going in a cave, or closing your eyes and ears and saying something over and over and over again to shut the world out. It makes you very peaceful, but the problem is that when you are done, you leave the cave or you stop meditating and you go back to drive on the freeway or to the supermarket, and there you are again, and you get upset again easily.

The second class of meditation, including Vipassana, and Zen, and a number of other practices, fall in a group in which one seeks to find stillness in the midst of activity; so you look for stillness not by shutting the world out, but by finding a centeredness or an ease or a peacefulness, even though you are hearing and seeing and smelling and tasting. That is a kind of practice that you can do when driving or speaking with someone.

In other words, you might be meditating right now.

JK: I might be meditating right now, if I was any good at it, that's right. There is another part to your question, because many people have used meditation as a kind of escape, and anything can be used as an escape. Television can be used as an escape; eating can be used as an escape. Meditation has also been used or misused in that way; you meditate a lot and try to get rid of your troubles by escaping.

There is a teaching in Buddhism called "the Near Enemies" which is relevant to this. It says that the near enemy to love is attachment; the near enemy to compassion is pity; and the near enemy to equanimity is indifference. Let me take just one of those to illustrate it – equanimity, because it's so important. Many people think that if you become meditative you become passive like a jellyfish, and you don't care – "Who cares? It doesn't matter" – sort of from the hippie days; "Well, if it happens it's OK; if it doesn't I can change jobs, try a new wife, a new relationship. It's all impermanent, it's all a passing show." That's indifference. It is a non-caring, a withdrawal from the world. True equanimity, which is taught in meditation, is a kind of balance in which you let the world come in, you engage in the world, and find an ability to be with the world without fear. Meditation helps one, through centering with the breath, getting quiet in the body, and then opening to what is inside, to learn a kind of fearlessness or openness

One of the key things in meditation that people learn – and this is why it is helpful in their lives – is how to sit and be with all the kinds of things within them, things that might otherwise be difficult. Some people are afraid of boredom, some are eating compulsively because they are lonely or hungry for love, but it comes out through food. Some people are afraid of being quiet, of being still, or of past things that arise in their minds, that they keep themselves busy to avoid thinking about – guilt and so forth.

Ultimately I suppose in meditation one is confronting oneself.

JK: That's exactly right; and in doing that you can learn to relate with kindness, with love, with more awareness, than if you don't look inside. It is actually kind of practical. Most of the people I know who have developed somewhat in meditation can play tennis with more concentration, can be with another person more fully, because they have trained themselves to be more present and a bit more open.

But many people are really afraid of themselves. They're afraid that if they meditate they are going to learn the terrible truth about themselves. They just are not ready to confront themselves.

JK: In twelve or thirteen years of leading retreats in this country now, teaching some thousands of people, I have found that half of the work people do in meditation in the West is work of self-acceptance – seeing the places where their hearts are closed, where they have held in their bodies, where they are afraid, that need acceptance. Acceptance doesn't mean following every whim or indulgence, but it means not to be afraid and not to close oneself off. There is a whole process in meditation of learning in a deep way to care for oneself – one's body, one's feelings, one's heart, one's mind. And then, when you do that, you have the resources, the happiness inside, to begin to care for others.

Another piece which is critical is not being so afraid of what is painful. Our lives are a duality. There is light and dark, up and down, sweet and sour, pleasure and pain. Yet our culture is really afraid of that. We put freeways around ghettos and old people in old-age homes. We dress our corpses up as if they were going to some kind of party or banquet – unlike India, where someone who has died is honored and some flowers are put there, but they don't pretend they are still alive. Our culture is almost phobic about pain. We have air conditioners and heat and everything to keep us comfortable.

Mother Teresa was interviewed one time about her life, and they said, "It's so good what you do, but somehow it must be easier for you. After all, you don't have a car and you don't have insurance policies and all the bills to pay like we mortal people do. You don't have a family, you don't have children or a husband, and so it's easier." She said, "No, no," and she held up the ring which symbolizes the wedding of the nuns in her order to Christ. She said, "I'm married too, and he can be very difficult sometimes." If it is hard for Mother Teresa you can bet that in some ways spiritual practice will be hard for anyone. So your question is right; but the possibility through meditation is to learn in a gentle way how to open to things that are closed, how to touch places that have been hurt or fearful or wounded in us with a gentle awareness, and to release them to heal ourselves, and find a way to live in the present more fully.

Let's step back just a second, because we haven't quite defined meditation. Within

Buddhism there must be a hundred or more different kinds of meditation. Given that there are so many different techniques and styles, how can we describe it?

JK: There are a couple of major parts to all meditation. The first is just a quieting. The mind tends to be very busy and filled with thoughts of past and future anxieties and plans and delights and memories – so much so that we may walk down the beach and not smell the ocean or feel the sand, because we are thinking about something else all the time. So the first piece of all meditation is just to learn to quiet ourselves and become a little more aware in the present. There was a sign in a casino in Las Vegas that a friend of mine took and now has in his therapy room; it says, "You must be present to win." It's true in Las Vegas, and it's true in therapy, and it's true in tennis, and it's the starting point of meditation. So the first thing is the calming. You can use the breath, feeling it go in and out, or becoming aware of the breathing through the heart; or you can say some prayer over and over again, some word, some mantra, over and over, as a way to let the heart and the mind and the body come to rest in the present.

Then the second thing in meditation, once you become quiet, is a process of awareness or discovery. You become a little still, and then you begin to observe. What is going on in the body? Where is it tight, or where is it held, and is it possible to release that? What is going on in the heart? What are the barriers or the fears there? What forgiveness may be necessary? What things in the heart haven't been listened to? And then, how is the mind working? What am I getting caught up in too much? Where is there too much fear or attachment that I could let go of and live more peacefully? So it is a process of quieting first, and then of a discovery of how the body and the heart and the mind work, and the laws which let us relate a little more wisely and kindly to them.

As a psychologist, how would you distinguish this from self-hypnosis or autogenic training or other more Western practices?

JK: Somebody asked one of my teachers if meditation wasn't kind of like self-hypnosis. He replied that actually it is de-hypnosis. In a way we live in a very conditioned reality, mostly on automatic pilot. We eat three times a day; we cook, make our meals, and shop for the food, and we do that primarily unconsciously. We talk for hours, usually not so mindful or aware of what we do. The process of meditation begins with the simple activity, while sitting, of noting the breath, or what sensations arise in the body, or moods, or feelings of the heart, and trying to bring them into a fuller, more conscious awareness.

That can be painful.

JK: Sometimes it is painful, sometimes it is pleasant. Meditation isn't to make it all pleasant, but to find a place in our being and in our heart which can open to that with gentleness and kindness, so that it is free, so that it is released.

I suppose what we're getting at are the things that we have chosen for one reason or another not to be conscious about. One would expect that one of the first things that you would become aware of in meditation is the tension in our bodies.

JK: That's right, and it is actually a beautiful process for people who do it even for a short while. If you sit and you are quiet and you pay attention to your body, you can feel the places where you chronically hold your tension. For some it is the jaw or the neck or the belly. It doesn't matter. As you get quiet, those patterns of holding start to reveal themselves. Initially our response is, "Well, let's distract ourselves. Let's have an Oreo cookie, or let's turn on the TV." But if you stay with it and bring a gentle awareness to it, even though it hurts a bit at first – because as it starts to come alive, all the pain that's stashed in there starts to open – if you bring a gentle awareness to it, gradually it will soften and open, and the jaw relaxes, and the neck and shoulders drop, and you find if you do it daily, that you can really open your body.

You seem to be saying that meditative awareness has a healing quality to it.

JK: Exactly right. In fact there is a healing in all the dimensions of our being – first in the physical dimension, the body; secondly in the heart, because there are a lot of feelings that through awareness we can release and open. Similarly in the mind, there are old ideals and concepts that we hold that don't serve us anymore, and those can be released. Most importantly, in the deepest levels meditation can touch places that go beyond our limited sense of our self to connect with the mystery of the earth and life and the kind of universal laws of birth and death and impermanence that give us a sense of grace and ease in living.

Attainment in Buddhist meditation and most meditative traditions is associated to some degree with psychic abilities.

JK: In many meditative traditions there are particular practices to tune or refine those abilities. In fact, everybody has intuitive or psychic abilities, and there are all kinds of circumstances where they come into play. Sometimes in great difficulties in life one all of a sudden gets a hunch or an intuition that's based on a connection other than just our normal thinking; and by becoming quiet and training concentration in meditation we get more access to those levels of intuition.

Some Buddhist teachers practice a walking meditation, walking in circles. Other times you see people sitting in lotus position, or sitting on little pillows. Is there any posture or position that's better than another?

JK: What is most helpful is that you sit up relatively straight. You can sit in a chair or cross-legged or on a bench. You can keep your eyes either open or closed; if they are open, just downcast in front of you so that you're not looking around too much. But for the posture, you sit relatively straight, so that your breath can move easily; if you lean back or slump, there is a tendency to go to sleep. Sleep is wonderful; it's just a different state than meditation. If you want to sleep, it is better to lie down; you get a better sleep than sitting.

So would you not recommend meditating lying down?

JK: It can be done, but it's harder; there is such a tendency to go off in sleep. Then when you have found a comfortable posture – sitting cross-legged, or sitting up in a chair – then you could begin very easily by closing your eyes at first to minimize distractions, and just feeling the breath as it moves in and out of the body, as a way to center or quiet or calm yourself. You could note in and out as you do that, or count your breaths, but most important is to actually feel the breath – the coolness in the nose, the movement of the belly – and in doing so it's bringing the mind and body together, so the mind isn't off at Disneyland or Las Vegas or New York or tomorrow's appointment, but you really train yourself to be here a little more. When you train yourself in that way, over many days of doing it, then when you decide to feel and pay attention to your body, you can do it. Or if you want to talk to someone, you do that more than thinking about the dinner that is planned afterward or some event that happened in the morning.

So you suggest that people just pay attention to whatever is happening to them. It's not as if they have to focus on beads or a mantra or something particular.

JK: It is actually a combination. In this style we start first by using the breath just as a way to quiet. So if you had twenty minutes to meditate, maybe you would do ten minutes of just following your breath until you were here more in the present and felt your body. Then as you followed the breath, if sensations or sounds or strong feelings or anything strong arises, you let that be received in your awareness and make that part of the meditation, being conscious of it or mindful of it without reacting or judging it, and letting things come and be released in that way.

Is there a point at which you become conscious of yourself becoming conscious of yourself – an awareness of awareness?

JK: It seems like that, but what is actually happening is that there is a succession of thoughts. In the moment you may be breathing, and then another moment later you think, "Now I'm aware of my breath." Another moment later you say, "I was just thinking about being aware of my breath." And then another thought comes that says, "I was thinking about thinking about it." So if you look closely, you see that really there is just awareness and our experience, and that awareness includes thought, and the thought is what complicates things. It makes it seem as if there are lots of layers, but actually there is just this moment.

If you want to do a quick exercise, you could close your eyes for thirty seconds and try to count your thoughts, and see what kind of thoughts you see. You observe they are picture thoughts or word thoughts, sad thoughts, happy thoughts, tricky ones that say, "Now I am observing my thought." See if you can count, in thirty seconds or a minute, ten or twenty thoughts, and if you do you begin to get a sense that there is this whole inner world which can be observed and related to without being lost in it. You can use meditation to discover, in your body and your heart and your mind, the whole workings of your inner life, and maybe relate to it with greater kindness and greater awareness.

THE PSYCHODYNAMICS OF LIBERATION

WITH KATHLEEN SPEETH, PH.D.

Kathleen Speeth is a clinical psychologist and co-editor (with Daniel Goleman) of THE ESSENTIAL PSYCHOLOGIES. *She is author of* THE GURDJIEFF WORK *and* GURDJIEFF: SEEKER AFTER TRUTH. *She is a faculty member of the Institute for Transpersonal Psychology in Menlo Park, California.*

Beneath the apparent separation of individuals there is a level of unity and interconnectedness. True liberation, suggests Dr. Speeth, involves attaining an awareness of this level. In this interview, she enters into a dialogue on the nature and meaning of liberation as viewed in both Eastern and Western traditions.

We *get stuck; we get limited. Every form of psychotherapy has its own diagnosis of what is the problem; and then they all offer a way to get around it. What I'd like to explore with you are some of the commonalities, the larger things that we can say about the issue of liberation. Maybe a good way to lead into that is just to ask, what is your definition of liberation?*

KS: Well, I don't know if we can hope to find complete liberation in this lifetime from whatever traps we are in. But we can move toward liberation if we can find ourselves freer rather than less free, by whatever we understand about ourselves, or whatever techniques we use from psychotherapy or from religious tradition, or any other technological helps we can find in the culture – political ones even.

We are caught in so many veils of illusion. There is no end to the ways in which our perspectives are limited by our particular situations. I suppose at some level maybe that's healthy. Maybe it would not be good for a human being to be fully liberated. How would one function?

KS: Well, I suppose the most liberated person from that point of view is a neonate – a tiny baby, just born, who experiences the world as a booming, buzzing confusion, who doesn't have any concepts to clot the world into observable things and repeatable experiences. But perhaps a free and developed human being isn't like that. Perhaps they can be free without giving up conceptualization.

Well, we certainly have ideal models of what this might be, especially from the Oriental traditions when they talk about spiritual liberation, unfettered by the bonds of karma or samsara or illusions of various sorts. And yet every time a so-called enlightened, liberated guru comes over to the West, it's like the emperor wearing no clothes. It is easy to see their foibles.

KS: So you are disappointed. You feel betrayed.

I wonder if there is such a thing as enlightenment, really, or if it is a goal we all should strive for, but which is not really attainable. We are all born alone; we have to deal with death and alienation, and no matter how much we practice yoga or meditation we will always be in these bodies, at least while we are alive.

KS: Well, that is undoubtedly true. There is a Sufi story about that. Basically, the story is about Bahaudin Naqshband, who was the founder of one of the major Sufi orders. He materialized an apple – I don't know why; as some demonstration of competence – and the apple had a worm in it. They said, "Well, Bahaudin, you're so powerful that you can materialize an apple. How is it that you can't materialize a perfect apple?" He said, "In this context, nothing can be perfect."

But it isn't just the Eastern meditative traditions that give us some help with liberation. I think that Western psychotherapeutic approaches are even more appropriate for us, although I certainly have participated a lot in both.

My sense is that the Western approach is to say, "Well, look, the world isn't perfect; we've got to live with its problems." And psychotherapy is often oriented towards adjusting, coping, dealing with how bad life really is.

KS: Well, that's one form of psychotherapy. But you practice psychotherapy; do you have another view?

Well, I tend to think that underlying the basic alienation, the separateness, the fundamental ground of reality is one of connection; and for me, liberation is becoming more and more in touch with that dimension of being interconnected with everything. As we move towards that, we get closer to what we might think of as our divine reality.

KS: The way you are talking now, you sound like Freud talking about eros as opposed to thanatos – the idea of a life instinct, something that moves toward life, and away from dying, away from entropy; something that makes form out of chaos. And you feel that is development, and of course so do I. So then, what keeps us from that? What holds us back? What do we need to be liberated from so that we could make connections instead of break connections and get hot rather than cool?

I would say it's our attachments.

KS: What attachments?

It could be an attachment to a habit pattern that we have or to a belief system. We have a million excuses for not always resonating at that level of connectedness.

KS: Or for not living enthusiastically. And what do you think holds people back from that? Wilhelm Reich would call it an anti-pleasure bias in a character. Where does it come from? We are talking about being liberated from some kind of net we throw around ourselves.

Well, in many people it's clear to me that they have been traumatized in one way or another, and they are kind of stuck. They haven't worked through their trauma.

KS: And how does trauma stick people? What really happens? Let's talk about it as deeply as we can. What do we need to be liberated from?

I would say the basic thing is self-hatred. It's places where we feel that we can't love ourselves. If we have been traumatized, we think, "I deserved that. The universe is telling me I'm the kind of person who should be punished."

KS: You are saying two things; in this way I believe we've got a lot of wisdom in the Western psychotherapeutic tradition. One thing you are saying – and I of course agree with you – is that it is something about going away from entropy and toward life. And the second thing you are saying is that it has something to do with having been hurt. We have to somehow work through some nonmetabolized experiences. We need to liberate ourselves from something that has gripped us and grabbed us and is holding us back, something that happened very early. The wish we have to dissolve and to die hangs on. One extraordinary thing about liberation, it seems to me, is that the very things that hold us back are the things that hold us in the family structure.

For example, Mother doesn't want you to sit and play in your own way. She wants to have interaction with you, so she can feel like a good mother. That is one example. I just worked with someone today in a therapy session for whom that was true. He didn't dare, when he was with his girlfriend, be quiet and just look at the fire. He felt he had to keep entertaining her. And so he was ready to clear the decks of all girlfriends, because he didn't allow himself to be himself while in the company of a person who reminded him of his mother. So he is not a free man.

Another example is a woman I worked with whose mother was a Holocaust survivor. This patient was a happy, well-adjusted woman; she had four or five brothers and sisters who weren't, and a mother who was a widow and a Holocaust survivor. She couldn't give up her guilt because, it turned out, her guilt was the only link she had with her mother.

That's where they could communicate. Her mother felt guilty because she was a survivor, I imagine; therefore in order to enter into resonance with her mother, she had to be guilty too.

KS: Exactly; they could be connected. Even if they had a rotten time, they would be together.

The irony is that guilt is totally unnecessary. It serves no function whatsoever.

KS: Except the function of connecting one with a guilty subculture. So in order to be free, we have to be willing to be emotionally solitary.

What does solitary mean?

KS: It means that we have to dare to be objective and not to share the beliefs of other people in order to become a "we" with them.

To remove ourselves from the herd instincts.

KS: Yes. Perhaps to be really free, one can't be a healthy animal in a happy herd. Or perhaps one can; but one has to take the chance to find out, and that is a courageous step.

You have delved quite extensively into the Gurdjieff work. In your writing you make the point that Gurdjieff claimed, in contrast to Western psychotherapies, that all of the negative emotions – anger, hatred, and so on – were unnecessary, that it was possible to live a healthy, harmonious, happy life without any of those. And yet in our culture, we have so much reinforcement that says you should be getting angry, you should be feeling guilty, you should be negative a certain amount of the day. Otherwise you are not owning your emotions.

KS: Of course I think that is one of the mistakes that many therapists make. They render their patients unhappy. People come out of therapy feeling entitled to a lot of negative emotions. The fact is that those do have to come to consciousness, and to be worked through, and then to be put aside; because they are really not necessary.

So for you, part of the definition of liberation would be to be liberated from negative emotions.

KS: One could still have them, but probably the perverse sustaining of them would be gone. As we sit here, there are probably bombers going overhead with nuclear warheads on them. We live in a very dangerous, explosive world. It would be difficult to simply accept that without a certain amount of what you might call negativity – but we need not dwell on that.

Of course psychotherapy deals with an individual person rather than the whole political scene. And within an individual that same thing is true. There are many I's and many subpersonalities.

We are often at war with ourselves.

KS: And that war has to be ended.

You know, the Muslims have a term, the holy war. It often refers to an internal war between the personality and the spirit, or various parts of ourselves. It is treated as something that we have to engage in; we can't avoid these things. The psychologies say the same thing – that you can't just ignore your anger.

KS: It is certainly not at all an invitation to repression or suppression to think that it might be possible to live in a very deeply content way without that.

Kathleen Speeth | **317**

Negative emotions are a little analogous to other substances that are misused, like cocaine, marijuana, or alcohol. It is an addiction to feel negative. And one meaning of the holy war inside might be to feel no need to have the rush that a negative emotion produces – the rush of, "I'm entitled," of feeling vindicated.

We become polarized to such an extent that we think that good and evil are at odds with each other inside of us and that one must totally vanquish the other. But, there is no vanquishing of that kind; they really have to come together.

KS: So there is that feeling of wanting to be a whole person, a dappled person, a 3-D person – not a person split into black and white. That is part of moving toward liberation – to be free of the sense of being split inside, into a part of me that I love, and a part of me that I despise. So that is another aspect of what it is necessary to do. Another thing that seems to me very important is that we need to be free of the necessity to take and defend one position. Why should I see everything from a narcissistic point of view? Why couldn't I be objective and see myself as the same as other people? That would be a big liberation – if I didn't polarize myself and aggrandize this little one that I am.

The Sufis have a nice way of saying it: "Let go of your preconceptions, and accept your destiny." What is the reason to be liberated? What are we being liberated from? We are being liberated, basically, from conditioning that we received in early childhood, and also from anti-life aspects probably inherent in our biology. And for what reason? It seems to me, so that we can live out some kind of personal destiny. And how will we ever know about that if we are going through the motions in order to continue some family tradition, or some cultural tradition?

When we talk about liberation, we are talking about liberation from the perspective of our own personal ego so that we can see from all points of view. And that is divinity.

So it's the ego that separates us from that.

KS: It's a kind of trembling, paranoid clot of attention inside. Trungpa Rinpoche called it the basic contraction of ego.

The basic contraction of ego; I like that. And I suppose that's also what is responsible for selfishness and greed and clinging of every sort.

KS: Right. And of course to the degree that one is getting free of that, then it's possible to have empathy with others. If I am not in a fortress protecting myself, maybe I can have a sense of what your situation is.

I should think there must be a difference, though, between this kind of egoistic clinging, and when a person is on a real mission – when they are following their destiny, when they are attached to something greater than themselves – a life purpose, a creative work of some sort.

KS: Right – a heroic life, a life like that of Theseus, who was able to go through the labyrinth and kill the Minotaur; or like the life of Einstein, who was able to lock himself in a room for two weeks and come out with $E = mc^2$, and so forth. That is a heroic life.

Now how does this relate to the dynamics of liberation? How do we free ourselves from the petty clinging, and enter into the heroic life?

KS: How do we work through enough so that our actions come not from deficiency, not from fear, not from conditioning, but from what Longhenpa called lucid awareness and consummate perspicacity – that sense of doing just the right thing at the right time? How do we get there? I think as Westerners we get there on the psychotherapeutic path. Jack Engel, a psychiatrist in Boston, reported on a study in Burma in which both Westerners and Burmese sat with a Theravadin Buddhist teacher. After six weeks the Burmese had the first level of enlightenment, and the Westerners had developed a transference neurosis on the teacher. So we are different from the people for whom those meditative traditions were developed.

We should note that is where one projects one's own emotions onto the teacher.

KS: Right, and one is acting toward the teacher as if he were a loved, feared, or whatever, parent. So for us, we could do the two-person meditation called psychoanalysis, in which the therapist sits with evenly hovering awareness, and the patient sits or lies with free association of thought. What could be more likely to produce self-awareness than that kind of working through? In my experience, the people that I know, and also my own self, have profited by understanding their minds in the therapeutic manner. That just means conducting your own analysis of your life with the companionship of a therapist.

My sense is that maybe therapy does get one through certain stages, but there are certainly stages on the heroic journey that go beyond what Western psychology is equipped to deal with.

KS: In fact a hero wants to face his destiny without a cane. So at some point he will have to stand alone and make it, and meet whatever is coming toward him.

COMPASSION IN ACTION

WITH RAM DASS

 *Ram Dass (a.k.a. Richard Alpert, Ph.D.) is a spiritual teacher who, subsequent to his academic career as a psychologist, studied yoga and meditation with his guru in India. He is founder of the Hanuman Foundation which serves prisoners and the dying and is a co-founder of the Seva Foundation, an international service organization. He is author of BE HERE NOW, THE ONLY DANCE THERE IS, GRIST FOR THE MILL (with Stephen Levine), JOURNEY OF AWAKENING, MIRACLE OF LOVE, AND HOW CAN I HELP? (with Paul Gorman).*

In this interview, Ram Dass probes deeply into the nature of helping relationships, examining the delicate state of awareness in which one acts compassionately for social change while also accepting the world exactly as it is.

At the root of things, the spiritual premise is that we are all one; therefore, politically we would want to treat the whole world as if it were our own body. That would seem to be the basic premise of spirituality and politics.

RD: Yes, but there are many levels to understanding that. You can understand it with your intellect, or you can understand it because you are that, and that is a very different place to act politically. It's like Mahatma Gandhi said: "When you make yourself into zero, your power becomes invincible." Any politician, anyone trying to institute change in society, would like to have that power of the invincible. But you have to die in a way into "Not my will but thine" to have that kind of potential impact on social change.

There is a paradox there, because if we totally bow to the will of God, we might not want to resist the current situation.

RD: That is an incredibly interesting risk. You've got to trust that when you have surrendered, you will hear clearly. The Tao says, "The truth waits for eyes unclouded by longing." Your longing to have it different than it is, is ultimately a trap, because it keeps you from hearing the whole gestalt, the whole way things are. And as you hear the totality of it, you trust that out of that will come an appropriate action, a dharmic action. That is the trust of dharma, the trust in the wisdom of the universe that is greater than your own personal egoism. We are so used to working out of "I ought to do it, I should do it" – getting behind ourselves and pushing. The whole idea of trusting – that if we didn't push, something would still happen – is very interesting to explore.

There must be a fine line between trusting and not pushing on the one hand, and on the other hand being really passionate about social change.

RD: But it's a question of where passion comes from. If passion comes out of what I call milking the drama, out of identifying with the emotions, it falls short of what the possibility is. There is, for example, what is called dharmic anger, where a Zen monk will beat his student out of the incredible amount of love and compassion he has. If you are deeply enough in love with the universe, then the passion that arises out of that is different than if you aren't, and I think the passion is one that comes out of joyful involvement in the universe. But I think it's the passion of a river or a tree; I don't think it has to be like, "Aahhhh!" although it could be.

You seem to be suggesting that the quality of one's actions in a political-social arena, or any arena for that matter, is really determined by internal factors. It seems that would make it impossible to judge the actions of anyone else, even a Stalin or a Hitler.

RD: It's a pretty tricky business. I think that you can make judgments about actions; you don't judge beings, you judge their actions. And actions are good or evil, in the sense that actions increase paranoia and separateness, or they increase unity. So you can judge actions and you can be opposed to them. I can say, "I don't agree with that action you are going to do, and in fact I am going to stop you from doing the action," but as Kabir said, "Do what you do with another human being, but never put them out of your heart." If I have to harden my heart in order to oppose you, I have lost, we have both lost.

That is part of the art of the inner and the outer dialogue.

George Orwell in 1984 *refers to Big Brother. The game is that he is this loving tyrant, or at least his people believe that all of the cruelties are done out of some kind of benevolence. People seem to have a longing perhaps for a benevolent tyrant who will come in and straighten things out for us. Dostoyevsky said that people long to take their freedom and lay it at the feet of a benevolent church that might act in a tyrannical way.*

RD: I think the deeper issue is whether the universe is benevolent or not, because when you invest in an institution or another person you are investing external to your own deepest inner truth, and you've constantly got to be running that back against your inner truth. You can't just join a club and then say, "I surrender to the club." The whole misconception about a guru is that you surrender to a person. You surrender only to that which is the truth where God, guru, and self are one and the same thing. I could never imagine surrendering to something that would invalidate my intuitive wisdom. As long as you keep connecting to that, you don't have to judge whether it is benevolent or malevolent; you just judge, "Is this harmonious with my inner being?" I don't have to judge you. I just have to keep my own game on a straight path.

There is a strong trend among existentialists, and among behaviorists, atheists, and left-wing political people to suggest that the universe is fundamentally indifferent, and it is up to us to create our own reality. And often people feel that it should be created from the intellect, from rationality.

RD: Well, I think that is giving us really short shrift, because to me the intellect is a very small system within a much larger context, and to deny the context in which the intellect functions is to leave one little segment of nature trying to subsume everything under it. It is a lot like the drunk looking for his watch under the street lamp, although he lost it up in the alley, because there is a light here. The intellect also makes the whole world objects; you always think about things. And that always puts you one thought away from where it is; so you are always an alien in your own universe when you mediate everything through your intellect. As Ramakrishna said, "It's a wonderful servant, but it's a lousy master." I think that is probably true.

You spoke a little earlier about making political decisions and judgments in terms of how it fits with one's heart.

RD: Not heart in the sense of emotional heart but heart like the Chinese hsin-hsin, or the Atman, meaning the deepest place of truth, the deepest intuitive place in one's being.

That notion would seem to contradict what we see today in religious-political movements such as the Moral Majority or Islamic fundamentalism. In the name of a particular religious dogma certain political planks are established, and everyone within that organization or within that tradition is expected to support a particular political attitude.

RD: When there is a lot of fear, there is a lot of uncertainty. When there is a lot of uncertainty, there is usually a lot of fear attendant to it. How people react to fear is interesting. Some people just consume more. They say, "I'll get it while I can, because it's all going to blow up anyway." They become more and more materialistic. Some people want to be on the right side when the doors close, so they become fundamentalists in one sense or another. They grab onto right as opposed to evil. They want to be one of the 144,000 that gets in the door. Another group uses the uncertainty as a way to deal with their inner relationship to uncertainty, and they go inward. You can see the society dealing with fear that way, and so the real thrust of that kind of righteousness is to stay at the plane of good and evil, at the plane of polarities – not seeing, as G. Manly Hall said, that "he who knows not that the Prince of Darkness is the other face of the King of Light, knows not me." It is interesting that all these Western religions – Christianity and Judaism and Islam – are really monotheistic. They believe in the one. And yet they always live within the two. It's like it's all one except for me, or except for us; but it is chutzpah in exoteric Western religions to think that you are one with the one. We say it is all one, but we don't really act as if it were all one, which is much more like holography.

You seem to be making a clear distinction between spirituality and religion.

RD: Religions do provide exquisite practices to get deeper into the spirit. The problem is that every practice is entrapping. I don't care whether it is meditation or Catholicism or the Torah or yoga or drugs, or whatever it is.

They are all traps. The game or method is that you've got to use the trap and risk being entrapped, with the expectation that it will self-destruct if it really works. The problem is, if it self-destructs the whole priest class is out of business in institutional religion; so the game has a false top on it, because any institution that starts to have salaries and institutional structures and all that, immediately can't self-destruct. It is not designed that way.

In your book How Can I Help? you suggest that through service one finds a path to realization, to God, or to enlightenment. In all religions there is this path of service, and that seems to come as close as religion gets to political action.

RD: The difference is where you do the service from. There are an awful lot of religious organizations that do service, but they do service like, "We'll help the poor." That's not exactly karma yoga, or the use of serving somebody to transcend the dualism between the server and the served. I am talking about it as a very precise method of enlightenment – of serving where there is no server. As the *Bhagavad Gita* says, "Be not identified with being the actor, and be not attached to the fruits of the action." But still, you do it. Now, how do you help somebody where you are not attached to how it comes out, and you are not busy being the helper? That's the art form; then you're just doing what you're doing because you're doing what you're doing. You are the help. You are not the helper, you are the help, and who is getting helped remains open to question. If you are not getting helped by being a helper, forget it. You must be standing in the wrong place.

It seems that the Bhagavad Gita really puts the issue in its starkest form, when you consider that what is being discussed here is warfare – in fact, warfare against one's own family.

RD: You also can take that metaphorically, as the warring between the ego and the higher self, the whole internal battle. The fun of the *Bhagavad Gita* is that you can play with it at so many levels, like any good holy book. Any good holy book is a multi-leveled smorgasbord of possibilities of interpretation.

It seems that some people take almost a religious attitude that they are going to do what they think they have to do, and if they have to kill people, God will figure out who goes to heaven and who goes to hell, and they are not to blame.

RD: What they are saying is that they are going to kill all the "thems." There are two ways to kill the thems. One is you go da-da-da-da-da-da with a machine gun, and the other is you extricate yourself from a world of us and them in your own mind, and you have killed all the thems, and there is only us left.

I was in Guatemala, and one of the women, a widow whose husband had been murdered before her eyes, said to me through a translator, "Thank you so much for leaving your home and family to come and help us." I said, "I didn't. You are my home and family." And I felt the truth of that at the moment. She was defining it in terms that she was them, and I didn't see her as them. She was us. That is part of the excitement of being willing to risk in service – seeing the beloved in all the forms and yourself in all the forms. Instead of averting your eyes from pain and suffering, turn around and embrace it into yourself, without being afraid you are going to be drowned by it, because you know you can say no without closing your heart. These are all a part of a piece, the beautiful services a yoga is.

If one carries your position to its logical extreme, it means being willing to look at the grossest, most hellish misery on the planet, and embrace it.

RD: All of it, all of it. You learn how to keep your heart open in hell. You see the horrible beauty of the universe. I remember once I was teaching down at the Esalen Institute in Big Sur. They gave me a house to house-sit, and it came with a cat. The cat and I became buddies, and every day the cat would come in when I was meditating in the morning, and bring in its breakfast, a lizard or something, which was usually still alive. It would sit down between my legs to eat, to be with me. I would be sitting there being with God, and I would hear, "Squeak, squeak. Crunch, crunch," and I didn't know who to hate. I mean, I loved the cat, but suddenly the cat was a killer. And I loved the lizard, because I identified with it. I went through all the changes, and I saw it as the phenomena of nature. You've got to be able to look at it all and say, "Yes, I acknowledge it," without being so busy reacting to it that you don't even understand why it is that way. My ability to see, as Rilke said, around the edge of the billboard at the edge of town, to see just around the edge of the veil – and I can just see a teeny little bit, just like we all can – leads me to understand that the game is much farther out than I thought it was. I can understand the term, "Suffering is grace." I can't live it. I can live it at moments, with little sufferings; but I can understand that there is a beautiful unfolding of awareness through suffering. That is what my work with the dying is about.

Once when I was a teenager I heard a rabbi talk about what he felt was the essence of Jewish ethics, and he said, "If I saw another man and he had no clothes, and all I had was a pair of pants, I would take off my pair of pants and give it to him." It struck me that, well, that's very beautiful, but I don't live my life that way, and I don't know anyone else who does. And yet I think I hear that coming from you – that when we recognize the One as being ourselves, how can we not want to share our last pair of pants?

RD: You and I have a unique predicament, a karmic predicament, that we were born in this time in this place with these potentials and these opportunities. I am not sure all people have the same game in life. I am not sure that I have to be just like everybody else. But I know, like my guru said to me, "God comes to the hungry in the form of food." Now, if I am worrying about my survival every day, there is no way I can be here with you, and if I can't be here with you, all of us can't be sharing. So in a way, we are part of the microcosm of human consciousness. We have a part to play, which means we have to have the pants in order to play. So I am not sure I would give away my pants at that level. I would explore it. I would stay with the moment. I either would or I wouldn't, is the way I would deal with that. I don't think I am a bad Jew for not giving away my last pair of pants, by the way.

That's an extreme example; but how about, for example, building elaborate houses of worship – cathedrals, synagogues, and churches?

RD: You can look at those both ways. I wouldn't do it, but at the same time I can see that for people in very poor countries who have very little mythic identity to give them joy, when they go into their cathedral, and they look up, and they worship and light incense, and there is the beautiful Christ, I can see that they get their lives enriched in a way that a lot of the regular daily stuff of their life doesn't do. You could say that the Church is milking it so that they are not getting an extra meal, but maybe it is feeding them in another way, which is its justification. I don't think it is a black-and-white issue in that way.

It seems to me what you are expressing here is a willingness to accept reality as it is.

RD: That's a big one, isn't it? To accept our humanity. And to accept that an institution could be serving, and it could also be a corruption of what it was intended to do, and it is probably a little of both; and so are we, and we've got to deal with that. We've got to accept our own humanity first – really accept it and not judge it so much. I have shifted from being a judger of everything to being an appreciator of it – just appreciating how it is. It brings me to a much more intimate relationship. The judging mode is always distancing myself from everything; so I am not even judging judging now.

THE WAY OF THE SHAMAN

WITH MICHAEL HARNER, PH.D.

Anthropologist Michael Harner is a leading authority on shamanism and shamanic healing who has pioneered their return to contemporary life. He is founder of the Foundation for Shamanic Studies in Norwalk, Connecticut, and conducts shamanic training worldwide. A former professor at Columbia, Yale, the University of California at Berkeley, and the New School for Social Research, he is author of THE WAY OF THE SHAMAN, HALLUCINOGENS AND SHAMANISM, and THE JIVARO, and coauthor of the novel CANNIBAL.

Shamanism is practiced among native peoples throughout the world and has common features that transcend differences of culture, place, and time. In this interview, Dr. Harner explores the landscape of the alternate reality in which the shaman operates and its relevance to the needs of our modern world.

You *are unique in the field of anthropology in the sense that you started out as an objective student of shamanism, and eventually transformed yourself into a practitioner.*

MH: That sometimes happens to anthropologists, they go native to some degree; I think it is a respected and revered tradition in the field. But perhaps this is unique – that more than going native in a sense, I have decided that some of the things the natives have are very pertinent to our daily life today, and badly needed. And so part of the work I am doing is attempting to bring back shamanism to modern society.

Can you explain what the word shamanism means?

MH: One of the reasons we use that word is because it doesn't have previous connotations for many people. The word itself, *shaman*, comes from the

Tungus tribe of Siberia. The Europeans who first saw much of shamanism saw it in Siberia, and described it. The shaman is a kind of medicine person, but with some very specific characteristics that one should note. The shaman goes into an altered state of consciousness when doing his or her work – either men or women may be shamans – and this is often brought on by monotonous drumming. The shaman is a person who makes journeys, you might call them out-of-body journeys to use current terminology, or journeys of the imagination, though many of us think there is more to it than that – to an upper world, to a lower world, or here in the middle world. These journeys are done for very practical purposes, such as to gain knowledge; shamans are often called persons of knowledge. Shamans work to help solve problems in the community – healing and other problems of daily life.

People might think of them under such terms as witch doctor or sorcerer.

MH: The problem with those terms is that they have ancient histories in Europe and mean many different things, often of a pejorative nature. So it is best to wipe the slate clean, use the word shaman, and look closely at what the person really does. Not all witch doctors or medicine people are really shamans. Many of them are tribal priests who do very beautiful, valuable work for their peoples, but don't necessarily fit into the category of shaman.

You began a lot of your research in the Amazon region of South America working with the Jivaro, who used to practice headhunting.

MH: Yes, of course that is widespread in many parts of the world, and not unknown in Europe, as a matter of fact. But in that part of the world, when I first went down there, shamanism was still quite strong. It is still strong in many areas there. Just as a matter of course, as an anthropologist, I had to study this part of the local culture, and I found it fascinating; but for some time I remained just an outside observer. Then, on a later expedition to the Conibo Indians in eastern Peru, the Indians said if I really wanted to learn about what they were talking about, that I had to actually do it, and they gave me a certain drug that they use. In that part of the world, unlike most parts of the world where they do shamanism, they use psychedelic drugs, and I discovered in just a few hours that there was a whole amazing world that we in anthropology hadn't realized existed. That was back in 1961, and I knew nothing about psychedelic drugs then; in fact, very, very few people had even heard of them at that time.

That was the ayahuasca plant, I believe.

MH: Right, the ayahuasca; the vine of the dead, it is sometimes called. It is sometimes called the little death, because it gives you entrance into what we now call a near-death experience. But it also was an opportunity to increase your own knowledge of what Castaneda called non-ordinary reality, and in that way improve your own life and permit you to help other people in certain ways that wouldn't be possible if you were just stuck in an ordinary state of consciousness.

In THE WAY OF THE SHAMAN, you say that after you had this drug-induced experience, you met with one of the elder shamans, a blind man, and described your experiences to him, quite detailed, visionary types of experiences. He seemed to understand exactly where you had been, and what you had experienced.

MH: Yes, that was a critical point for me, because here I had these experiences which were so incredible, and then I went to the shaman, and he dealt with them quite matter-of-factly. There were certain creatures who said certain things about how they were really running the planet, and he just smiled and said, "Oh, they're always saying that." I realized, from that and many other things, that he was quite familiar with the terrain that I had been to.

You also remarked in your book that the same terrain was covered at least in part in some sections of the book of Revelation in the Bible.

MH: Through the years I have followed this more and more intensely, and it is clear to me, although there are obviously cultural differences in mytholo-gies and cultural differences in experiences in journeying in shamanic cultures, that there are remarkable uniformities in this hidden reality – uniformities that are beyond culture, beyond individual experience. You will find great similarities between experiences of great Christian mystics and experiences of shamans, experiences of the near-death situation, and so on. This is fascinating to me, because I was trained as a cultural anthropologist, and I was told that culture did everything. And now it looks as if maybe culture isn't the last word about everything. It is standard anthropological knowledge that you have the same system for using the mind in a place like Tierra del Fuego, at the tip of South America, or in Lapland in northern

Europe; these things are known in Europe too, or over in North America or Siberia or Southern Africa. So we are dealing with a remarkable consistency of knowledge about how to use the mind and the heart and the spirit for healing and other purposes.

And these are cultures that have been separated from each other for tens of thousands of years.

MH: Yes, the Australian aboriginals have the same system, basically, and they were separated for thirty or forty thousand years from other peoples. So we can't ascribe this thing to anything except that it works, because these people were very inventive when it came to peculiar kinship systems; they were inventive when it came to making special adaptations to difficult environments. But this one thing stays very consistent – how to use the mind and the heart for healing and helping.

Doesn't it strike you sometimes as ironic that our modern culture has had such a negative attitude toward shamanism? In fact, I think up until rather recently anthropologists assumed that shamans were schizophrenics.

MH: Yes, there was a tendency to feel that shamans were psychotic individuals – in other words, crazy; but they had the good fortune to live in crazy cultures, i.e., cultures other than our own, which of course is very sane. There also was the point of view that they were fakers – that when they claimed to go into a trance, which is the word they often used in the literature, they couldn't possibly be going into the trance and having experiences they claimed to have. I have run into ethnologists from Germany and from Russia who in the course of field work stuck pins or burning embers under the skin of shamans while they were in a trance, to see if they were really faking or not. There was this kind of skepticism.

Mircea Eliade wrote that even if they were crazy, it was uncanny how they could dance all night long and maintain this incredible level of energy.

MH: Well, you are drawing on power beyond yourself. Shamanism looks like a lot of hard work; you know, dancing all night – my goodness, what terrible hours to be working. But as a matter of fact, the person who is doing this work is drawing upon an experience of power far beyond himself or herself. There is a thing called shamanic ecstasy where you are having ineffable experiences, difficult to describe, which make living very, very worthwhile. They are experiences connected with helping others too, and working in harmony. This power comes from harmony; some people might say God, some people might say love. But this power has tremendous strength, and so when you draw upon it, particularly for good purposes, then this energy is there.

Shamans are sometimes referred to as wounded healers. Eliade points out that in the training of shamans, sometimes illnesses occur, and the shamans have to learn how to heal themselves as part of the process.

MH: Often in Siberia and some places in South America, some of the shamans became shamans through a very simple process. That is, a person would become very, very ill. Sometimes it was an illness of a very physical nature as we would ordinarily call it, like smallpox. Everyone expected the person to die. Then suddenly the person experienced a miraculous recovery. When that happens in a shamanic culture, they say, "Ah! A miracle has occurred. The person has received power to fight that illness and succeed." Now, since other people also would suffer from similar illnesses, or sometimes the same illness, it was only natural for them to seek out this person, and say, "You have the power to fight this illness. Could you please try to help me?"

That was one way for a shaman to be born, but there are many other ways. I was in one tribe, the Suara or Jivaro of eastern Ecuador, where all the shamans had bought their power from other shamans. There was quite a trade in spiritual power in exchange for things like hunting dogs and blowguns and so on. In other cultures, you may inherit it in your family. Other times, you may learn it from a tree; in fact, my first main teacher was a tree. What is important is not how you become a shaman, just as it is not really that important where you went to school – it is how good you are when you do your work.

In your book THE WAY OF THE SHAMAN you actually have a set of exercises and practices so that Western people, without even meeting with a shaman face to face, can induce this ability in themselves.

MH: Of course the best thing, if possible, is to work firsthand with somebody; but the book was written to help people for whom this was not possible. What I found was that we are not introducing something exotic, we are just going home. Europeans had shamans up to a few thousand years ago; in fact, the Laplanders had shamans up to the 1930s. So we are not talking about something exotic, but about some ancient capacity that is right there; it only needs to be waked up by certain proven techniques. It is quite practical, and it is sometimes almost embarrassing how easy it is to do this work, because you ordinarily think you should be wearing a hair shirt and be suffering in a cell for thirty years to do it. But in fact it is really not that difficult for most people.

It is very important that a tradition which has developed over tens of thousands of years not be exterminated by our modern civilization. You seem to be taking great steps in the direction of preserving the essence of the tradition.

MH: Well, in anthropology we have had a long tradition of trying to save a record of disappearing cultures, and in more recent years especially there has been an attempt to save the culture as it exists, not just to make a record of it. Now this is another step – to recognize that many of these people in these tribal cultures are potentially great teachers for us, and particularly in something as universal as the use of the mind, so that we see them as custodians of ancient knowledge. So we can do two things: we can learn from them, but we also can reaffirm to them that they have something of value, because they are in a state of great crisis in many of these societies. Missionaries and many other people have spent much effort and much money to persuade these people that they are nothing but savages, that they have nothing of value, that they should change and get with it and be like ourselves. So it is very important for a few of us to go to them and sit at their feet and say, "We are studying at your feet. We need to know what you know." And it's quite honest; they know a great deal – things that were stamped out long ago in most of Europe, for example.

I suppose the very fact that the native cultures didn't possess our technology led them to delve deeper and deeper into the powers of the mind.

MH: Well, one could think that; but the fact is that today, when we have the highest level of technology, when we have the highest development of the medical healing arts, this is just the time that people are turning to shamanism, or the rediscovery of some of the principles in shamanism – to develop what they call holistic health, to develop many shamanic techniques that already were present for thousands of years, such as visualization. So I think the high level of technology has been proven to be inadequate. And the reason that shamanism went out of fashion was more for political than technological reasons. The shaman is inherently a subversive person. The shaman believes that each person can directly contact this hidden, spiritual universe, and receive information; every shaman is his or her own prophet.

When the first kingdoms arose, and the empires arose, it was necessary for the priests to be consolidators of the political power, and shamans then were persecuted – not just by Christianity, but by many other state religions. They had to go, and they went underground, and they finally disappeared in most of these cultures. Now, when we have essentially the age of science, ironically science makes it easier to do shamanism. For example, shamans anciently claimed that we were related to the animals and the plants. Only with Charles Darwin have we again had permission to reassert this understanding. There are many other things I could point to as well that science gives us permission to inherit once again.

In your work you use simple techniques such as drumming to help people begin to enter these other realms in a space of perhaps ten minutes.

MH: Absolutely. It is an amazing thing. We are ready to go, basically, and the drum is an incredibly underestimated instrument. We go to wars to the beat of a drum; we have our highest moments of social dancing to the beat of a drum. The shamans have been using the drum in a monotonous, steady way for thousands and thousands of years. And yet I have located only four papers in the scientific world on the impact of drumming on the human nervous system. Drums are so close to us, and so natural, that we underestimate their power. But when you use them in the proper, ancient way, and use them with a certain discipline, things happen that are truly profound.

In this work you train people to enter into a realm that you call non-ordinary reality – a realm that would seem to be a fantasy from our logical, awake state.

MH: Yes. Well, I sometimes define fantasy as something that I have been told by somebody else that I never saw myself. Much of the news, for example, or claims by politicians, I often consider to be in the fantasy realm. What I don't consider to be fantasy is what I have seen for myself. A lot of people make the mistake of assuming that if other people haven't voted on it, it isn't real. But in the spiritual reality, the information you get is very specific and tailor-made for you. It is perfect for you, and you don't have to wait for other people to vote on it and say, "Ah yes, I saw that too." If you experienced it firsthand, the shaman says it is real. If you heard it firsthand, the shaman says it is real. If you smelled it firsthand, it is real. No one can take that away from you. So for us, non-ordinary reality means that in a non-ordinary state of conscious-ness you are encountering things firsthand, and that is your reality. Now sure, we can use the word fantasy, or imagination. It doesn't much matter, because once you do enough of this work, you arrive at your own conclusions about what it really means. It is not a belief system, it is a method.

You also note that people who practice shamanism are still quite capable of functioning in the world of ordinary reality; they keep their feet on the ground, so to speak.

MH: That's right. Years ago among the Jivaro, there was a man who wandered the forest day and night, talking with the spirits. Now everybody in that culture had had experience with the spirits; they had taken psyche-delic drugs, gone on vision quests, and so on. They all knew the spirits were there. I said, "Is that man a shaman?" They said, "No, he's crazy." The reason was that he couldn't turn it off. The shaman is a person who knows when to enter that other reality, that sacred ground, with discipline; and who knows what to do there – a mission such as a journey of healing – and then when to return. All shamans are part-timers; if you were full-time, you couldn't do shamanism. I mean, how could anyone be full-time in the world of spirits unless they were dead?

You focus quite a bit on the role of the shaman as a healer, and how the shaman gets in there and struggles with the patient to fight against the disease, or against the evil spirits that may be contributing to the disease. Somehow that motivates the patients, perhaps to get in touch with their own inner healer.

MH: From a psychological point of view I think you are absolutely right; but there is another aspect too. The shaman, from the shamanic point of view, is offering himself or herself up as a sacrifice on behalf of the person. In other words, another human being cares enough that he or she is interceding on behalf of that human being. The person who is ill is no longer alone; and not only the shaman but the family, the whole village, maybe the tribe, is gathered there together, working intensively together with their wills, asking for help for this person. So there is already this harmony in the group, this will, and it seems that great results then ensue. The person is not left alone, as we often do here in the West with the so-called self-healing process. Now, I think one should make an effort to help oneself, but why not have other people work with you in this process? The shamanic view is that we are not alone, and that we can call upon vast resources to help, including other humans who have training and ability to move in realms that we normally don't move in. In fact the shaman doesn't just treat people who are ill; the shaman also looks after them after they die. A shaman is a psychopomp, a conductor of souls. One of the jobs of the shaman is to move people at the time of death into realms where they will be content.

Let's talk a little bit about the world of spirits. One of the universals that comes through in every culture is that shamans interact with spirits.

MH: You know, for a while I was wondering if the word spirit was out of date. Carl Jung wrestled with this; he suggested a word that was similar, not identical, called archetype. But that doesn't quite do the job, and I come back to spirit again and again. As I study cross-culturally, the bottom line seems to be that spirit is something you see when your eyes are closed. Now, that's not all there is to it, because people who have done visualization work in healing know that these images have tremendous power. So if you see something with your eyes closed or in complete darkness, don't dismiss it as unimportant. It could be so important that it could help save your life.

The shaman believes that these spirits live in a kingdom of their own, like the animal kingdom – that they are actual entities.

MH: Well, if you talk to entities and they give you advice, and you interact with them just as you are doing with me here, you come to believe they exist, just as I believe you exist. Naturally, if they give you wisdom, and they give you help, you regard them in a serious way. That is what happens with shamans. Many people in our present society take up shamanism because they are skeptical; they don't really have a belief system, but they would like to see what's there. Then as they work, they come not to a belief system, but to a system of knowledge based upon firsthand experience. And so it has been

Michael Harner | **337**

since ancient times – that people in shamanic practice come to the conclusion there are such things that they call spirits, though you could give another name to them, I suppose.

Are there good spirits and bad spirits?.

MH: It is not that simple, actually. For example, illness often presents itself to the shaman as some sort of horrible insect or something. But the insect is not evil. Take termites, for example. Do you consider termites evil? Probably not; but you probably wouldn't want them in the foundation of your house either. The shaman is busy moving entities around without making value judgments about their being good or evil or whatever, because they in fact aren't. They are part of that universe, and the shaman is simply trying to move them where they should be. And the shaman finds the universe in fact is much nicer than is often advertised. There have been various caveats prohibiting us in recent centuries from exploring that on our own; and as a matter of fact, when you go there, what do you find? You find cosmic unity, you find a sense of love, you find what is called shamanic ecstasy where tears of joy exist. It's the same world of the Christian mystics of medieval times, the same world of the great Eastern saints.

LIVING AND DYING

HEALING AND THE UNCONSCIOUS

With W. BRUGH JOY, M.D.

Brugh Joy is an internationally known teacher, seminar leader, and speaker, and the author of Joy's Way: A Map for the Transformational Journey *and* Avalanche: Heretical Reflections on the Dark and the Light. *Formerly in practice as a medical doctor, he presently conducts year-round residential workshops in the Arizona desert.*

The unconscious, according to Dr. Joy, is far more extensive and powerful than is generally acknowledged. It contains multiple, autonomous personalities which are beyond the control of the conscious mind. In this interview, Dr. Joy discusses the importance of esoteric rites and initiations in calling forth particular personalities from the unconscious at appropriate stages of human development.

F*reud once likened the mind to an iceberg which was one-tenth above water and nine-tenths below water – the unconscious. You seem to be suggesting that the unconscious mind is vastly larger than Freud suggested. And yet, people initially argued against Freud, that it didn't exist at all.*

BJ: It is still argued that it doesn't exist. I am really quite struck by the degree to which the unconscious mind is unavailable to us. Carl Jung pointed this out when he said that the trouble with the unconscious is it's unconscious. But the more you probe into consciousness, you begin to suspect that the other mind is like a little dot on a vast ocean of beinghood. We could say that the outer mind is 99.999999 percent comatose. It simply does not realize the unconscious forces that dominate or direct the life of the individual. A lot of my work with people on health and disease, or spiritual awakening, or whatever, has to do with first introducing them to the realization that who and what they are is far vaster than they know. It reminds me of being in a television studio where the television camera is only allowed to see so much, and so the audience only sees so much of what this room is actually like. But when you begin to move into deeper ranges of consciousness, you become aware that that is a limited, controlled view, sort of like the outer mind; and there is actually a much larger context in which this whole setting exists, some of which is ego-enhancing, and some of which is not ego-enhancing.

Sometimes I hear people say that you create what your life is, as if the part that you know about had any sort of resource to do that. We are talking about much richer, deeper, more awesome states of consciousness, for which one can no longer use the word mine or yours. We're talking about a total shift in consciousness, a sense of a multiplicity inside that is still within the range of you as an individual; but there are many more of you than you or I may know about, that are within your personal sense of beinghood.

I am very much impressed with some of the material coming out of the National Institute of Mental Health that addresses multiple personality. My feeling is that the human psyche may well be multiple, and the illusion of self – and I call it an illusion – is what gets us into trouble. We have the sense that we are a singularity, but I can demonstrate over and over again in working with people that oftentimes maybe two, three, four parts of them are speaking in the same sentence. You can hear the presence of these parts, but we have a final common pathway, which is called the voice structure or the body movement. People make the assumption that they are in a singularity of beinghood, when indeed it is easy to demonstrate that they have more beings inside than just one. There are many eyes and ears sitting in this room, far more than the number of bodies. You have a number of eyes and ears, I have a number of eyes and ears, and the outer mind may be totally oblivious to their cognitions and their experiences of the same material. But as you begin to find ways to expand, to pull the camera eye back further, to be able to see more and more of what is going on, you begin to discover these components and take advantage of them.

One of the great spiritual realizations one has as one matures is that the outer level, one's most personal sense of self, is not *numero uno;* it is way down on the totem pole of what I call an internal community. Whether or not this is an exact representation of the human psyche at the unconscious level, it is a good working hypothesis. It is a good way to go in and begin to take on these forces which act quite autonomously, independently of who and what we think we are. We don't know about that if we are living a relatively unconscious, sleepy sort of life, going through life doing the nice things and the right things. We don't bump up against it until we either encounter major stress in life or we come up against a life-threatening illness. Then we begin to understand we are not in charge, we haven't been in charge, and that there is something else operating that we have to get in touch with. This is a good opening to begin to explore these forces that I describe as like entities – but not as discarnate in the sense that they come from the Pleiades, or from somebody who died; I don't believe that at all. I believe that we are a rich composite of what I call patternings and forces, and that just as the personality is a pattern of energy, these are patterns of energy also, and some of them are far more resourceful and far richer in their content than is the outer level.

The research you mentioned earlier suggests some striking things. If one personality comes to the fore, allergy patterns may change, or definite physiological character- istics, such as eye coloring, might change. This suggests that these subpersonalities, or autonomous energies, have quite a bit to do with our wellness.

BJ: In my exploration over the years, the most dramatic shifts in illness that I have ever encountered were in people who underwent a total change in their consciousness. It is as if they were "born again" and a whole new being was present. Even though the name and the historical data are still part of the memory bank, it is an entirely different energetic that you are dealing with.

Certainly the material you referred to about multiple personality is star- tling. It suggests that the consciousness that is in charge of the body determines the body's response to stimuli. They can test one personality when it is in, and they come up with diabetes, and it carries a certain patterning. They test it when another personality, or what I call an entity, is in charge of the psyche, and they don't find the diabetes. You begin to wonder what is primary – tissue and disease, or something about consciousness? And what is the relationship between mind and matter.

All of this is bringing us right to the threshold where a conscious state changes the whole possibility of what a body responds to. I have often thought that some of the more dramatic "healings" I have encountered were not because I did something to the body tissue per se, but because some psychological induction took place. It's as if the pattern or part that was tied up in the conflict, and which was leading to the disease and participating in the disease patterning died; something else pops in, and it doesn't carry that patterning, and the disease dissolves.

You mentioned earlier that it is a big mistake to think that our ego can ever control all of this dynamic.

BJ: Who would want it to? It is so limited in its dimension and its scope and its understanding. I see some material that disturbs me a lot. The teaching of lucid dreaming disturbs me because it is teaching a way for the ego awareness to go in to control something that is far vaster and far richer and in contact with a far vaster reality than we grok at this level. It is like the subatomic quark in the molecule in the cell in the hair – the tail of the dog wagging the dog. Who would want a quark wagging the dog? That is what the ego does when it goes in.

The ego takes its place. This is the key, critical process, the key development to the mysteries. This is why the mysteries aren't brought forward until after thirty-five. There is that whole process of, "I too am important. I too can contribute to the world. I too can make a meaningful stance. Those are all part of our earlier stages of development that have to do with development of me and mine, family, service to the self. That is an aspect of beinghood, but it isn't its totality. At some point most of us reach a stage, midlife, where we begin to realize that that doesn't bring us the fulfillment, that there is something lacking. This is where we have to pass through if we are going to enter mystical or spiritual paths. It may take the form of the surrender of the ego, at which time one has to be in relationship to something else. I find it very limiting to talk about being in relationship to God, or something like that, when there are so many stages before you need to evoke such a statement.

"Know Thyself" is an ancient aphorism over the temple at Delphi. To know oneself is a profound path, and much of what we are talking about is not going in to look at somebody else's material; but rather the journey, the struggles, the dangers of going into the unconscious. It has been said that the journey into the unconscious is more dangerous than stripping down naked and walking through the Amazonian jungle. It is potentially overwhelming, and unless there is some way to handle the entry – perhaps through centering, or through an intent to look at only a part of the unconscious, such as disease – one can be overwhelmed and collapse the ego structure, and then we have insanity.

This needs to be done in stages; it needs to be done carefully. If we're on a path of growth towards beinghood in this sense, we want to be looking at what we might think of as the demonic side, the dark side, the shadow, but never more than we can handle at any given time.

BJ: This gets us back to multiple dimensions and multiple entities. It depends on which one is in charge of the consciousness when you bring forth the disowned material. If the child is in charge of the consciousness it is terrorized. I can't tell you how often I have to tell people, "If you bring that child out, I'll eat it," because they lose all capacity to hold their center when they are in a very critical shift in their development. It also needs to be understood about the shadow content of the unconscious, or the unconscious parts of ourselves, that when we say demonic, or dark, it doesn't really mean evil. It means that which we do not identify as self.

You said that if somebody you were working with brought their child up, you said you would eat them. What did you mean by that?

BJ: I mean if they bring it out, they won't survive very long. The child cannot come out. In the mystery trainings the children are never brought into the temple; they are never brought into certain arenas. The child has a wonderful place; unfortunately, it is deified in our society until you wonder whether or not our society will ever get over being a child; parent-child material particularly, is deadly to later stages. I find that we haven't done the initiations in our culture that closed off these stages, so they are left wide open, and we run back and forth between these various parts of our psyche, not realizing the consequence of regressing under the impact of a particularly devastating revelation about oneself – something that's very humiliating, let's say, as you probe the deep unconscious, and you have to take on the realization. Let's say you have a feminine part that is almost diametrically opposite to what you perceive yourself as being, and you have to realize that that is you, it exists in you, it has a place in you. Usually what happens is that people become overwhelmed under this, and they immediately begin the defense, and then they regress to an earlier stage such as a child. The key is to hold the development, to hold the state of consciousness that can actually entertain the new idea or creative thought, and has resources to engage it and live it and celebrate it and welcome it, rather than saying, "Oh, I don't want to know about that," or "Oh, oh, that terrorizes me." What rites and rituals do we have that teach us how to take on these?

You seem to be suggesting that for any given predicament we find ourselves in, there is within this vast unconscious a particular being who is appropriate to call forth; and the mystery traditions and some of the esoteric traditions have initiations for calling forth at different stages the quality of beinghood which is appropriate to the individual at that time.

BJ: Exactly; and this is what we lack in our culture, and we need to close the door. It's a good thing the vagina closes and we can't get back in, because people would go clear back into the womb if they could get back into it. It's interesting how at the times when we really want to hold our development, our resources, our richness of being and life experiences, how quickly within an eyeblink these earlier stages can seize us. This is true not only for an individual who is faced with a life-threatening process or an initiation – because that's what initiations are; they are life-threatening to earlier stages – but this also holds true for collectives, it holds true for nations. Whenever we are stressed we regress, we become more fundamental – "Go back to the old ways," and so on. That is a regressive tendency, and very difficult to prevent in a collective sense. The only thing one can do is hold one's own development.

I do believe that in our culture we will develop and bring back the initiations that allow childhood to die, to close off, and to induct the next stage. In true initiations, there was always a possibility one would not survive them; one had to be stressed. If everybody just gets moved through, as we do through our educational system, it means nothing. Even some of the wonderful initiations that have been lost in our culture, such as the Bar Mitzvah, or the Catholic confirmation, which is just social now, have lost their real depth, which was to birth and incarnate an aspect of that individual and close off the previous stage. But this means mother and father have to let them go too, and that isn't what our culture is all about. In our culture, we stay children until our parents die. But I think the initiations will come back.

I think they come and they go in the long cycles, and we are in a time period where there is a yearning to return to some of the richness of the initiations, to touch upon collective forces that help to induct certain states of consciousness, to transcend the differences that divide us today.

THE NATURE OF HEALING

WITH STEPHEN LEVINE

Stephen Levine is a meditation teacher and poet whose work with the terminally ill has led him to evolve an expanded definition of healing. He and his wife Ondrea served as codirectors of the Hanuman Foundation Dying Project. He is author of Who Dies?, A Gradual Awakening, Meetings at the Edge, Healing into Life and Death, *and coauthor (with Ram Dass) of* Grist for the Mill.

Genuine healing, according to Stephen Levine, occurs when we take ourselves mercifully into our own hearts and accept the totality of our lives. This healing of the soul and spirit is independent of bodily healing. Conscious living and conscious dying require that we bring our pain into our own hearts, rather than wall ourselves off from it. In this interview, Levine illustrates this point by referring to case histories of dying individuals with whom he has worked.

Y ou have done an enormous amount of work with the sick and the dying. You have witnessed the healing process in operation thousands of times. Let's talk a little bit about that process to begin with.

SL: When you ask me, "What is healing?" I still don't know. When my wife and I were directing the Hanuman Foundation Dying Project, we worked predominantly with people who came to ask us for help in dying. Many people, at a certain point in their process, usually as they opened to the reality that death might well be in the near future, began to finish business. Our relationships are usually run like business: "I'll give you two; you give me two. If you only give me one, I'm going to take my bat and ball and go home; I won't play anymore." This kind of totaling of accounts is always going on with people. It's easy to think of finishing business as, "You forgive me, I forgive you; but I'm not going to forgive you until you forgive me" – always waiting for someone else to give you something. Many of these people started to see that finishing business meant no longer treating relationships as business. When I take you into my heart, our business is done. If you don't take me into your head, that is your pain; I feel it, but it really doesn't affect my business. We started to see people heal their relationships towards the end of their lives, really meeting other people with mercy and such care for their well-being.

Let me give a really extreme example. A woman we worked with never really got along with her mother. Her mother had been very judgmental, unkind, and abusive. The mother then became very ill, and the woman was the only one of the sisters who would even go and sit at her bedside. They had all had such contention and felt so judged that they had put their mother out of their hearts. This woman was a Zen student, and she decided that her work on herself was to be there for her mom. As she sat next to her, her mom would go into a light sleep and come out – in and out, as people do when they are very ill. She would just sit next to her mother and wish her well – not asking, "Why haven't you given me this? Why didn't you do that for me?" She was not trying to total the accounts, but trying to let her mother, as is, into her heart. This is the basis of relationship – as is; because if I want you to be the least different, then you become an object in my mind instead of a subject of my heart. Where is the healing there? It is just separation. The mother had been very nasty in her lifetime, and it wasn't ending just because she was dying. Day after day the woman sent loving-kindness to her mother. On the day that she died, the mother looked up at her and said, "I hope you roast in hell. I hope that you have the worst possible life." The mother died cursing her, and she died with her daughter sitting next to her, looking at her with soft eyes, and with an open heart saying, "Ma, I hope everything is OK for you." For her mom it was terrible, but for her it was wonderful. She had really finished her business. She was just with another human being who was having a hard time.

That is really an extreme story, and hopefully we can all get some glimpse of how that would be. But that is enormous healing. The woman who was dying died; the woman who was sitting next to her was healing.

Who was she healing?

SL: Herself. That is all we can heal. If we are not working on our own healing, we certainly can't be contributing to anyone else's healing.

You use the phrase, "take somebody into our hearts." That seems to have a lot to do with your sense of the healing process.

SL: Yes; here is another story. A woman is dying in the hospital. She has lived her life in a great deal of separation. She has a cancer that has infiltrated her bones. Interestingly, this is a lot like the mother who was dying. Six weeks into the hospital, she has been so unpleasant to the doctors and the nurses that they don't even want to come in her room. One night she is in a real quandary, her pain is so great. She has been a person who was always able to control. In fact, her controlling quality has been so extreme that she hasn't seen her children in years and has never met her grandchildren. She is dying alone in the hospital. The nurses and doctors don't want to be there; they walk in the room and she blames them for her pain, for her illness, for not being able to cure her. She is able to take very little of her own experience within herself; she is pushing it away.

One night the pain is so great there is nothing she can do about it. She comes to a point where it is almost like a drowning person who just says, "I'm going down. This is it; I'm just too exhausted to fight anymore." And maybe for the first time in her life, she surrendered. Perhaps for the first time in her life she let go of her separation, of her idea of herself as opposed to the whole world. In that moment something happened. Her bone cancer was mainly in her back, her hip and her legs; she was lying on her side, in kind of an embryonic state. All of a sudden, she was no longer herself lying in the hospital. She was an Eskimo woman lying on her side, dying in childbirth, with enormous pain in her back and her legs and her hips. An instant later, she was a woman lying on her side by a river in some tropical environment, her back crushed by a rockfall, dying alone, with enormous pain in her back, her hips and her legs. A moment later after that, she said she thought she was somewhere in Biafra. Her skin was black. She had a slackened, empty breast, at which was suckling a starving child. They were both starving, perhaps dying of cholera, she later thought; there was enormous pain in her back, her hips and her legs. Over the next hour or two – she said she couldn't really gauge time – she experienced ten thousand woman dying in pain at that moment. She said as that happened it went from being my pain to being the pain. She said, "I had no room in myself. My pain is in the mind; but the pain is the pain we all share, and it can be touched, it can be experienced in the heart – the heart we all share, the heart of common experience, the heart of common concern for the well-being of all sentient beings.

In the next six weeks, up until the time when she died, her room became the center of love in the hospital. The nurses would hang out there sometimes on their break. A few weeks after this experience, there were her grandchildren, whom she'd never met before, sitting on the bed, playing with grandma, and there were her children, her son standing next to her. The day or two before she died, one of the nurses brought in a picture of Jesus in the form of the Good Shepherd with the children and the animals; and this woman, whose heart had been like a stone, whose mind had been blocked to all but self-concern, looked at this picture and at the children and she said, "Oh Jesus, forgive them, they are only children."

Hers is one of the most amazing healings I have ever seen. And that is why I really can't say I know what healing is, because I have seen people's bodies get well whose hearts were not as healed. There is a healing we took birth for. When we look around this world, and we say, "How can there be so much greed, so much cold indifference, so much suffering?" It is because this is the place where we come to heal, and not everybody takes responsibility for the healing they took birth for. Some people may not even consider it until they find that they may be dying soon.

You seem to be saying that healing of the body is really unimportant.

SL: Healing is not limited to the body. In fact, I have seen parallel situations, where two people had similar diagnoses and one fought the illness. It was them against the illness, and contention filled the room. When they were in pain, they didn't think they were OK. Just when they most needed mercy, it was least available to them, from themselves. They pushed everybody away, and whether they lived or died, what they did was create schism and judgment and guilt in the family, feelings of unworthiness in those who loved them most, because nobody could help. And I have seen other people in the same situation – the same pain in their body, the same pain in their mind – say, "I don't have a moment to lose. I can't stand to live a moment longer with my heart closed. Too much pain for me, too much pain. The world doesn't need another closed heart."

Maybe the sign of real healing is, what are the people at bedside left with when someone dies? Are they left with their hearts full and a sense of connectedness to that person; or are they left frightened of death, scared of that person, with much rumination about how things didn't work out, how they might have helped more? Did they leave a legacy of mental suffering behind? So I see people heal into death. I have seen people who died with their heart open and left more healing behind than someone who lived and continued the judgment and aggression in the family, so that the family was unhealed although the body was healed.

Are the people who do experience physical recovery from a serious disease ornery kinds of people who are fighting for their lives?

SL: Aggression can be a very strong part. When people fight their illnesses, it can become me against my illness – separation and anxiety. Our sense is that when you touch that which is in pain with mercy and awareness, there is healing; where there is awareness, there is healing. The word healing is used in an odd way. To heal is to become whole, to come back to some balance. I know one doctor who helps people heal through modern methods, who says that the patients who heal are his superstars. Another doctor says that patients who heal are the exceptional patients. Well, what does that make everybody else – a second-stringer, a loser?

The very conceptual framework in which you are a good person if you heal, makes you a bad person if you die. Who needs to die with a sense of failure? Those ideas are very dangerous. They are very well intended; they are good fellows, and they sincerely want to help and they have helped many. But many people have been injured by the idea that, for instance, you are responsible for your illness. You are not responsible for your illness. You are not responsible for your cancer; you are responsible to your cancer. If you are responsible for your cancer, then how are you ever going to heal? If my conditioning caused it, do I have to get rid of all of my conditioning to be well? I know people who have meditated for fifty years and are still not done with their conditioning; when their time is short and their energy is low, it just strains them, and may cause schisms within. When we see that we are responsible to our illness, then when pain arises we can send mercy and kindness.

You and I are conditioned. We walk across a room and we stub our toe. What do we do with the pain in our toe? We are conditioned to send hatred into it, to try to exorcise it. We cut the pain off. In fact, even many meditative techniques for working with pain are to take your awareness, your attention, and put it elsewhere. Just when that throbbing toe is most calling out for mercy, for kindness, for embrace, for softness, it is least available. In some ways it is amazing that anybody heals, considering our conditioning to send hatred into our pain, which is the antithesis of healing.

You have developed a number of guided meditations for healing, and part of that process is to really feel the pain, explore it, and know how we protect ourselves from getting at it. There is sort of a wall of deadening around it, to keep us away from our own pain.

SL: The way we respond to pain is the way we respond to life. When things aren't the way we want them to be, what do we do? Do we close down, or do we open up to get more of a sense of what is needed in the moment? Our conditioning is to close down – aversion, rejection, denial; and so nothing heals. That is the very basis on which unfinished business accumulates, putting it away – I'm right, they're wrong – with no quality of forgiveness. Many people we know are working on sending forgiveness into their tumors, into their AIDS, into their degenerative heart disease. It sounds bizarre, because our conditioning is to send anger and fear into it. Where can there be healing in that?

Carl and Stephanie Simonton have developed visualization exercises where you imagine the white blood cells being like cowboys chasing the Indians; there are these little battlefields in the body, and the white blood cells are out to win so that the immune system overcomes. You are suggesting that that's not appropriate.

SL: Well, that system does work for people, and I certainly wouldn't want anyone who finds it a feasible means of working with illness not to do it. But I think we need to watch what it means to add aggression to this mind that already is so aggressive in moments of fear and aversion. Imagine those people who have cultivated all that aggression, and the cancer doesn't go away; what happens? My experience is that the aggression turns inward, and they often die in self-hatred and a feeling of failure: "I really am a rotten person. I really am dying and abandoning my wife and children. I really am a terrible person. I really am abandoning my lover and my friends." The mind takes so quickly to self-negation. Anything that reinforces that has to be watched really closely, because all self-negation seems to slow and limit healing.

I think it is very important in such methods as the Simontons' method, that one finds the imagery that is just right for them. Here is a story: a fellow was going to do the Simontons' technique, and he was a pacifist minister. He said, "I have spent most of my life trying to make peace instead of war. I can't have white sharks eating black gerbils, or whatever it is. This is not appropriate for me; it's not going to work for me." So he was told, "Why don't you take some time, and find the imagery that's right for you?" And what did he come up with in a week? The Seven Dwarfs, going in, singing "Whistle While You Work," digging the cancer up in buckets and carrying it away. And he healed.

So you must ask if the imagery is not appropriate for you, and also, how are you using it? Is there more armoring in you? That is really the diagnostic device. Are you tightening your belly? Is there more holding? Is there more separation? If your belly is tight, you heart is probably going to be closed, and your mind is going to be painting you into a corner.

In your meditative work, you suggest that if one can soften the belly, the heart, and the breathing, that creates a state of surrender to an essential healing that is available for all of us.

SL: The word surrender is funny, because most people, particularly in the case of illness, equate surrender with defeat. But surrender is letting go of resistance. Most of what we call pain is the resistance that clenches down on the unpleasant. A lot of the people we work with, if they take medicine, look at it first; they don't just swallow it automatically. They are not trying to take healing from outside. They look at the pills, and as they take them in, they guide them with loving-kindness into the proper area, because they have put so much attention into that area that they know it from inside. They direct it into that area, and they find, for instance with pain medication, that once the resistance has been gone through, they can decrease the medication. I think a lot of medications get used up by the resistance before they ever get to the place that they are being taken to.

We suggest that people treat their illness as though it were their only child, with the same mercy and loving-kindness. If that were in your child's body, you would caress it, you would hold it, you would do all you could to make it well. But somehow when it is in our body we wall it off, we send hatred and anger into it. We treat ourselves with so little kindness, so little softness. There are physical correlates to the difference between softening and hardness around an illness – blood flow, availability of the immune system, etcetera. If you've got a hard belly and your jaw is tight, and that hardness is around your eyes, it is very difficult for anything to get through.

You seem to be suggesting healing not just for the sick, but as a way of life in general.

SL: The hardening has become involuntary, and the softening takes remembering priorities – that this is the only moment there is, and this is the moment to open. If we are not doing it now, how will we do it at any other time? That is why we suggest you not wait until you get a terminal diagnosis to give yourself permission to be alive. Now is a good time.

LIFE AFTER LIFE

WITH **RAYMOND MOODY, M.D.**

Raymond Moody is a psychiatrist and author of the classic LIFE AFTER LIFE, *which sold more than ten million copies and inaugurated research in the field of near-death studies. A professor of psychology at West Georgia College, he is also author of* LAUGH AFTER LAUGH *and* THE LIGHT BEYOND.

In this interview, Dr. Moody describes the common characteristics of near-death experiences among people with whom he has worked and explores the significance of these experiences for our understanding of life, death, and the power of love.

When you first began investigating the phenomenon of people coming back from near-death experiences, there was almost no literature in the field at all.

RM: That's right. I kept hearing from these patients who had almost died, who had had really dramatic experiences that had profoundly altered their lives. And yet I couldn't find anything in the psychiatric or medical literature that could give me any clue as to what was going on with them.

Can you summarize what a typical near-death experience would be like?

RM: Well, a very typical pattern reported by the patients is that they have a cardiac arrest – no heartbeat, no detectible respiration. During this time, very often their physicians will say something such as, "Oh my God, he's dead, we've lost him," or something to that effect. The patients tell us that from their perspective they feel more alive than ever. They say they float up out of their bodies and watch the resuscitation going on from a point of view just below the ceiling. They can see exactly what is going on down below, they can understand the remarks and the thoughts of the medical personnel. After a while they realize that although they can see clearly and understand perfectly what is going on, no one seems to be able to see or to hear them. They then realize that this is something having to do with what we call death, and they experience what we might characterize as a turning inward of the sense of identity. One woman said, "At this point, you are not the wife of your husband, you are not the mother of your children, you are not the child of your parents. You are totally and completely you."

At this point, at this moment of isolation, on realizing that this is what we call death, very unusual, transcendental experiences begin to unfold. The patients say that these later steps of the near-death experience are absolutely indescribable. Try as they may, they can't find any words in ordinary language to describe the amazing feelings and experiences they are going through. They say they become aware of what they describe as a tunnel, a passageway; they go into this tunnel, and then they come out into a brilliant, warm, loving and accepting light. People at this point describe amazing feelings of peace and comfort. In this light they say that relatives or friends who have already died seem to be there to meet them and help them through this transition. At this point they are often met by some religious figure – Christians say Christ, Jews say God or an angel. This being, in effect, asks them a question, and they say that words can't convey it; communication does not take place through words such as you and I are now using, but rather in the form of an immediate awareness. The way they try to put it into words is that he asks, in effect, "What have you done with your life? How have you learned to love?" At this point, they say, they undergo a detailed review of everything they have ever done in their lives. This is displayed around them in the form of a full-color, three-dimensional panorama, and it involves every detail of their life from the point of their birth right up to the point of this close call with death.

Interestingly enough, the patients often report that during this life review they view the events of their lives not from the perspective they had when they went through the event, but rather from a third-person perspective. Their perspective is displaced out to the side or above, and as they watch themselves go through these life actions, they can also empathetically relate to the people with whom they have interacted.

In other words, if some of their actions have caused pain in another person, they feel that pain.

RM: Absolutely; they take the perspective of the person that they have been unkind to. And if they see an action where they have been loving to someone, then they can feel the warmth and good feelings that that has produced in the life of that person. All of the patients who go through this tell us that one thing comes up in these reviews as the most important feature in their lives. It doesn't have anything to do with earthly success; no one asks them about their financial well-being, or how much power they have had, or any of the other things that our society suggests we should be paying so much attention to. Every single person has told me that they were faced with the question of how they had learned to love, and whether they had put this love into practice in their lives.

What a powerful message for those of us who get caught up in thinking that our identity is contingent upon whether we get a raise or a promotion.

RM: And certainly one of the prominent after-effects of these experiences is that people have exactly the kind of realization that you are talking about – that those are not the important things in life.

At one point in your book you say that as they review their lives they realize that it is the little things that count, not the big things.

RM: Yes, and living in the moment – not worrying obsessively about what is going to happen next week, about deadlines, and so on.

Some of the patients see little glimpses of things even beyond what I have described so far. Sometimes they report beautiful pastoral scenes, heavenly scenery, places of amazing beauty. After a time in this, though, all of them have to come back, and people differ a little bit in how they describe how they got back. Some say that they suddenly found themselves back without knowing why. They say at first maybe they were out of their bodies watching this resuscitation, then suddenly they just found themselves back in their bodies, perhaps after the paddles had been put on the chest during the resuscitation procedure. Others will tell us that someone there – either the religious being, a relative or friend who has died – tells them, "You've got to go back. It's not your time yet. You have things left to do, and you can't come here yet." And so they go back.

Another group of people say that they were given the choice – that someone there told them, "You have a decision to make. You can go back to the life that you have been leading, or you can come on in this experience you are having now." Obviously all those that I have talked with who were given that choice have chosen to come back; and when they do, the reason that they give for returning is almost universal. They say, "From my own point of view I would rather have stayed, but I had children left to raise, so I decided that I had to go back to take care of them." The one exception was a young woman who at the time of her experience was in the last part of her training as a nurse. She told me, "All my life I had wanted to become a nurse and to help people." And so she chose to go back to resume her nursing training and career. It should be fairly obvious that when people do return from this experience their lives have been totally transformed.

The description that you just gave us is an amalgamation of thousands of people who you have now interviewed.

RM: Yes, absolutely. Not every person necessarily has every element of that experience. We found that some people who have a relatively brief cardiac arrest may report only one or two of these things, whereas people with more extensive cardiac arrest can report the full-blown picture.

It seems to suggest that there is a world beyond which is a very pleasant world indeed.

RM: I'm glad you used the word suggests because it certainly doesn't give us rigorous scientific evidence, or proof that we live after we die. But I don't mind saying that having talked with over a thousand people who have had these experiences, and having heard many times some of the really baffling and unusual features of these experiences, has given me great confidence that there is a life after death. As a matter of fact, I must confess that I have absolutely no doubt, on the basis of what my patients have told me, that they did get a glimpse of the beyond.

And they themselves come back with an enormous conviction that they know what death is like.

RM: Oh yes, certainly, and it gives them a great sense of peace. Never again do they fear death – not that any of them would want to die in a painful or unpleasant way, or that they would actively seek this out. As a matter of fact, they all say that life is a great blessing and a wonderful opportunity to learn, and that they don't want to die anytime soon. But what they mean is that when death comes in the natural course of events, they are not going to be afraid. They don't fear it in the least anymore as being a cessation of consciousness.

A Gallup poll has indicated there may be as many as eight million Americans who have had this experience. And yet, only a little over a decade ago it was simply not discussed; it was literally unknown in our culture.

RM: I suspect that the enormous strides in resuscitation technology over the past couple of decades are a factor here. Just in the past twenty years we have developed devices that can bring people back from a state that a hundred years ago would have been called death; and cardiopulmonary resuscitation is widely taught, even to young people. Due to the advances in medicine, we are seeing a much greater number of people who are brought back from the verge of death. In fact, if we look back into history, we find these experiences going way, way back; some reports are literally thousands of years old. In medieval times, there was great interest in this phenomenon. One of the Popes of the medieval church became very fascinated with near-death experiences, and actually wrote a book about them. So this goes way back. But I think that because there are so many more now, we have just reached a point where something had to be said; we had to understand how to talk with these eight million Americans who had had this experience.

I should add also that that figure of eight million in Dr. Gallup's poll dealt only with adults since his sample was limited to adults. We now know, from some fascinating work by a pediatrician and some other physicians and researchers, that children have experiences identical to those of adults. Dr. Melvin Morse of the University of Washington School of Medicine, who is now a pediatrician in private practice in Seattle, has published three articles in the American Journal of the Diseases of Children on his studies of over fifty children who have had near-death experiences. They report exactly what we hear from adults.

Prior to the publication of your book LIFE AFTER LIFE, people who were having these experiences had very little to relate to in the literature. I would imagine also that they were afraid to discuss it with their doctors or even their relatives.

RM: It is interesting how many of my patients over the years, before there was any widespread publicity or public knowledge of this, would relate to me that they had tried very hard to tell their physician, or a minister, a friend, or a relative, but that no one paid any attention to them. They tried to dismiss it. That was very distressing to the patients, I am sure, because this was such an overwhelming, meaningful and touching personal experience, and the patients had no one to listen to them.

With these experiences being discussed commonly now in books and research, it would seem as if a whole new context for spirituality is being created, because I gather that these experiences are relatively similar regardless of a person's religious denomination.

RM: As far as I know, yes. I haven't done a lot of research in other cultures outside the Judaeo-Christian tradition, so I have to rely on reports that I read in the literature. I have talked with people from over large areas of the world – Western Europe, South America, even the Orient – but most of these people were raised in Judaeo-Christian traditions. But certainly, from reports I have heard from other people looking into this, we get identical accounts from other cultures as well. David Hallowell, an anthropologist working back in the late twenties or early thirties, wrote a most fascinating paper on his research among the Salto Indians in Canada. He found that the Salto were very intrigued with near-death tales, and they had accumulated a large number of them in their oral tradition. Again, he encountered the same kinds of reports that we hear from contemporary Americans.

You described the people who have had this experience as being truly transformed in a very deep way, that they become more spiritual – not more religious, necessarily. You say being religious means following the teachings of your church, whereas being spiritual means following the promptings of your soul.

RM: Oh, absolutely, that's a very good way to describe it. They come back saying that it is not denominational religion that counts. I once talked with a very wonderful man who told me that he had his near-death experience during the last year of his seminary training. He characterizes himself as a very narrow person; up to that point he said he was absolutely convinced that only the members of his specific denomination were going to be in heaven, and that everybody else was going to hell. He said during his near-death experience after seeing his body, he went up through this tunnel into a brilliant light, and was there in the presence of a being whom he identified as Christ. His interesting remark was that he found this Christ to be a much more affable fellow than he had imagined; he said, "I was very surprised to learn that God wasn't interested in my theology." Generally, the patients who return from this will say that it is not denominational religion that counts, it is commitment to the basic spiritual truths that are embodied in religion – the love of oneself and of others, and the attempt to expand oneself and to be harmonious with God and one's fellow human beings.

You reported on another case, a fundamentalist preacher whose sermons had frequently dealt with the fire-and-brimstone kind of theology.

RM: Oh yes. This fellow said that when he went through the review of his life, it was pointed out to him in a very gentle and loving way that that was not the way to be with people, to try to frighten them. He changed very dramatically. And we see this again and again – no more fear of death; renewed commitment to loving others; a feeling that what is important is to live in the present and not worry about the future; a great sense of contentment; and so on. And interestingly, very often they describe a renewed interest in learning. I have had quite a few patients who had near-death experiences, even patients of advanced age, who said that one of their first impulses when they recovered was to go back to school; some even entered college for the first time. In their life review, these people say, they saw events in which they had been developing themselves by learning, and it was pointed out that that was a plus for them.

Do you feel that this experience is affecting our culture as a whole now that so many people are talking about it in this way?

RM: No doubt about it. It has been portrayed in a number of really excellent films, such as *Resurrection*. It has even been on soap operas. In my own field of medicine every year now there are a number of articles in the medical journals about near-death experiences – not from the point of view of proving that there is a life after death, but rather in the sense that it has a genuine relevance to clinical medicine. There is a study which indicates very strongly that between, say, forty-five to sixty percent of the people who undergo a cardiac arrest from which they are resuscitated will have an experience of that nature. And so, from the point of view of a physician, whatever one might believe about the origin and the nature and the cause of it, it is certainly important for us to be able to reassure these patients: "Look, you are not alone; we don't fully understand what happened to you, but we know that it was a very important thing, and we want to help you to try to integrate it into your life."

FURTHER READING

JANELLE M. BARLOW, Ph.D.
The Stress Manager

JAMES BUGENTAL, Ph.D.
The Art of the Psychotherapist. Norton, 1987.
The Art of Psychotherapy. Santa Rosa, CA, author, 1982.
Challenges of Humanistic Psychology [Editor]. McGraw-Hill, 1967.
Psychotherapy and Process: The Fundamentals of an Existential-Humanistic Approach.
        Addison-Wesley, 1978.
The Search for Authenticity: An Existential-Analytic Approach to Psychotherapy.
        Holt, Rinehart & Winston, 1965; Irvington, 1981.
The Search for Existential Identity: Patient-Therapist Dialogues in
Humanistic Psychotherapy. Jossey-Bass, 1976.

JOSEPH CAMPBELL
The Hero with a Thousand Faces. Princeton Univ. Press, 1990.
The Masks of God. Viking, 1991.
Historical Atlas of World Mythology. HarperCollins, 1988.
The Inner Reaches of Outer Space. HarperCollins, 1988.

FRITJOF CAPRA, Ph.D.
Belonging to the Universe (with C. Spretnak). Harper, 1991.
Green Politics (with C. Spretnak). Bear and Co., 1986.
The Tao of Physics. Shambhala, 1991.
The Turning Point. Bantam, 1987.
Uncommon Wisdom. Bantam, 1989.

RAM DASS
Be Here Now . Hanuman Foundation. Distributed by Crown Publishing. 1978
Grist for the Mill (with S. Levine). Celestial Arts, 1987.
How Can I Help? (with P. Gorman). Knopf, 1985.
Journey of Awakening. Bantam, 1982, 1990.
Miracle of Love. NAL-Dutton, 1979.
The Only Dance There Is. Doubleday, 1974.

ALBERT ELLIS, PH.D.

The Art and Science of Love. Carol Publ. Group, 1960.

Executive Leadership. Carol Publ. Group, 1972.

Growth Through Reason. Wilshire, 1971.

Guide to Personal Happiness (with I. Becker). Wilshire, 1982.

Guide to Successful Marriage (with R. Harper). Wilshire, 1961.

How to Live with a Neurotic. Wilshire, 1957.

How to Stubbornly Refuse to Make Yourself Miserable About Anything, Yes Anything.
Carol Publ. Group, 1988.

Humanistic Psychotherapy. McGraw, 1974.

New Guide to Rational Living. Wehman, 1975.

Sex Without Guilt. Carol Publ. Group, 1966.

What to Do When AA Doesn't Work for You . Barricade Books, 1992.

Why I Am Always Broke. Carol Publ. Group, 1991.

JAMES FADIMAN, PH.D.

UnLimit Your Life: Setting and Getting Goals. Celestial Arts, 1989.
Chinese Edition, 1991.

Personality and Personal Growth (with R. Frager). Harper and Row, 1976.
Second Edition 1984. Third Edition 1992.

Health for the Whole Person (edited with A. Hastings, J. Gordon). Westview Press,
1981. Bantam 1981.

Holistic Medicine (edited with A. Hastings and J. Gordon). National Institutes of
Mental Health, 1979.

Be All That You Are. Westlake Press, 1986.

The Proper Study of Man: Perspectives on the Social Sciences. Macmillan, 1971.

MATTHEW FOX, PH.D.

The Coming of the Cosmic Christ. Harper and Row, Scranton, PA, 1988.

Creation Spirituality: Liberating Gifts for the Peoples of the Earth. Harper
and Row, 1991.

On Becoming a Musical, Mystical Bear. Paulist Press, Mahwah, NJ, 1976.

Original Blessing: A Primer in Creation Spirituality. Bear and Company,
Santa Fe, 1983.

WILLIS HARMAN, PH.D.

Changing Images of Man (with O.W. Markley). Pergamon, 1982.

Global Mind Change. Knowledge Systems, 1988.

Higher Creativity (with H. Rheingold). Tarcher, 1984.

An Incomplete Guide to the Future. W.W. Norton, 1979.

Paths to Peace (with R. Smoke), Westview Press, 1987.
The Study of the Future. World Future Society, 1977.

MICHAEL HARNER, Ph.D.

Hallucinogens and Shamanism. Oxford Univ. Press, 1973.
The Jivaro. University of California Press, 1973.
Way of the Shaman. Bantam, 1982; Harper and Row, 1990.
Cannibal (with Alfred Meyer). Morrow, 1979.

W. BRUGH JOY, M.D.

Joy's Way: A Map for the Transformational Journey. Tarcher, 1979.
Avalanche: Heretical Reflections on the Dark and the Light. Ballantine, 1990.

PIR VILAYAT INAYAT KHAN

Toward the One
The Call of the Dervish
The Message in Our Time
Counseling and Therapy
Introducing Spirituality into Counseling and Therapy. Omega, 1982.

JACK KORNFIELD, Ph.D.

Living Buddhist Masters. Wisdom, 1989.
Seeking the Heart of Wisdom (with J. Goldstein). Shambhala, 1987.
A Still Forest Pool. (with P. Breiter). Theos, 1985.

U. G. KRISHNAMURTI

Mind is a Myth
The Mystique of Enlightenment

GEORGE LEONARD

Education and Ecstasy. Delacorte, 1968; North Atlantic, 1987.
The Transformation. Delacorte, 1972; Tarcher, 1986.
The Ultimate Athlete. Viking, 1975; North Atlantic, 1990.
The Silent Pulse. Dutton, 1978; Arkana, 1991.
Adventures in Monogamy. Tarcher, 1988; originally published as *The End of Sex,* Tarcher, 1983.
Mastery. Dutton, 1991.

STEPHEN LEVINE

A Gradual Awakening. Doubleday, 1979.
Grist for the Mill (with Ram Dass). Celestial Arts, 1987.
Healing into Life and Death. Doubleday, 1987, 1989.
Meetings at the Edge. Doubleday, 1984.
Who Dies. Doubleday, 1982, 1989.

GAY GAER LUCE, PH.D.

Body Time. Pantheon, 1972.
Sleep. Coward-McCann, 1962.
Your Second Life. Delacorte, 1979.
Longer Life, More Joy. Newcastle,1992.

ROLLO MAY, PH.D.

The Courage to Create. Bantam, 1984.
Dreams and Symbols.
Existential Psychology. Random, 1990.
Freedom and Destiny. Norton, 1981.
Love and Will. Norton, 1969; Dell, 1974; Doubleday, 1989.
Man's Search for Himself. Dell, 1973.
The Meaning of Anxiety.
Psychology and the Human Dilemma. Norton, 1980.

RAYMOND MOODY, M.D.

Elvis After Life. Bantam, 1989.
Laugh After Laugh. Headwaters Press, 1978.
Life after Life. Mockingbird, 1981; Bantam, 1988.
The Light Beyond. Bantam, 1989.
Reflections on Life After Life. Bantam, 1985.

JACOB NEEDLEMAN, PH.D.

The Heart of Philosophy. Harper 1986.
Lost Christianity. Tempest Brookline, 1990.
Money and the Meaning of Life. Doubleday, 1991.
The New Religions . Doubleday, 1970.
Sorcerers (a novel). Mercury House 1986; Viking, 1990.
A Sense of the Cosmos. Viking Penguin, 1988.
The Way of the Physician. Arkana, 1992.

HELEN PALMER, PH.D.

The Enneagram: Understanding Yourself and the Others in Your Life. Harper, 1991.

JOSEPH CHILTON PEARCE

The Crack in the Cosmic Egg. Crown, 1988.
Magical Child. Bantam, 1981.
Magical Child Matures. Bantam, 1986.

KARL PRIBRAM, PH.D.

Brain and Perception: Holonomy and Structure in Figural Processing.
    Erlbaum Assocs., 1991.
Languages of the Brain. Brandon House, 1982.

LEE PULOS, PH.D.

Beyond Hypnosis. Omega Press, San Francisco, 1990.
Miracles and Other Realities (with Gary Richman). Omega Press,
    San Francisco, 1990.

THEODORE ROSZAK, PH.D.

The Cult of Information. Pantheon, 1986.
The Making of the Counter Culture. Doubleday, 1969.
Where the Wasteland Ends. Doubleday, 1973.

VIRGINIA SATIR

Conjoint Family Therapy. Science and Behavior, 1982.
Meditations and Inspirations. Celestial Arts, 1985.
New Peoplemaking. Science and Behavior, 1988.
Self Esteem. Celestial Arts, 1975.
Satir Step by Step. Science and Behavior, 1984.

RUPERT SHELDRAKE, PH.D.

A New Science of Life. Tarcher, 1962, 1988.
The Presence of the Past. Vintage, 1989.
The Rebirth of Nature. Bantam, 1991.

JUNE SINGER, PH.D.

Androgyny: The Opposites Within. Boston: Sigo Press, 1976; 1987.
Boundaries of the Soul: The Practice of Jung's Psychology. New York: Doubleday,
    1973.
A Gnostic Book of Hours: Keys to Inner Wisdom. San Francisco: Harper and Row,
    1992 (forthcoming).
Love's Energies. Boston: Sigo Press, 1983; 1990.

Seeing Through the Visible World: Jung, Gnosis and Chaos. San Francisco:
	HarperCollins, 1990.
The Unholy Bible: Blake, Jung and the Collective Unconscious. Boston:
	Sigo Press, 1986.

SAUL-PAUL SIRAG

Hyperspace Crystallography . World Scientific Publications. Forthcoming in 1994.

HUSTON SMITH, PH.D.

Beyond the Post-Modern Mind. Theos, 1989.
Forgotten Truth: The Primordial Tradition. HarperCollins, 1985.
The Religions of Man (revised and reissued as *The World's Religions*). Harper, 1991.

KATHLEEN SPEETH, PH.D.

The Essential Psychologies
Gurdjieff: Seeker after Truth
The Gurdjieff Work. Tarcher, 1989.

HAL STONE, PH.D.

Embracing Heaven and Earth. DeVorss, Los Angeles, 1985.
Embracing Our Selves: The Voice Dialogue Manual (with S. Winkelman). New
	World Library, 1985, 1989.
Embracing Each Other: Relationship as Teacher, Healer, and Guide
	(with S. Winkelman). New World Library, 1988, 1989.

CHARLES TART, PH.D.

Open Mind, Discriminating Mind. Harper, 1990.
Waking Up: Overcoming the Obstacles to Human Potential. Shambhala, 1987.
Learning to Use Extrasensory Perception. Univ. of Chicago Press, 1976.
Altered States of Consciousness. Wiley, 1969; Harper, 1990.
Transpersonal Psychologies. Harper, 1990.

IRINA TWEEDIE

Daughter of Fire. Dolphin, 1986.

FRANCES VAUGHAN, PH.D.

Awakening Intuition. Doubleday, 1979.
Beyond Ego: Transpersonal Dimensions in Psychology. Ed by R. Walsh and F. Vaughan.
	Tarcher, 1980.
The Inward Arc: Healing and Wholeness in Psychotherapy and Spirituality. Shambhala/
	Random House, 1986.

ARTHUR M. YOUNG

The Bell Notes. Delacorte, 1979; Robert Briggs, 1984.

The Geometry of Meaning. Delacorte, 1976; Robert Briggs, 1984.

Mathematics, Physics and Reality, Robert Briggs, 1991.

The Reflexive Universe. Delacorte, 1976; Robert Briggs, 1984.

Which Way Out? Robert Briggs, 1980.